Real Native Genius

Real Native Genius

· ·

*How an Ex-Slave
and a White Mormon
Became Famous Indians*

· ·

ANGELA PULLEY HUDSON

The University of North Carolina Press
Chapel Hill

© 2015 The University of North Carolina Press
All rights reserved
Designed by Rebecca Evans
Set in Miller and Clarendon
by Westchester Publishing Services
Manufactured in the United States of America

The paper in this book meets the guidelines for permanence
and durability of the Committee on Production Guidelines
for Book Longevity of the Council on Library Resources.
The University of North Carolina Press has been a member
of the Green Press Initiative since 2003.

Complete cataloging information for this title is available from the
Library of Congress.
ISBN 978-1-4696-2443-3 (paper: alk. paper)
ISBN 978-1-4696-2444-0 (ebook)

**with a subvention by
Figure Foundation**

native to origin stay

··· FOR JONATHAN ···

Contents

Illustrations

Real Native Genius

Prologue

> There is nothing so certain to succeed
> as imposture, if boldly managed.
>
> —*Buffalo Courier*, 1851

In 1852, when Sarah Marlett pressed charges in Toronto against her Indian husband for bigamy, the news became a tabloid sensation, reaching across the Canadian border to Buffalo and Brooklyn, throughout the Great Lakes region, and as far away as Kentucky.[1] Marlett was a white woman from New York, and she had met her ill-fated beau on a canal boat. After a speedy courtship, they were married next to the roaring cataract of Niagara Falls. But Marlett soon learned that her new husband, known to audiences across the region as the virtuosic Choctaw flutist Okah Tubbee, already had an Indian wife and family.

Even more shocking, however, was the discovery that Marlett's "tawny lover" might be an impostor. Papers began to spread the news that the popular performer was actually a "negro barber" who had managed to "humbug" his way across the United States, performing his Indian show for unsuspecting audiences from Missouri to New Hampshire.[2] Like other penny-press celebrities whose salacious stories kept antebellum newspaper readers titillated and horrified, the tale of Okah Tubbee's charade made great copy.[3] Sarah Marlett was depicted as a romantic fool, while Tubbee's Indian wife, Laah Ceil, was regarded as a poor, deluded "squaw."

The truth of it all was far more complicated.

As dramatic as it seemed at the time, the scandalous Marlett affair was just another brief episode in the life of a fascinating antebellum couple known by over a dozen aliases. Okah Tubbee and Laah Ceil came from widely divergent backgrounds, but both before and during their marriage they shared a particular history of performing as Indians in a variety of contexts: from Mormon meeting houses to packed concert halls, temperance rallies to doctors' offices. Their story ranges across the nineteenth century from the deep South through the Great Lakes region, to the

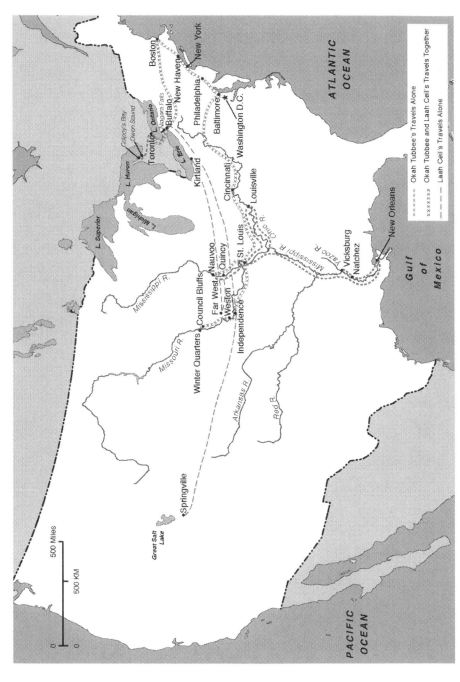

Points of interest during the life and travels of Okah Tubbee and Laah Ceil, 1810–1878. (Map drawn by the author, 2014)

Midwestern frontier, across the northern border with Canada, and into the Mountain West (see map showing points of interest during the life and travels of Okah Tubbee and Laah Ceil, 1810–78). Along the way, they entertained Americans from many backgrounds, penetrated the inner circle of the nascent Church of Jesus Christ of Latter-day Saints, and fled all sorts of legal jeopardy. Through it all, their performance of Indianness was the key. Following their journey reveals how Americans thought about Indians and how those ideas influenced nearly every aspect of antebellum culture, often in surprising ways. It is a story of pain and suffering, but also one of marvelous ingenuity—a twisting tale of real native genius.

• • •

The man who would become Okah Tubbee was born into slavery around 1810 near Natchez, Mississippi. Known by the name Warner McCary, he became the property of his free black family members at the death of his owner, James McCary. McCary's will stipulated that four of his slaves, Sally, Franky, and Franky's children Bob and Kitty, were to be freed. But Franky's youngest child Warner would remain in bondage, the proceeds of his labor designated for the benefit of his apparent half-siblings.[4] He spent his youth being hired out in and around Natchez, often suffering in want and humiliation, while his family went free. To escape the literal and emotional poverty of slavery, he began performing. He learned he could provide for himself by imitating animal sounds, whistling tunes, and later playing the fife and flute. By all accounts, he had exceptional natural talent as a musical entertainer. McCary would later put these skills to use in a wide variety of forums, performing a shifting Indian identity both on and off stage.

The woman later known as Laah Ceil was born Lucile (Lucy) Celesta Stanton in 1816. Although she, like Okah Tubbee, would later profess to be descended from Native royalty (frequently performing as the Mohawk princess Laah Ceil Manatoi Elaah Tubbee), she was raised as a white woman. Born in central New York, Lucy Stanton grew up on the southern shore of Lake Erie in the community of Kirtland, Ohio. In 1830, the Stanton family converted to a new religion introduced by missionaries passing through from New York. The missionaries had been sent by home-grown prophet Joseph Smith Jr. to preach a new gospel—later called Mormonism—and were on their way to the "Lamanites," a term they used to refer to American Indians. Although many antebellum denominations were interested in proselytizing Native peoples, one thing that set the early "Mormonites" apart was the centrality of Indians to their theology.[5] For Lucy Stanton, ideas about Indians were a central feature of her new faith. In time, performing Indianness would become not only an occasional register for expressing her spirituality, but also a path to personal empowerment and financial stability.

Together, McCary and Stanton crafted an elaborate traveling Indian act that included a short-lived religious sect, a variety of musical stage shows, a medical business, and three editions of their composite autobiography. Their professional Indian personae helped conceal their interracial relationship, as well as other secrets they may have wished to hide, like unorthodox religious beliefs and marital practices.[6] They carved out alternate lives for themselves by capitalizing on, reinforcing, and sometimes subverting popular antebellum beliefs about American Indians. To do so, they drew on many sources, like captivity narratives, frontier romances, Indian dramas, ethnic autobiographies, sectarian theologies, and the performances of Native people themselves.[7] That they were successful in a wide variety of cultural contexts suggests both the popularity and currency of ideas of the Indian in nearly every corner of antebellum American life.

What would drive, compel, or inspire Warner McCary and Lucy Stanton to become professional Indians? Perhaps profit, protection, or even pleasure. The range of possible answers to this question exists against the backdrop of a central paradox in antebellum attitudes toward identity. On one hand, broad social changes connected to the market revolution, the growth of a global system of capital, an explosion of print culture and popular entertainment, the emergence of new social classes, and the expansion of transportation networks inspired a belief, albeit fraught, in the flexibility and fluidity of individual identities. Such beliefs underlay the contemporaneous fascination with both self-fashioning and public performance. On the other hand, a new "science" of race grew rapidly during this era. Scientific men were busy measuring and codifying differences among the races they believed composed humanity. Although they disagreed on the relative positions of Indians and blacks within their schema, these race scientists were unanimous on two points: that whites were innately superior and that race was fixed, immutable, and visible on the body. Simultaneous debates on the proper place of men and women in society reflected concerns about the increasing number of women wage earners and sparked widespread legal and social reforms, often focused on narrowing the roles of women in the public sphere.

Indianness, a wide-ranging set of ideas about how American Indians looked, talked, lived, and loved, provided Okah Tubbee and Laah Ceil a way to navigate the contradictory impulses toward fluid and fixed identities that shaped their world. The period between the Indian removal era (1830s and 1840s) and the Civil War was arguably the most generative in U.S. history with regard to the popular representation of American Indians. These representations took many forms and had many sources, including the celebrity of Native people, as diplomats, orators, activists, writers, and artists. Okah Tubbee and Laah Ceil drew on this deep well and exploited their audiences' fascination with Indians to make money, to protect their marriage, and to fulfill their personal longings. As they capitalized on others' desire for Indianness, they too were fascinated, perhaps even seduced, by the idea of the Indian. Despite considerable differences in their backgrounds, both of them were liberated in some senses by their performance of Native personae.

The social and cultural circumstances that enabled Warner McCary and Lucy Stanton to transform themselves into professional Indians requires us to consider the broader context of what one scholar has called the "crisis of social identity faced by . . . men and women who were on the move both socially and geographically" and the central role that Indianness played in it.[8] The increasing availability of travel, particularly on steamboats, connected once distant locales and enabled people across the antebellum United States to travel farther and faster than before. Steamboat travel inspired new possibilities for the presentation of self—memorably depicted in Herman Melville's 1857 novel *The Confidence Man: His Masquerade*, in which the title character imposes on a host of steamboat passengers by shifting his identity as they proceed along the Mississippi River. Such possibilities captured the imagination of antebellum Americans.[9] Spectacles of masquerade were obsessively rehearsed on the stage and breathlessly recounted in pulp fiction and yellow journalism, capitalizing on the public's simultaneous fascination and discomfort with pretense. It was the era of humbug, of "confidence men and painted women," of Christy's minstrels and Fiji mermaids, crackpot prophets and lying seducers. Entertaining as they were, these widespread examples of imposture generated a sense of unease and gave rise to new regulations designed to properly categorize and discipline race, gender, religion, sexuality, class, and status.

As a complex of popular ideas within this midcentury milieu, Indianness was remarkably resilient and surprisingly persistent.[10] From sects that regarded Indians as descendants of a Lost Tribe of Israel to the fetishization of Native botanic knowledge in the patent medicine business, and seemingly everywhere in between, ideas about Indians coursed through American cultural life. Okah Tubbee and Laah Ceil paid close attention to the beliefs and desires of their audiences (broadly conceived) and learned through repetition and revision to adjust their performances accordingly. They were not simply impersonating Native people—they were helping to shape the popular cultural phenomenon of Indianness.

Some audiences may have suspected or known that the pair were not the Indians they claimed to be. Their performative career peaked in the late 1840s, years during which thousands of theatergoers paid nightly to watch white men perform, caricature, and subordinate blackness on stage by applying burnt cork to their faces in blackface minstrel shows. Some scholars have suggested that the "racial cross-dressing" apparent in both the minstrel shows and practices of playing Indian helped mitigate white audiences' deep-seated anxieties about their complicity in slavery and colonization.[11] Eastern audiences might also have liked the idea of a flute-playing Choctaw chief and his surprisingly articulate Native wife, not only because Indians were thought to be rapidly disappearing and thus increasingly rare and exotic, but also because their abilities registered a sort of cognitive dissonance. That an "unbettered" Indian was an accomplished musician and an Indian princess could wax poetic on temperance was a sort of curiosity.[12] The surprise audiences felt upon witnessing the refined talents of performers like the Tubbees was rooted in their ideas about what Indians were like.

That said, Indianness was not an infinitely flexible signifier. Ideas about Indians went through an important transformation during the first half of the nineteenth century. The first of these was a turn from *culture* to *race* as the chief explanation for differences between American Indians and European-descended people. During George Washington's administration, the new United States had faced the expensive prospect of continual border warfare with the indigenous peoples on whose homelands they now presumed to build a nation. To avoid constant violence while expanding the nation's territory, the first official U.S. federal Indian policy had been to "civilize" eastern Native peoples by teaching, coercing, and equipping them to abandon "savage pursuits" like hunting and become settled cultivators (their long history as sedentary agriculturalists notwithstanding). Despite the seemingly humanitarian intentions of the "civilization" plan, it was in fact an effort to shrink American Indian territories from the vast tracts necessary for hunting to small plots suitable for subsistence farming. Conversion to Christianity was also desirable, so long as it did not interfere with the project of reducing the Indians' landholdings. Although the "civilization" plan was equal parts self-preservation and dispossession, it was nevertheless rooted in Enlightenment thinking that all human beings were capable of improvement through education. In other words, many proponents of this mindset believed that American Indians were culturally distinct from European Americans, but nevertheless capable of learning to behave differently if provided the proper tools. One day perhaps they would even be eligible for inclusion in the national body politic.

By the 1820s, however, the idea of Indian improvability was giving way to another mode of thinking about difference. Whereas Native people had once been viewed as capable of becoming "civilized" through influence and instruction, an ascendant way of thinking held that humans were divided into races, whose traits and characteristics were fixed and immutable. According to the burgeoning nineteenth-century science of race, even "improved" Indians were still Indians, and no amount of education could change their innate inferiority. Rather than render them suitable for amalgamation, these proponents argued, the "civilization" plan had emboldened Native people to fight for their land and sovereignty using the very language, laws, and logic that the federal government had encouraged them to embrace. Emergent pseudoscientists argued that American Indians were a biologically distinct race with inherent traits that could not be changed—with pride and stubbornness chief among them. Although at one time, they had been deemed eligible for inclusion in the nation, many European Americans now concluded that Indians were a fundamentally unassimilable other that stood in the way of national improvement.

Scientific racism rationalized white supremacy through putatively objective and frequently physical measures of nonwhite inferiority. Phrenologists and anatomists joined ethnologists and theologians in debating the genesis of humankind and the "capacity" of the races. Beyond their concerns with the origin of the human species, proponents emphasized the body as simultaneous marker of racial identity and evidence of intellectual capacity. As Indian removal and the rapid westward expansion of slavery unfolded during the 1830s and 1840s, beliefs in the biology (and thus the immutability) of race provided convenient justification for the hierarchy that put whites in control of black bodies and Indian land. Thus, despite the veneer of objectivity, the science of race was never disinterested; it was used and, some argue, created to defend racial hierarchies.[13]

Although white superiority was never questioned, the relative positions of American Indian and African American people were sometimes in flux. Some argued that, unlike people of African descent held in slavery, Indians had resisted and were rapidly "receding" as a result. Such self-serving logic concluded that since blacks had allowed themselves to be enslaved, they would survive but remain in a state of permanent inferiority to the whites who had enslaved them. Meanwhile, the Indians who had resisted enslavement (and by extension, civilization) were doomed to extinction.[14]

As a consequence, by midcentury, a belief in the eventual and inevitable disappearance of indigenous peoples had pervaded many corners of American thought. The Indian Removal Act (1830) itself referenced such thinking when it guaranteed western lands to the expelled tribes only until they should "become extinct," at which time these lands would once more revert to the United States. In the South, where events like the Creek and Seminole Wars provided ample opportunity for whites to impugn their Native neighbors as bloodthirsty savages, the idea that Indians could be civilized rapidly lost ground to the American school of ethnology that provided "scientific" evidence to support white supremacy. Even committed philanthropists and well-intentioned reformers outside the South, such as those northern activists who campaigned against Indian removal, increasingly seemed to agree that efforts to intervene in the "plight" of the Indians were just forestalling their unavoidable extinction.

The period immediately following the mass expulsion of indigenous peoples from their eastern homelands inaugurated another turning point in thinking about Native North Americans. By the 1840s, with many eastern American Indians believed to be extinct or safely segregated in western lands, images of Indianness were being used to sell everything from hair tonic to tobacco. In addition to their ubiquity in advertising, Indian characters "skulked in and out" of popular drama, comedy, and fiction. Even when Native people graced stages and pulpits across the country and across the Atlantic as dancers, orators, and missionaries, they were often regarded as the last of their race.[15] Nostalgic portraits of American Indians appeared in traveling shows, folio pages, and public buildings. Native peoples were perceived to be literally fading away, receding into both the western territories and the pages of history. As their physical presence in the East diminished, images of American Indians gained increasing prominence in the art, letters, theater, and iconography of the United States.[16]

In other words, the widespread belief that Native American people were a vanishing race generated an explosion of Indian representations. Romantic writers and artists who regarded American Indians as people of the past fixated on traits of "Indian character" that, like cranial size and skin color, were increasingly believed to be unchangeable. They produced stories, novels, poems, dramas, paintings, and sculpture that attributed to Native people a set of characteristics that persist in some stereotypes to this day, such as stoicism, mysticism, innocence, and pride. Authors and playwrights capitalized on Native themes, emphasizing melodrama, romance, and heroic but doomed figures like Pocahontas, Metamora, and Uncas. Particularly in the northeastern United States, American Indians were considered "sufficiently remote" from everyday life to be profitably exotic and potentially sympathetic figures.[17]

Native people themselves also worked to capitalize on (and in turn helped to shape) some of these ideas. Indigenous missionaries and activists like Peter Jones and his protégé George Copway, as well as many less famous figures, employed the trope of "the poor Indians" to solicit political and financial support for their tribes or themselves, publishing autobiographies and often appearing on stage in their Native garb as curious living remnants. Others, like dancer, medicine man, and author Maungwudaus, dispensed with the pretense of missionary zeal and marketed Indianness to audiences eager to consume it, both at home and abroad.[18] In launching their career as professional Indians, Okah Tubbee and Laah Ceil drew on the examples of these and other Native entrepreneurs who were active participants in shaping ideas about nineteenth-century Indianness.

• • •

Real Native Genius examines the lives and careers of Okah Tubbee and Laah Ceil to better understand the role that Indianness played within antebellum culture in the United States (and to a lesser degree, Canada). I argue that ideas about American Indians were deeply enmeshed with social and cultural forces, including the regimes of chattel slavery and settler colonialism, and played a powerful role in the expression of racial, gender, sexual, class, and religious identities. Though the question I am most frequently asked relates to my subjects' "real" selves, I have tried not to get bogged down in questions of authenticity that emphasize the genuine or spurious nature of individual claims to indigeneity. Instead, I am interested in analyzing how Indianness, as a complex of ideas and practices, was understood and performed by Native and non-Native people during a period of rapid social and economic transformation.[19] The lives of Okah Tubbee and Laah Ceil provide a useful window on how categories of identity were lived and experienced in the mid-nineteenth century and the role that ideas about American Indians have played within and across these categories. Although their experiences may seem exceptional or even bizarre—and in some ways, they certainly were—the ubiquity of Indianness in such a wide variety of contexts suggests its centrality to antebellum American culture in ways not heretofore fully considered.

Scholars have written a great deal on the figure of the Indian in American art and letters. Such studies have frequently focused on the practice of "playing Indian," a phenomenon wherein primarily non-Native people imagine, create, and don Indian costumes and engage in real or imagined Indian activities.[20] With a few notable exceptions, these analyses tend to focus on white men who have played Indian for a variety of social, cultural, and political reasons, from the Sons of Liberty at Boston Harbor to the Boy Scouts, hobbyists, and genealogists of our own time.[21] Because they do not conform to our expectations about who plays Indian and why, Okah Tubbee and Laah Ceil complicate academic narratives about the performative uses of Indianness, even as their pretensions underscore the centrality of "the Indian" in shaping American identities.

In contrast to the scholarly emphasis on playing Indian as primarily the pastime of white men, the practice of passing has been theorized almost exclusively in relation to the African diaspora and remains closely linked with regimes of slavery.[22] In antebellum usages, "passing" implied upward movement within a hierarchy; it was a form of imposture in which one could theoretically transcend a particular identity in order to access privileges reserved for another group. In its most common nineteenth-century usage, passing denoted a slave of African descent attempting to be accepted as white or free. The very word "pass" could signify both the literal passes that permitted some slaves and free blacks the freedom of travel and the practice of pretending to be free (or white).

Despite the utility of playing and passing as scholarly tools for understanding antebellum identity practices, I have applied them to Okah Tubbee and Laah Ceil infrequently, hesitantly, and cautiously. Playing Indian has mostly been deployed to describe low-stakes, low-risk behavior, like that of privileged white men who don Indian costumes to enact fantasies about political power or ancient history. Passing, on the other hand, is almost always seen as indicative of high-stakes, high-risk behavior in which discovery could lead to ostracism, imprisonment, or death. One might argue that although Warner McCary was already free when he assumed an Indian persona, he nevertheless did so to escape the constraints of the racial identity that had been imposed upon him and to access real or perceived benefits associated with "Indianness." In that sense, his actions might be regarded as passing according to its traditional definition. But uses of the term "passing" as it applies to race rarely allow for pleasure and enjoyment, two apparent aspects of Okah Tubbee's Indian performance.

The question of Laah Ceil's Indianness is equally complicated. For example, we might describe her behavior of "Injun" tongue-speaking among the early Mormons as playing Indian. But in her later life, it would be more appropriate to say that she sometimes passed as Indian in order to disguise religious beliefs for which she had been persecuted and to deflect dangerous attention away from her interracial marriage, thus raising the stakes. And while she also earned an income from the practice, in both circumstances, adopting an Indian persona may also have satisfied less material needs, enabling her to fulfill personal ambitions for success, influence, and power. And as with her husband, we might reason that she too derived some pleasure or enjoyment from being regarded as Indian.

Rather than uncritically redeploying these terms, I see playing Indian and passing as Indian as practices along a broad spectrum of identity performance. Such an approach does not foreclose the possibility that some individuals were engaged in both practices simultaneously, as I believe Okah Tubbee and Laah Ceil sometimes were. In fact, the paradox of antebellum beliefs about the fluidity and fixity of identity makes such layering particularly likely.

· · ·

Having provided some tantalizing details, it is perhaps useful at this point to briefly map the narrative. Chapter 1 focuses on understanding Warner McCary's desire to escape Natchez and his own painful past by reinventing himself. It explores the brickyards and barbershops of the Mississippi River port and sketches the city's complex cultural milieu—its reliance on chattel slavery, its briefly flourishing free black community, its connections to other ports, its rich indigenous life and history, and its varied cultural venues. In this section, I show that young McCary's decision to represent himself as an Indian following his manumission and departure from Natchez must be evaluated not only in the context of slavery, but also with an understanding of the influence of Native people and affairs on life in the South, including the context of Indian removal.

Chapter 2 doubles back in time to explore the early life of Lucy Stanton, her role within early Mormonism, her time as a religious refugee during the 1830s and 1840s, and her own background as a performer. Through her experiences, we see the unique place of Indians within Latter-day Saint theology and the virulent anti-Mormonism that swept the nation during the era of Indian removal. Stanton's decision to remake herself as an Indian was rooted in both her experience of early Mormon fervor and the persecution she suffered because of it.

By the time Lucy Stanton and William McCary married in 1846, she was the divorced mother of three children, and he was already perform-ing an Indian identity. They soon crafted their own prophetic movement modeled on Mormon practices, but which also incorporated distinct ideas about American Indians. Chapter 3 thus opens in Cincinnati, where the "big burley, half Indian, half negro" and his "Delaware" wife led about sixty followers in a new religious sect.[23] Within a year, they were with the main body of Mormons settled uneasily among Native peoples at Winter Quar-ters in present-day Nebraska as they prepared for the journey further west. While McCary's identity as an Indian was unevenly received, charges of spiritual and sexual indecency imbricated with racial concerns were responsible for his subsequent ouster from the Mormon community. Although the Winter Quarters episode may have had lasting significance for policies of racial exclusion within the Mormon Church, it also had a transformative impact on the pair's later enactments of Indianness.

Chapter 4 charts the rise and fall of the McCarys' fortunes from 1847–50, as they transitioned from minor sectarian leaders to celebrated Indian performers, but then suffered a series of personal and financial setbacks. Taking the stage in eastern cities, the pair now performed as a Choctaw flutist "torn from his tribe when a boy" and his eloquent Indian wife, giv-ing wildly popular concerts with oratorical interludes.[24] Laah Ceil played an ever-growing role in shaping their Indian show, including the produc-tion of the first edition of their autobiography, *A Thrilling Sketch of the Life of the Distinguished Chief Okah Tubbee Alias, Wm. Chubbee, Son of the Head Chief, Mosholeh Tubbee, of the Choctaw Nation of Indians*, pub-lished in 1848.[25] Although they had become famous in the East, their for-tunes shifted when they traveled west for the birth of their son Mosholeh and faced theft and ostracism. These hardships motivated the Tubbees to again return to the East, leaving Laah Ceil's older children behind, and to remake themselves as purveyors of "real Indian medicine."[26]

As they traveled through the Ohio valley in 1850, Dr. Okah Tubbee and his wife stopped to treat patients and occasionally took the stage. But as chapter 5 explains, it was not a fortuitous time to be a person of indeterminate race traveling across the United States. This section contextualizes their downfall within tightening racial ideologies exemplified in the Fugitive Slave Act passed in September 1850, which codified the immobility of slaves and threatened free people of color with kidnapping. Like many others endangered by the new law, the Tubbees headed for Canada, but fear of racial persecution was only part of the reason they fled the United States. Okah Tubbee's racial claims were publicly contested in this era, and his brief and apparently bigamous marriage to Sarah Marlett intensified the scrutiny. Meanwhile, accusations about medical malpractice threatened the Tubbees' new livelihood as Indian doctors in Toronto. This chapter considers the last edition of the autobiography (1852) as a defensive effort to counter both a decline in the utility of their Indian guise and the spate of bad publicity. Shortly thereafter, records relating to Okah Tubbee evaporate; he simply disappears.

With her husband gone and no mention made of her young son, Laah Ceil made her way back to western New York. There she established a new career as "Madame Laahceil, Indian doctress" and provided services that included illegal abortion. Chapter 6 considers her subsequent arrest, trial, and incarceration for manslaughter in the context of changes in the American medical profession that accompanied the Civil War era, alongside shifts in popular ideas about Indianness. This final chapter examines how and why she maintained an Indian identity even in her husband's absence and why she finally let it go. The narrative concludes in Utah, where she died in 1878.

Not all questions about Okah Tubbee and Laah Ceil can be satisfactorily answered. And it is fitting that some mystery remains. They went to great lengths to shroud, to disguise, or to alter the circumstances of their lives, and some of their efforts remain successful to this day. But these uncertainties, although frustrating to the reader and maddening to the historian, must endure. Rather than a comprehensive biographical study of the pair, this book considers their lives as a way to explore antebellum notions of identity that coalesced around ideas about American Indians. To do so, it engages many of the important concerns of the period—the socioeconomic roots of religious awakening, the indeterminacy of race and gender as lived categories, the anxieties of physical and social mobility, and the importance of entertainment for the burgeoning middle class—linking them explicitly to popular cultural notions of Indianness, sometimes authored by Native people themselves.

. . .

Finally, a word on titles and names. Near the end of his stage career, an advertisement for one of Okah Tubbee's concerts advised readers, "No one who admires real native genius should lose this only opportunity of seeing and listening to the great Indian performer."[27] The writer used "real native genius" to signal a quality as opposed to a person. It referenced the antebellum obsession with defining a *national* artistic tradition worthy of keeping company with the ancient history, arts, and letters of Europe. Within literary circles, the effort to elevate "real native genius" frequently hinged on Indian themes as quintessentially American, earning real and imagined Native peoples a central place in American cultural nationalism.[28]

Newspaper readers would also have understood that the phrase was meant to refer to Okah Tubbee himself, noticing the play on words—the claim that the "great Indian performer" was not only a talented *American* virtuoso, comparable to any from the Old World, but that he was also, in fact, a "real native," meaning a genuine American Indian. That the word "native" still functions in both registers today, meaning "not foreign" in the sense of "nativist" political discourse, for example, and meaning indigenous to North America, is evidence of the continuing (though not unproblematic) centrality of ideas about Indians to notions of Americanness.

Although the phrase "real native genius" was not directly used to describe Laah Ceil, she, too, participated in and helped to shape American notions of Indianness, in her faith, in her marriage, and in her career. Like her husband, her performances of Indian personae changed over time in ways that were certainly ingenious and remarkably effective, even convincing many modern scholars that she was the Indian she claimed to be.[29]

Laah Ceil and Okah Tubbee's varied performances of Indianness worked in multiple, contradictory, and sometimes confusing ways, disturbing the ideas of "real" and "native." And in displaying such genius, were they not also making a claim to be quintessentially American?

Over the course of their lives, both before and after they were engaged in the business of nineteenth-century Indianness, the two people at the center of this work used a wide array of names. I do not know what they called themselves or each other in private. Therefore, throughout the book, I refer to my subjects by the names they used publicly (or those that were used to describe them) during the period under discussion. To help ease the reader's confusion, I signal the first use of each new name in the narrative. When referring specifically to passages from the autobiography and when discussing broad swaths of time, I use Okah Tubbee and Laah Ceil over other aliases for the sake of clarity and because these are the names that they seem to have chosen to represent themselves most often.

A list of their various monikers in more or less chronological order of their use:

given name: Warner McCary	*given name: Lucile Celesta Stanton*
James Carey	Lucy Stanton
William Carey	Lucy Bassett
William McCary (McCarey)	Luceil Bsuba
Andrew Carey	Laah Ceil Manatoi Elaah
William Chubbee	Laah Ceil Manatoi Elaah Tubbee
William McChubby	Laah Ceil
Okah Chubee	Lucy Okah Tubbee
Okah Tubbee	Adelaide Okah Tubbee
Dr. Okah Tubbee	Madame Laahceil
Dr. O.K.	Celeste La Salle
Wah-bah Goosh	Lucy Stanton Bassett

CHAPTER ONE

Coming of Age in Mississippi

· ·

The Life and Times of Warner McCary

Antebellum Natchez was a bustling city perched "on a most beautiful eminence" overlooking the Mississippi River. It had long been a hub of social, cultural, and economic exchange for southeastern Indians and newcomers from Europe and Africa, and in the first decade of the nineteenth century, the lively port was experiencing unprecedented growth. Most days, the water throbbed with boats almost a mile down the riverbank. In 1808, travel writer Christian Schulz estimated that there were about three hundred houses and nearly three thousand inhabitants, "including all colours." His impressions of the city—the swagger of the wealthy planters, the brawls between sailors over a "Choctaw lady," and the "misery and wretchedness" of the enslaved—suggest a vibrant but volatile atmosphere. The gentlemen of Natchez, Schulz surmised, "pass their time in the pursuit of three things: all make love; most of them play; and a few make money. With Religion they have nothing to do."[1]

Although Schulz overestimated the Natchez population—it was closer to 1,700 than 3,000 in 1810—his perceptions of the bustling port captured the city's economic and cultural vitality.[2] It was a place of opportunity, and though the population grew relatively slowly compared to other cities on the Mississippi River, it was home to an incredibly diverse array of people. In addition to the emergent American planter elite, Natchez and the surrounding area known as the Natchez district were inhabited by a variety of French, Spanish, and English immigrants and their descendants, Choctaws and other Native southerners, artisans and merchants from the eastern United States, a significant number of free blacks, and a large population of enslaved people.[3] Pennsylvania cabinetmaker James McCary was among the half million eastern migrants who entered the Mississippi Territory in the early years of the nineteenth century, seeking a new life and new possibilities.[4] He established himself by purchasing several slaves, at least one of whom would bear his children.[5] Just a few years later, a child named Warner would be thrust unceremoniously into this milieu. The difficulty of the enslaved child's early life would both inspire and equip him to remake himself as a street performer, militia fifer, and ultimately, an Indian.

. . .

Though its great waters were an undeniable fact of life, the Mississippi River was not a major commercial route until the 1790s. The first European colonists to settle the lower river valley were French, and they alternately traded with and abused the Natchez Indians in whose ancestral lands they insinuated themselves. After years of French insults and encroachments, the Natchez organized a surprise attack in 1729, but were ultimately defeated and scattered by combined Choctaw and French forces, who then took their land and their name for the town. Like many of the French colonial settlements in the southern part of North America, the frontier hamlet of Natchez limped along pitifully for much of the eighteenth century, often subject to the wishes and dictates of powerful neighboring Indian nations. At the conclusion of the French and Indian War in 1763, it was among the possessions that passed from French to British control, if only on paper, and then into Spanish hands in 1779. In the Treaty of San Lorenzo (1795), Spain ceded the territory that included Natchez and most of the remaining Choctaw homelands to the United States, without bothering to involve the Choctaws in negotiations. By 1798, Natchez was the capital of the newly organized Mississippi Territory, and by the time of the Louisiana Purchase in 1803, it had developed into an important stop on the Natchez Trace, an overland route connecting Nashville to New Orleans.

For much of the colonial period, the commercial potential of the region was hampered by European imperial competition intertwined with the determined efforts of Native people to maintain control of their homelands. But just before and after the establishment of the Mississippi Territory, the city experienced a mercantile transformation. To the existing trade in furs, livestock, timber, and indigo, new planters and merchants added incredible quantities of cotton and tobacco. As Natchez grew, it became an important trade depot between Ohio valley ports and the Gulf of Mexico, importing flour, whiskey, and slaves from upriver and sending agricultural products and naval stores downriver to New Orleans and

FIGURE 1 Antebellum Natchez. Painted by Henry Lewis during a tour of the
Mississippi River in the mid-1840s, this scene captures the bustle of the waterfront,
the city of Natchez sitting high up on the bluffs, and Natchez-under-the-Hill down
below. The image appears in Lewis's *Das illustrirte Mississippithal*, facing
page 392. (Courtesy Yale Collection of Western Americana, Beinecke Rare Book
and Manuscript Library)

beyond.[6] Until the era of steam navigation, most goods were moved down-
stream on flatboats that were destroyed upon reaching their final destination, their motley crews of Kentucky, Ohio, and Métis sailors returning
home on foot or by sea.[7] (See Fig. 1.) Schulz observed, "From the brow of
the hills before mentioned, you discover small fleets arriving daily, which
keep up the hurry and bustle on the flats or Levee below; while at the same
time you see detachments continually dropping off for New-Orleans, and
the slaves breaking up the hulks of those that have discharged their car-
goes, in order to make room for the new comers."[8] Nearly twenty years later,
the port was no less busy. In 1824, traveler Adam Hodgson remarked that
the landing at Natchez was perpetually "crowded with Kentucky boats,
and an odd miscellaneous population."[9]

During the intervening years between Schulz's and Hodgson's sojourns
in Natchez, the city had experienced a profound transformation specifically in the realm of agricultural commerce. Early successes in cotton cultivation inspired emigrants who arrived from the East, their numbers

growing steadily as new travel routes were opened through Indian lands.[10] Newcomers who didn't already own slaves generally aspired to acquire some and typically sought a parcel of the fertile land in the environs of Adams County. But unless they were extravagantly wealthy, the hopeful were often disappointed and forced to settle for smaller tracts in disputed areas, where they squatted in hopes that their "improvements" would overrule the need for legal purchase or Indian cession.

Migrants' hopes notwithstanding, the indigenous character of the place was undeniable. Still strewn with the massive earthworks erected by its earlier Mississippian inhabitants, the country showed "signs of having formerly cherished a population far exceeding any thing which has been known in our time," Schulz noted.[11] For example, Emerald Mound, situated just ten miles outside of town, was built by the ancestors of the Natchez Indians and is among the largest surviving mounds in all of North America. In addition to these topographical reminders of Native inhabitance, the city of Natchez itself had been the historic site of the Grand Village of the Natchez people from the late seventeenth century until 1730. Over the subsequent century, Native history would still loom romantically large in local memory.[12]

Situated along the western boundary of Choctaw territory, the Natchez district was a richly diverse borderland region where Indian, African, and European peoples shaped a social and cultural landscape as complex as any in the Atlantic world.[13] Choctaw stories, informed by the histories of other indigenous people with whom they fought, collaborated, or merged, narrated this place into being, and Native paths crisscrossed the land long before any Europeans had thought to blaze their own trails.[14]

The area's long history of ethnic intermixture was a matter of fact for inhabitants, but fascinating for outside observers. It became a key theme in popular literary representations of the place, from François-Rene de Chateaubriand's romance *Atalá* (1801) to the racially indeterminate cotton pickers of William Gilmore Simms's short story "Oakatibbee, or The Choctaw Sampson" (1845), which may have later inspired the name "Okah Tubbee."[15] This multicultural environment—a place where "Americans, Africans, and Europeans resisted one another, borrowed from one another, or simply found cultural resonances among one another"—not only inspired Chateaubriand, Simms, and much later, William Faulkner, but also shaped the world of the child Warner McCary who was born about 1810. Although it is impossible to say what precise set of circumstances attended his conception and birth, it took place somewhere in this sultry river valley, where sexual relationships across racial and cultural boundaries were more common than not.[16]

When James McCary died in Natchez in 1813, his will bore evidence of just such a complicated relationship. It stipulated that four of his slaves, Sally, Frances (or Franky), and "the children of the said Franky, that is to say one called Bob [Robert], and the other called Kitty," be granted "their freedome forever." Bob (age 6) and Kitty (4) were to be educated and "brought up in . . . the principles and practice of true religion and morality." But "the youngest child of Franky," a three-year-old boy "called Warner," was to remain enslaved, his "labor and Services, and the proceeds of the same shall be solely for the use and benefit of the aforesaid Bob and Kitty, the children of Franky, Share and Share alike."[17]

Although it may at first seem capricious, McCary's decision to free some of his slaves but not others was not terribly unusual. As one historian notes, "Slaveholders saw no contradiction in doling out liberty with one hand and tightening the chains of bondage with the other."[18] James McCary died a bachelor, but wished to provide for his illegitimate children by bequeathing them wealth in the form of real estate, cash, and slaves, including their apparent half-brother. The young man known as Warner McCary would later describe his "first recollections" of childhood as "scenes of sorrow," and above all else, it was perhaps the incredible injustice of his being kept a slave and made to serve his own siblings that led the young man to imagine a new family for himself, a new life, and ultimately, a new identity.[19]

According to Okah Tubbee's later autobiography, "Mosholeh Chubbee . . . a Chief of the Choctaws, who inhabited a scope of country on the Yazoo River, about one hundred miles west of the Mississippi River" was his father. Tubbee claimed to have been stolen from the Choctaws at a very young age.[20] (See Fig. 2.) Although clearly intended to establish Okah Tubbee's paternal ancestry, the autobiography's claims on this point are grossly imprecise. "Mosholeh Chubbee" apparently meant Mushulatubbee, a Choctaw chief of the eastern division and noted cattleman, a leader in the tribe's early national embrace of stock-raising.[21] And although the Choctaws did historically inhabit the Yazoo River region in present-day northern Mississippi, it runs to the east of the Mississippi River joining its waters near Vicksburg. Before Indian removal, some Choctaws lived west of the Mississippi River, having agreed to settle in the Arkansas territory in the Treaty of Doak's Stand (1820), but no Yazoo River flows there.[22] The rest of the "Biography" is similarly interwoven with fact and fiction, including a purported covenant between the Iroquois Six Nations

FIGURE 2 Mushulatubbee. Painted by George Catlin in Arkansas following
Choctaw removal, this portrait captures the famous leader's distinctive appearance
and characteristic dress, both of which inspired Okah Tubbee's self-fashioning.
Mó-sho-la-túb-bee, He Who Puts Out and Kills, Chief of the Tribe, 1834.
(Courtesy Smithsonian American Art Museum, Gift of Mrs. Joseph Harrison Jr.)

and the Choctaws under "Chief Chubbee," who makes a dying request to the "Oyataw" nation to find his long-lost son.

Although Tubbee confessed in his later autobiography to having an "imperfect recollection" of his Indian father, he nevertheless described him thus: "a very large man, with dark, red skin . . . his head was adorned with the feathers of a most beautiful plumage." He was supposed to bear "a strong personal resemblance to his father, except the father was taller and heavy built," the "Chubbee" in his name indicating that the chief was "big and fat." But the youth was forced to acknowledge a "new father, or a man who took" him to a new home in Natchez. He soon determined that this white man was not his "own father, neither in appearance nor in action" and began to understand that he "could have but one father." Faced with a family he repudiated, the enslaved youth sought solace in dim memories and comfortable fictions.[23]

Although it is possible that Warner McCary's real father was Choctaw, it is less likely that his father was *the* Mushulatubbee. It stands to reason that a man of such prominence would have complained, petitioned, or at least alerted someone that his cherished young son had been kidnapped.[24] It is also possible that Warner was the child of an enslaved woman and an unknown Choctaw man. Another possibility is that he might have once belonged to Mushulatubbee or another Choctaw slave owner. The eastern district chief had more slaves than most other Choctaws, and observers asserted that by the early national period, enslaved people in the Choctaw nation tended to be mostly of African descent, having been purchased or stolen from slaveholding American neighbors. But there is little certainty about any one bondsperson's particular lineage because some of the slaves imported into Choctaw territory had come more or less directly from Africa, whereas others were brought from the Upper South or West Indies.[25] And, like their American counterparts, Choctaw masters were sometimes both owner and father to their slaves. Whether Warner was a missing child, stolen property, or something in between, there is still no evidence that Mushulatubbee ever looked for the boy. Early southern writer Gideon Lincecum lived near the Choctaw chief during the 1820s and recalled that, in addition to his slaves, the chief had two wives (one fair and one not) and a house full of children, all of whom "seemed to be very happy."[26]

Acknowledging the possibility of Choctaw beginnings does not necessarily clarify the question of Okah Tubbee's origins. But it is an important reminder of the role of slavery in the colonization of the American South, intertwining the lives and fates of Native, European, and African-descended people.[27] Local whites reportedly confessed that "it was not unreasonable" to think that Warner was an Indian child kidnapped into slavery and "asserted they had heard of such circumstances. . . . It was easily done, where there was such a diversity of color as there is in the South."[28] Indian captivity narratives helped keep such possibilities alive in local and national imaginations. One popular story told the tale of John Marrant, a free black evangelist taken captive by the Cherokees. He became so immersed in their customs that he was unrecognizable to his friends and family. Like others, Marrant's narrative had a strong religious theme, but it also emphasized his ability to seemingly *become* Cherokee through language acquisition and costuming.[29] Despite these intriguing possibilities, however, legal records from Adams County suggest less exceptional circumstances surrounding Warner McCary's childhood.[30]

According to James McCary's 1813 will, Warner was the youngest child of Franky, a "negro girl" in Natchez. McCary stipulated that "Franky, and her children, Bob, and Kitty" be sent to Pennsylvania, "there to be manumitted agreeably to the laws of that State." As noted, Warner McCary was to remain a slave for all his life, with his labor profiting his putative half-siblings.[31] Although the later autobiography focused on the question of his father, the question of his mother's identity would have been more important for the purpose of determining not only his origins, but also his status as enslaved or free.

In order to distance himself from Franky McCary, Tubbee later referred to her in the autobiography as simply "the slave woman." He further repudiated his connection to her by saying she was his "unnatural mother," a phrase historically applied to women who sought abortions, committed infanticide, or were otherwise deemed unfit for motherhood because of their neglectful or malicious temperaments.[32] By invoking this term, the autobiography participated in the representation of enslaved women as inherently poor mothers, being less susceptible to the "natural" maternal feelings believed to be common among white women.[33] The phrase underscored the absence of any familial link between Franky and Warner, a truth allegedly revealed to him by a "black woman" when he was about ten years old. According to the autobiography, she told him she was his "first black mamma" (at which he thought, "one black mamma was too many and . . . wished to be off"), and that she knew his real identity, having been present when he was brought from the Choctaws.[34]

Franky McCary's harsh treatment of young Warner, from daily humiliations to brutal beatings, was also offered as proof that she was not his real mother. For instance, Franky was not content to whip him for disobedience; the boy's very despondency incurred her wrath. He recalled that when "she found my pillow wet with tears, she whipped me for that." But such incidents also purported to reveal key information about his identity. He said, "This woman when angry called me different names . . . which, besides her evil treatment, gave me every reason to believe she was not my mother." In one angry outburst, Tubbee claimed she cursed his very presence and said "she wished she had never seen me or the man who had brought me there," suggesting that she was either not his mother or wished she weren't. In yet another scene, he alleged that Franky forgot herself, saying that he was untameable and suggesting that "this was the way Indians and all wild savages lived . . . that the white people could not make as much service of them, as they could of the blacks" and that "what is bred in the bone will be in the marrow."[35] Whether or not they were true, these recollections served to communicate Franky's unfitness for motherhood by capitalizing on the degradation of slave mothers as a whole. They also reiterated popular beliefs about race and biology, reinscribing the idea that although Indians were inherently (that is, biologically) unsuited to slavery, it was in fact the natural condition of African-descended peoples, and also implying that such realities were entirely unchangeable, having been "bred in the bone."

The autobiography's second edition elaborated further on Franky and Warner's dysfunctional relationship in a new section titled "Cruel treatment of the Colored woman in whose hands I had been placed by her master," a description that further repudiated Franky's maternal skills, while underscoring her status as a former slave.[36] In this chapter, Tubbee referred to her as the "slave woman who had the management" of a white man's house, "as well as her two older children, a boy and a girl." He explained, "She was very fond of them, but was never even kind to me, yet they obliged me to call her mother."[37] And it is certainly possible that Franky was not, in fact, Warner McCary's mother. Indeed, official records from Adams County offer no evidence that would contradict his assertion; aside from the brief reference in James McCary's will ("the youngest child of Franky, called Warner"), he is never referred to as her child elsewhere. By contrast, in the same document there were nine direct references to Bob or Kitty McCary as "the children of Franky," who were to be manumitted, clothed, financed, educated, and instructed in proper morals.

Young Warner, like Bob and Kitty, could have been Franky's child by James McCary, a possibility that would make McCary's manumission of the latter and not the former more difficult to understand. When he died, he left no wife and legitimate children, bequeathing his entire to estate to a handful of friends, their children, including other free blacks, and to Bob and Kitty McCary, implicitly acknowledging his paternity.[38] Alternatively, Warner could have been Franky's child by another man, and it is tempting to believe that James McCary's decision was intended to punish her for infidelity or dalliance. But she was otherwise well provided for in the will, and it is difficult to discern anything much about their relationship.[39] In other words, acknowledging that Bob and Kitty were born from a liaison between James and Franky McCary does not clarify whether or not their sexual relationship was consensual or ongoing, nor does it shed light on Warner McCary's relationship to either of them.

As noted, despite the autobiography's emphasis on the identity of Tubbee's father, establishing his mother's status was essential. As early as the 1660s, colonial legal codes prescribed that the condition of the mother (slave or free) determined the condition of the child, a legal principle known as *partus sequitur ventrum*, and subsequent laws and policies served to affirm the principle.[40] This concept was widely acknowledged in antebellum society and invoked in the autobiography itself.

On one occasion, a gentlemanly visitor informed young Warner that his mother was in fact a slave. He told the child that his father was "probably a white man," but since he never came forward, the child was "consequently given over as a slave to [Franky's] children."[41] In addition to obscuring the way women's sexual choices were policed within the regime of chattel slavery, emphasizing paternity in the memoir also confused the nature of southeastern Indian kinship that historically operated according to the logic of matriliny and clan, not patriliny and blood.[42] Despite his later claims about his race and status, the available evidence indicates that people of Natchez regarded Warner McCary as a mulatto slave.

What distinguished him most clearly from his half-siblings was not his race, but their freedom. Speaking of Bob and Kitty McCary many years later, Okah Tubbee related, "I was always made to serve the two children, though many times I had to be whipped into obedience." Emphasizing the injustice of his situation, he elaborated that Franky McCary's "children were well dressed and neat; I was not only in rags, but many times my proud heart seemed crushed within me, and my cheek crimsoned with shame because of their filthy condition."[43] He was compelled to go naked in order to wash his one pair of clothes, all while he was still a child "too young to work." These disparities highlighted the poverty and shame

associated with his bondage, but also provided an opportunity to emphasize his latent biological "Indian traits," suggested here by his "proud heart"
and his skin color, light enough to blush when embarrassed.[44]

The McCary family was enmeshed in a sort of racial caste system that
had developed in Natchez and other urban locales in the Lower South,
mirroring a similar hierarchy in parts of Latin America and the West
Indies. Whites, free blacks, and slaves each occupied distinct places in the
social and economic hierarchy of the Gulf South, despite the fact that skin
color and genealogy often varied only slightly between the three groups.
As one scholar described it, ties of "blood, friendship, or, in the case of
guardianships, the law" provided free blacks with status denied to enslaved people of color.[45] As the slave of free blacks, to whom he was ostensibly related, Warner McCary thus lived painfully within sight of the
advantages denied him.

Aside from freedom itself, there were only a few material differences
between the privileges afforded free blacks versus slaves in Natchez and
the surrounding county, but they were significant. Neither group could
vote in elections or officially serve in the militia. But free blacks could own
property, whereas slaves could not. Those who did own property, like the
McCarys, were frequently born from relationships between slaveholders
and enslaved women. They tried to increase and protect their property
whenever possible, but after Mississippi statehood in 1817, their ability to
secure and maintain wealth of any kind was increasingly threatened by
restrictive laws across the South. Protecting their assets meant crafting
mutually beneficial relationships with well-positioned members of Natchez white society, men (and sometimes women) who could vouch for their
good behavior before courts, provide testimonials and introductions, and
sometimes secure credit on their behalf.[46]

All of the McCary children relied on their relationship to local whites,
but their differing legal statuses predetermined their success. Bob and
Kitty McCary were not only manumitted but also provided with property
that would help sustain them. James McCary left real estate to each of
them (though Bob's was more valuable than Kitty's), and he made provisions for their education and upbringing, appointing his trusted friend and
executor, Walter G. Irvine, to be their legal guardian. When he came of age,
Bob McCary was to receive one thousand dollars and the children were
to share the remaining assets after estate debts were paid. Unlike manumitted slaves in other parts of the region, free blacks in the cities of the
Lower South were more likely to be favored with such provisions because

they were often the acknowledged or semi-acknowledged children of their owners.[47] By providing for them in his will, James McCary tried to secure his children's future and to protect them from the crushing poverty to which freedom without property would have otherwise consigned them.[48]

Legal and financial records from Adams County suggest that most of McCary's wishes were followed. Indeed, estate receipts tell a tale of the divergent paths that lay before Bob and Kitty McCary on the one hand and "Warner, youngest child of Franky," on the other. Under Irvine's direction and in accordance with the will, the estate paid for the older pair to board at various places in town and expended considerable sums for clothing, medical care, and schooling.[49] But receipts relating to Warner McCary's youth paint a different picture.

Although young Warner was tutored for one month and six days in 1823 (interestingly, six days more than Kitty), there are no other documents to suggest he received formal educational instruction, or at least, not at the expense of the McCary estate.[50] Receipts for his room and board show that when he lived with Franky, she was paid to "keep" him, though she often housed Bob as well. But other financial documents relating to his youth suggest the kinds of difficulties he faced. While Bob and Kitty were outfitted in fine Irish linen, silk, and shoes, Warner's clothing is never mentioned, suggesting that he did not exaggerate his poor attire.[51] Bob's washing was done by Franky or other women in town, and both he and Kitty were provided with pocket money, but Warner was not.[52]

Other documents shed further light on Warner McCary's tumultuous youth. On one occasion, the estate had to pay restitution to a local slave owner, including doctor's fees, for an assault on Lucian Adams, an enslaved teen whose face fifteen-year-old McCary had smashed with a brick—an episode that he recounted in the autobiography, claiming it resulted from the other boy having called him "nigger."[53] He used the incident to emphasize how he was misrecognized and therefore mistreated in Natchez. He insisted that his true identity was deeply rooted in his blood—his Indian blood—such that he could not control his impulse to show it, saying, "When this lad thus said, yonder comes the nigger, all my Indian nature was aroused, and my very blood boiled in every vein, and my feelings were so intense that I called upon the Great Spirit, and conjured Heaven and earth to know where I originated."[54] As painful as it must have been, at least so far as the rest of Natchez was concerned, he originated from the McCary family.[55] But as the slave of free blacks, he was little better off than if his owners had been white and in some ways much worse.

As the diary of free black entrepreneur William Johnson (who also happened to be Bob McCary's best friend) reveals, free blacks in Natchez initially experienced a wide variety of economic and social conditions. There was an identifiable "aristocracy," that included the Johnsons, the McCarys, and a handful of other notable families, most of whom owed their property to the legacies of white men and all of whom owned slaves.[56] If Johnson can serve as an example (and the dearth of available writings from Mississippi free blacks fairly requires it), then it is reasonable to assume that many slaves of free blacks were assigned to the same sorts of tasks and subject to the same sort of treatment they might have encountered under white owners.[57] Indeed, as one historian put it, "The degradation of slave life in the Lower South elevated the [position of] free" blacks.[58]

Although the young enslaved boy sometimes accompanied employers like lawyer Joseph Davis (brother of Jefferson Davis) to outlying plantations, the city of Natchez itself was where Warner McCary spent most of his childhood.[59] He occasionally apprenticed in trades, but also "did errands" and "hired out to doctors and lawyers to sweep their offices, &c."[60] These odd jobs provided him with both individual mobility and vital social connections, liberating him from the daily control of "the colored woman" and allowing him to establish important relationships with leading white men of the town, the so-called "Natchez Nabobs." This form of networking would continue to have an impact on his life long after he left Natchez.[61] Although his "industrious habits and talents" were reportedly admired by local elites, when he glimpsed the "highest circles of society," it must also have underscored the distinctions that persisted between enslaved and free. The ability to accumulate property was something his white employers shared with his free black relatives, which was made painfully clear to him throughout his childhood. Indeed, according to the autobiography, it was his inability to possess anything of his own that inspired him to begin performing.

As a child, Warner McCary learned that he could please white passersby with his animal imitations, "such as the mewing of a cat, the barking, howling, and growling of a dog, &c." He soon began to practice ventriloquy for the amusement of the locals, but Franky McCary took whatever small change he earned and spent it on her children. To protect his income, he stashed money wherever he could. He soon realized that by performing imitations and whistling (since, he boasted, "by this time I had become quite a whistler"), he could earn enough money to buy a fishing hook and line, which would in turn enable him to make more money by catching and selling fish. Bursting with the pride of self-reliance and ingenuity, he declared, "My bank was the brick pavement, my banker was my fish hook and lines, my cashier was my own hands, and my associates my own brains."[62] He learned he could profit from his talents and "was so delighted with the money" he received that he could hardly contain himself, not, he claimed, "because I loved money, but because it secured my wishes." Whatever else may be said of his beliefs about his true birth, his fascination with Indian blood, and his exposure to the diverse cultural influences of early Natchez, young Warner was driven to perform by the literal and familial poverty of slavery.

Despite the hardships he experienced, Warner McCary was not entirely without friends during his youth. In addition to his elite acquaintances and employers, he had other relationships across the Natchez social spectrum. Among his less prosperous friends was an unnamed African American man who was a preacher and "the only true friend" Warner had in the world. The older man's impact on the enslaved child must have been profound and may have influenced the boy's conceptions of religion and spirituality. As the child "watered his pillow" with tears each night, he thought of the old "colored man" who had taught him "to pray and hope for better days." Whether or not Warner McCary directly participated in formal religious worship during his youth, his recollection of the old man's friendship suggests that he learned early on how to draw strength from the example of spiritually-inclined people around him.

Although there is no direct evidence that young Warner ever attended church in Natchez, a handful of religious establishments thrived there. Methodism had good success, among both the white and black inhabitants of the city; though for enslaved people, worship was more likely to take place in the forests than in the pews.[63] In his earnest prayers for "better days," Warner McCary was not unlike many other enslaved and free black individuals across the South who sought solace from the pain of the present by anticipating deliverance in the future. He had witnessed at least one such miracle.

During McCary's adolescence, Natchez buzzed with the news that a long-lost African prince had been discovered living as the slave of a local planter. Fulbe prince Ibrahima (Abraham) lived and worked on the plantation of Thomas Foster in the mid-1820s. Once his royal origins were uncovered, interested locals made sporadic efforts to manumit him and return him to his native land. In 1828, the aging prince was finally liberated to considerable fanfare. Just before his departure for Africa, Ibrahima, along with his wife (but not his children, most of whom remained enslaved in Mississippi), was paraded through the streets of Natchez, dressed in a colorful and ostentatious "Moorish" outfit, complete with a white turban, gleaming blue coat, white pantaloons, smart yellow boots, and a scimitar. The costume was apparently conceived by well-intentioned white supporters to both signal Ibrahima's royal status and appeal to charitable white donors, on whom he would rely for the completion of his journey.[64] A procession followed the Fulbe prince down to the river landing, where he boarded a steamboat and left Mississippi behind. The extraordinary story was told in Natchez for many years afterwards and must have made an indelible impression on young Warner McCary.[65]

Although McCary probably did not conceive of his own "royal" status quite so early, he might have wondered what combination of secret histories could be uncovered to liberate him from the physical and social bonds of slavery. His interest in devising an alternative genealogy was probably not unique among enslaved children who grew up separated from their relatives.[66] He was shuttled about from job to job, insulted, and physically abused. He experienced hunger and shame, made worse by his proximity to well-known and relatively prosperous free blacks. Not unlike other despairing bondspeople, he ran away—or more properly, engaged in truancy—in search of brief respites from his condition.[67] More than once, he disappeared "into the back part of the city," likely ending up in the raucous multicultural jumble along the bluffs known as Natchez-under-the-Hill, where he would have rubbed shoulders with other local slaves and free blacks, sailors and laborers, musicians and peddlers, including Choctaws.[68]

Indeed, young Warner McCary's world was shaped by the continued presence and influence of Native people in Natchez and throughout the South. As one historian has put it, Natchez was "a locus of American Indian activity . . . well into the nineteenth century."[69] The Native South was alive and bustling during McCary's early life; it would have been nearly impossible for the young man to avoid the presence of Indian people, stories, food, and music. And it is clear from his later descriptions that even chance encounters with Native people made quite an impression on him. On one such occasion, he became "wild with delight" and was suddenly inspired to speak Choctaw, though he had never been taught, a practice popular among certain religious sects and known as xenoglossia. While these meetings were certainly embellished in his later life narrative, the youth was probably familiar with a variety of Native southerners.

Warner McCary would have had frequent opportunities to see and to meet Choctaw men and women in and around Natchez. As they adjusted to and helped shape the new realities of an emergent market economy, Native people frequented the area to sell game and produce, to work as day laborers, and sometimes to beg. They traveled from their towns to engage in the river city's active cash and exchange market, selling baskets, livestock, moccasins, and medicinal herbs. During the early national period, Choctaws and other local Indians also worked as seasonal laborers on area farms and plantations, making up "the cotton economy's first migrant workforce." And they kept the city's tables supplied with meat, including wild game like venison and turkey, and reflecting their embrace of American husbandry, plenty of pork and beef.[70]

In the autobiography, Tubbee would later admit that he saw Indians frequently in Natchez, but was "closely watched" whenever they came near because he "had threatened to run away with them." Temporarily forgetting his claims about his Indian father, he prefaced one such encounter by saying, "Permit me to describe my feelings the first time I ever saw Indians." Gazing at them in the street, he stood still and speechless until the men of the Choctaw company approached him.

> I thought I was their child, that they were seeking for me; I started and held out my hands, tears gushed from my eyes, I addressed them in a language to me unknown before; it was neither English, Spanish, or French; astonished, they spoke kind to me, smoothing my hairs with their hands; an explanation now took place, as one could speak English; he said I had asked in Choctaw for my father, saying he had gone and left me, and I was with bad people.[71]

The amazed Indians announced to a crowd of onlookers that the child was one of their own: "'White man lie, he no good, him no slave no, bad white man steal him, his skin is red.'" As apparent in the autobiography's descriptions of Mushulatubbee, as well as in tales of Tubbee's own "untameable" Indian passions, such episodes emphasized innate markers of Indianness, even unwittingly signaling an obsession with the texture of his hair that continued throughout his life. Reflecting on the incident, Okah Tubbee later insisted, "They did not even ask for or look for other blood in me."[72]

This particular meeting probably did not take place, at least not in the way it is described in the autobiography. But Warner McCary undoubtedly interacted in one way or another with Native people in and around

Natchez. In addition to delegations of Indian diplomats in town to discuss treaties and "gangs of idle Choctaw, Natchez, and Muskogee Indians, who stroll about the city," many other Native people in Natchez were probably relatively invisible to white observers—working as domestics, peddlers, sailors, prostitutes, and occasional laborers, and often of mixed ancestry. One traveler noted a motley group of Indians greeting arriving boats by playing flutes, drums, and hand-crafted stringed instruments and confessed that "the harmony produced by such an unpromising collection of instruments and performers, exceeded all my expectations." The variety of flutes and flute-playing was of exceptional interest to both audience and observer. It seemed clear that this was no mere spontaneous welcome; the Indian entrepreneurs had carved out a niche in the riverside market economy and expected to receive "money, whiskey, or provisions" in return for their musical talents.[73]

Warner McCary's early realization that audiences would pay to be entertained may have owed something to the success of strolling Choctaw players like those serenading boats at the bluff. It is possible that the young performer even learned some tricks of the trade by observing itinerant and professional musicians who made their way through town, some of whom were clearly Native people as well.[74] Indeed, all sorts of cultural exchanges took place in and around Natchez among visiting Indians, local slaves, free blacks, and whites of all classes, particularly in the brothels, taverns, and rum shacks of Natchez-under-the-Hill where they lived, loved, and let off steam.

In addition to informal interactions with Native people in Mississippi, McCary and other slaves who operated in close proximity to elite Natchez whites—running their errands, cleaning their shops, cutting their hair—would have had ample opportunities to learn how they regarded American Indians.[75] As one writer provocatively put it, "The Natchez country was pre-eminently a land of rumor," and the Choctaws and other southeastern Indian nations were a central—and sometimes *the* central—topic of conversation among Mississippi government officials, planters, merchants, and travelers during Warner McCary's youth.[76] Working among whites in Natchez would have exposed him to current events and taught him the names of notable Indians who signed or spurned treaties, fought with or against their white neighbors, and made regular appearances in Natchez. In addition to the ancient mounds that loomed over the landscape and the indigenous names that blanketed the region, by the early nineteenth century, the fate of Indian southerners was on everyone's mind.

Listening to the conversations of their employers, Warner McCary and his peers would have undoubtedly learned of the ongoing campaign to extinguish Indian title to valuable lands in the region. Early debates largely turned into unanimous calls for removal in the period following the violent and divisive Creek War (1813–1814), in which American-allied Choctaws (including both Mushulatubbee and widely heralded orator Pushmataha) fought alongside Andrew Jackson and Davy Crockett to defeat the Red Stick Creeks, a party that hoped to wrest tribal control from leaders they viewed as politically and spiritually corrupt.[77] Enormous Indian land cessions followed in the wake of the war and carved the interior South into alternating parcels of American and indigenous territory. After Mississippi became a state in 1817, the push to consign southern Indians to a region west of the great river gained momentum and through the 1820s, a wholesale removal of the South's Native peoples was widely discussed.[78]

Besides his chance meetings with Indians, his exposure to debates about Indian removal, and the ever-present reminders of indigenous people in the Natchez culinary offerings, market wares, and archeological monuments, McCary grew up in a time when southern Indians were an increasing presence in both regional and national popular culture, including the writings of William Gilmore Simms and the old Southwest humorists. While these authors are often referred to by modern scholars with a certain degree of disdain as primarily "southern writers," Simms and his contemporaries enjoyed a broad readership, particularly in the North, and a central feature of their fiction was story-telling about Indian southerners, albeit often of the tall-tale variety. Although Warner McCary was probably not able to read these stories (evidence exists that he was illiterate well into later adulthood), they shaped and were shaped by both the region's indigenous history and its increasing acceptance of racial determinism.[79]

Another aspect of popular culture that had an impact on McCary's youth was the growth of theatrical entertainment catering to an emergent middle class. By the time he was a teenager, several professional companies had made their mark in the city. Although the first permanent theater was not completed until 1828, stage performances of all kinds had been taking place since the time of the Spanish dons, including at least one "floating theater" that presented a series of wobbly shows on a boat at the bluffs.[80] By the mid-1830s, nightly theatrical performances by touring stars were common and most actors passing through the region would stop for a show or two in Natchez, despite the fact that local audiences were known for spitting steady streams of profanity and tobacco juice at the players.[81]

A key factor that contributed to the development of the Natchez theater—and to the growth of the city and the region more broadly—was the progress of steamboat travel. Starting in the 1810s, regular steamboat service was available between Natchez and New Orleans, and more boats were added year by year. Although it was often dangerous and unreliable, particularly in the early days, steam power nevertheless accelerated the rate of downriver transport and enabled travelers to move upstream at a pace that was, if not rapid, at least steady, especially in comparison to the slow, laborious work of rowing a flatboat or keelboat against the current.[82] By the mid-1820s, advances in transportation technology, including not only faster steam travel, but also canalling, multiplied the importance of interior commerce, which, in turn, linked inland ports like Natchez and Cincinnati with Atlantic and European capitals.[83] All of these innovations meant that more and more people were traveling into and out of riverside cities like Natchez, including entertainers interested in capitalizing on the emergence of a new middle class with money to spend.

One such figure was Solomon Smith, later known as "Old Sol" after a character he frequently played. Smith first came upstream from New Orleans in 1828 under the auspices of a company headed by James Caldwell, an actor and theatrical manager who had been producing shows off and on in Natchez since 1823. Many years later, Smith recalled that he had been the victim of theft during his engagement at the Natchez theater. The culprit, he claimed, was seventeen-year-old Warner McCary, "who afterwards became somewhat notorious as an Indian chief."[84] The case was dismissed when Justice Henry Tooley, a determined foe of "vulgar" theater (among other nuisances), concluded that the loss of his pocket watch served Smith right for being in the theater business in the first place.[85]

As tempting as it is to imagine young Warner McCary lurking about the Natchez theater, pilfering valuables from dressing rooms, and learning tricks of the acting trade, Smith's memoirs are notoriously embellished and chronologically unreliable.[86] It seems likely, however, that McCary was familiar with, and in some sense influenced by, the presence of actors, theater managers, agents, and professional entertainers in the city. Natchez was a locus of intense, if often coincidental, cultural exchange, centered on the river and the people it carried to and from the bluff landings. Its rising importance on the southern theater circuit ensured that all sorts of thespians, musicians, and charlatans would be among those disembarking. And for a young man hoping for better days, the lure of the stage and its alternate identities may have been irresistible.

Although the emergence of a middle class and its particular amusements reflected what a contemporaneous observer called "the most prosperous period in the history of Natchez," the possibilities of social advancement were not equally shared. During the first decades of the nineteenth century, social mobility had been possible almost entirely on the basis of accumulated property, enabling even those without elite status, including some free blacks, to attain some prominence on the basis of their wealth. But by the time Warner McCary was about twenty years old in 1830, broad societal changes had taken place in Natchez; property alone was no longer the full measure of social standing, and "the urge for status among the aspirants for the genteel level could no longer be fulfilled merely by the acquisition of wealth."[87]

Although prosperous entrepreneurs like William Johnson proved that people of African descent could flourish financially, new regulations soon emerged that would foreclose free blacks' paths to social advancement. Just at the time Warner McCary was entering adulthood, state and municipal governments began restricting the freedoms of free blacks and further tightening controls on the lives of slaves. Starting in the early 1830s, even comparatively wealthy free blacks like Johnson and Bob McCary faced new obstacles.[88] In response to the Nat Turner slave rebellion in Virginia (1831) and the growth of the abolition movement in the North, many southern states passed harsh laws limiting the rights afforded free blacks, in some cases prohibiting their very presence within state boundaries. By 1832, even well-regarded free people of color like Bob and Kitty McCary had to appear before the Natchez Police Court and provide evidence of their good behavior in order to remain in Mississippi.[89] Others were hauled before authorities to prove their free status, and some succeeded in using either white or Indian ancestry as a legal defense.[90] Such harassment increased throughout the 1830s, such that by the end of the decade, a veritable crusade against free blacks was under way in Natchez. Johnson referred to this campaign, led primarily by middle-class and aspirational middle-class whites, as "the Inquisition."[91]

During this era of stricter racial and legal codes, Warner McCary was hired out to a blacksmith and was savagely beaten by the shop master. Reeling from the abuse and the repressive atmosphere, he walked down to the river and boarded one of the boats bobbing along at the landing. Although it is unclear precisely when this first departure took place, he later maintained that he found a captain bound for the western reaches of the Red River who offered him passage to Alexandria, Louisiana. He "obtained sundry small jobs" that paid his way and then some, suggesting that he was operating on his own recognizance, although it was common for slave owners in western ports to hire out their slaves to boat captains for temporary stints.[92] Although their mobility was restricted upon landing, significant and surprising numbers of slaves and free blacks traveled on the nation's rivers despite concerns about escapes and kidnappings. Their circuits of travel and networks of information constituted what one scholar refers to as a "Pan-Mississippi Black Community."[93] When McCary decided to run away, he may have found the possibilities of this world intoxicating.

Indeed, his early experiences traveling the rivers made a lasting impression. Not only did he find the relative freedom alluring, but for a young man trapped in a cruel family situation, the anonymity may have also been attractive. He could use a different name, earn his own money, dress however he liked—even once donning a clumsy pair of "high heel shoes" that sent him sprawling overboard into the Red River or dressing in the "white linnen" he had been denied as a child, but which he felt "suited the redness of [his] skin."[94] The boats were also lively places of amusement, with gambling, music, and dancing—just the sort of environment to inspire a budding entertainer.[95]

The variety of fellow travelers he met must also have fascinated him. In addition to the enslaved and free sailors, servants, mechanics, and cooks who were a fixture on the riverboats, all kinds of interesting people thronged the ports, pouring onto and off of wharves, in search of their own fortunes and new beginnings. Among the travelers who moved upriver from New Orleans were religious pilgrims from abroad, including hundreds of recent Mormon converts from England. Starting in the 1830s, the port of Liverpool received bales of Mississippi cotton and returned boatloads of immigrants to the Gulf, many headed to their Latter-day Saint brethren then assembling in Missouri. Even if McCary did not have direct contact with the Mormon travelers bound for one of several designated "gathering" spots, he probably heard rumors about them. In Natchez, someone even set fire to a boat carrying Mormon migrants up the Mississippi, where the sojourners were called disdainfully "Joe's rats," a reference to the church's founding prophet, Joseph Smith Jr.[96]

During the remainder of the 1830s and after his return from the Red River adventure, Warner McCary continued to work at odd jobs in Natchez, occasionally apprenticing at various trades, but still legally bound to his family.[97] Toward the end of the decade, even as southern legal and social codes further inhibited slaves and free blacks, he embarked on a new avocation that would dramatically alter the course of his life.[98] Having already demonstrated his impressive talents with mimicry and music, he managed to garner the attention of local militia units, like the Natchez Fencibles, Natchez Guards, and Adams Light Guard.[99]

McCary's official participation in the militia was prohibited by law, but in testament to his musical gifts, he was allowed to perform as a fifer and parade with them on a number of occasions. His newfound notoriety did not go unnoticed by his "enemies," however, and he later claimed that he was verbally abused by "slaves and free, even [when marching] at the head of companies."[100] Despite vocal opposition to his visible role with local militia groups, whose public function in times of peace was largely social, his involvement with the Natchez units gave him the valuable opportunity to build useful, if paternalistic, relationships with men of note in the community, many of whom were also involved in Freemasonry, another social network that would become important in his later life.[101] A few of these notables would write testimonials on his behalf, introducing him to other militia companies and attesting to his immense musical talents.[102] It seems likely that his involvement with the militia would also have provided him additional opportunities to hear interested white southerners' thoughts on Indian removal.

Despite his colorful descriptions of convening with Native groups in Natchez, Alexandria, and Brandon (near present-day Jackson, Mississippi), the spectacle of removal during the 1830s and 1840s was just as likely to have shaped Warner McCary's lasting impressions of Indians during this era. The Choctaws were the first to sign a removal treaty (the Treaty of Dancing Rabbit Creek), under the terms of the Indian Removal Act passed in April 1830. A portion of the Choctaw population, as well as some Cherokees, Creeks, and Chickasaws, had already migrated west of the Mississippi following earlier treaties. But the Treaty of Dancing Rabbit Creek permitted removal of the rest, stating that "the Choctaw nation of Indians consent and hereby cede to the United States, the entire country they own and possess, east of the Mississippi River; and they agree to move beyond the Mississippi River, early as practicable." Choctaw signatories included the principal chief of each division, Greenwood LeFlore, Nittakaichee, and Mushulatubbee, each of whom was granted a handsome salary and a reserved parcel of land in Mississippi.[103]

Before removal began, the political elites of the bluff city port gathered to celebrate the new treaty. At a public dinner at Parker's Hotel in October 1830, assembled guests offered toasts to President Jackson, who found "half of our territory occupied by a few wandering Indians [but] will leave it in the cultivation of thousands of grateful freemen," to "our departing brethren," the Choctaws and Chickasaws, "destined where they are going, to learn the right of individual property, and self government," and to the "newly acquired territory—. The dawn of civilization now beams on its horizon."[104] The speakers expressed their earnest hopes that the Creeks and Cherokees would follow the example of the Choctaws and agree to leave their homelands for a territory in the West. In anticipation of the "flush times" to come, local citizen R. J. Walker rose and gave an ecstatic address.

> All classes of our community will feel the benefits of the new purchase [the Choctaw cession]—The enterprising citizen, who will commence a new plantation on these cheap and fertile lands—the monied man, in new demands for loans, and new opportunities of profitable investments—the state and other stockholders of our bank from the increased dividends, arising from the vast addition to the number of their notes which they will be enabled to keep in circulation—the professional man, in the new field for his skill and eloquence—the merchant who will furnish, the steamboat owner who will carry the supplies for every new farm and new inhabitant, the carpenter, the gin-weight, the blacksmith, and all our other mechanics, who will make the forest ring with the joyful hum of industry.[105]

A clearer statement of precisely how white southerners defined the benefits of Indian removal is hard to imagine. Every corner of the South, they believed, would be improved by the absence of Indian southerners.

Of course, not all Choctaws left Mississippi. Although many thousands of southern and Ohio valley Indians were forced into abandoning their homelands and removing westward, significant numbers of Native people remained. At the termination of the physical removal of the Choctaws in 1833, about 6,000 remained in Mississippi, some still making their way about Natchez.[106] When Irish actor Tyrone Power arrived at the bluffs in 1835, he encountered a party of Choctaw men, women, and children who impressed him with their wretchedness.[107] Indeed, those who remained tended to fall into one of three categories: a tiny handful of intermarried families who passed as white, a few hundred privileged recipients of reserved lands, and several thousand others who avoided removal by receding into the forests, emerging seasonally to perform agricultural wage labor.[108] The last and largest group was, as Power's observations suggest, extremely impoverished. Even those Choctaws fortunate enough to obtain reserved lands often lost their holdings in swindles and frauds that they were unable to contest in a court of law, despite having been forcibly made citizens of the United States following the extension of state laws over their territory.[109]

Whether they left the South or remained, Indians generally and Choctaws specifically were a fixture in regional and national newspapers between 1830 and 1840. The signing of the Choctaw removal treaty was front-page news, and it turned some Choctaw leaders into household names. Among them was Mushulatubbee, who said he would run for the office of U.S. representative from Mississippi. Addressing the state's populace, he explained, "I have fought for you [and] I have been by your own act, made a citizen of your state," and promising "with Indian sincerity" that "if you vote for me, I will serve you. I have no animosity against any of my white brethren." Whether his congressional bid was a political stunt designed to consolidate his influence within the Choctaw nation or demonstrate the duplicity of forcing U.S. citizenship on American Indians without ensuring their rights (such as testifying in court), it was reported in a variety of newspapers nationwide and added to the leader's notoriety. These stories ensured that broad swaths of the U.S. reading public became familiar with the Choctaws and with the name Mushulatubbee.[110] Some attentive Americans might have even recognized the Choctaw leader's likeness, since George Catlin's portrait of him (see fig. 2) was included in the artist's gallery tours during the removal era.[111]

Over the remainder of the 1830s, a period Tubbee later described by saying, "Time moved on in [a] pleasant manner, without much interruption," the removal of the Choctaws and their southern Indian neighbors unfolded before his eyes. He may have witnessed the heart-wrenching exodus of Choctaw people from their homelands to Arkansas. He almost certainly heard about the protracted Cherokee removal debates and the violent and disastrous efforts to relocate Creek and Seminole peoples. These episodes of Indian removal, and those that occurred elsewhere in the United States, may or may not have inspired sympathy in his heart, but when he left the state again at the end of the decade, he must have carried the memory of them in his mind.

Leaving Mississippi behind, McCary made his way downriver to New Orleans. Although much larger than his hometown, the Crescent City shared many similarities with Natchez, including its multitiered racial caste system, reputation for infectious disease, and murderous summer heat. Both cities had suffered financially in the national depression that followed the Panic of 1837 and were still struggling two years later as cotton prices slowly rebounded. But New Orleans was a place of excitement and diversity that far exceeded even the raucous river port of Natchez. Slaves, free blacks, Creoles, and a host of French, Spanish, Italian, Caribbean, and indigenous inhabitants worked and played alongside one another at the city's wharves, theaters, cockfights, horse races, dances, and parades. As former slave James Thomas put it, "New Orleans was the only city that I ever saw where nobody seemed to care about tomorrow."[112]

McCary must have reveled in the relative liberty he experienced in the bustling city. By the summer of 1839, he was familiar enough in New Orleans that a local paper casually referenced him (using the alias "Carey") in an unrelated story about the shenanigans of city slaves. While describing the "happy negroes" who worked at a popular restaurant, the writer remarked that some of them "whistle the Star Spangled Banner and Yankee Doodle just as correctly, note for note, variations and all, as Carey plays them on the fife."[113]

His growing fame as a musician was notable, but 1839 was an auspicious year for a far more important reason. Just days after the *Times-Picayune* referenced "Carey's" musical talents, Bob McCary took the first steps toward manumitting his slave and putative half-brother, transferring power of attorney to a lawyer in Cincinnati who would take charge of the legal details.[114] The reason for Bob's decision is unclear. Kitty had died in 1836, and Warner had apparently spent much of his time working at a foundry in New Orleans between 1837 and 1839, ostensibly having been hired out. The autobiography hints that he was pressured to purchase himself from his half-sibling, but there is no other evidence to that effect.[115] Perhaps Bob found his itinerant charge too costly or too difficult to manage and felt that freeing him would lessen the burden. Like his close friend William Johnson, Bob's financial situation suffered acutely during the national economic depression. Prospects for free black property owners in the Lower South were particularly dim. As Johnson put it, "Natchez is getting worse and worse."[116] Maybe Bob's new profession as a respectable schoolmaster also induced him to cut ties with his adventurous enslaved brother.[117] Regardless of the circumstances, within a few years, Warner McCary was a free man.

In February 1843, "Warner McCarey alias James Warner, a free man of Color of mulatto complexion, aged about 29 years, and five feet and four 1/2 inches in height," appeared before the Police Board in Natchez. Recent acts of the Mississippi legislature decreed that free people of color residing in the state had to periodically appear before local authorities and provide evidence of their lawful behavior and good standing. "Having satisfied the Board that he was of good character and honest deportment," he was licensed to remain in the state but apparently had little intention of doing so.[118] In addition to the foreclosure of opportunities for free people of color in Natchez, McCary had more personal reasons to seek a new beginning in New Orleans, as well. His last few years in Mississippi had been among his worst. During this period, he was lured back into Franky McCary's household. Feigning an interest in reconciliation, she then poisoned his coffee, tied him to a bed, and beat him mercilessly. His anger and bitterness at this humiliation grew to include the whole of Natchez. When a devastating tornado destroyed much of the city in 1840, he claimed he had sent it there himself.[119]

By the fall of 1843, Carey (or McCary) was operating full time in New Orleans.[120] An October newspaper advertisement informed readers that he was "prepared to furnish Music for Balls, Parties, and Military Parades," and although he ostensibly had testimonials from white men with whom he'd marched in Natchez, he nevertheless recommended himself in this ad, "being satisfied that he will be able to give satisfaction to all."[121] Perhaps owing to connections forged in Natchez, it was not difficult for him to ingratiate himself with area militia companies. But his participation was nevertheless unofficial. Although he later asserted that he was "appointed Fife Major of the Field Music of the Regt. Louisiana Volunteers" by Col. James Dakin in 1844, the official minute book of the company (kept by Dakin himself) makes no mention of Carey or his "appointment," instead obliquely referring to the company's music as "informal and contrary to military law and regulations."[122] But even without the official recognition he claimed and craved, he was nevertheless permitted to appear with this and other militia units. One Louisiana writer rhapsodized that Carey could draw more music from his fife and play it, "longer and stronger . . . put more twists in it, and play lower, and go up higher, and give more octaves, and crotchets, ketches and sky-rockets, change the keys, and gingle them with better grace, imitate more partridges and young chickens, and come the high notes shriller, and the low notes softer, and take off his hat more gracefully while he is doing it, and look at the people while it is going on . . . better than any other man living."[123] The popular fifer saw his star rising.

Carey's music was quite the talk of the town by the time he departed New Orleans later that year, but he was not yet performing the Indian persona that would dominate his later life. By 1845, the thirty-five-year-old musician had made his way upriver to St. Louis, where a local paper declared that he possessed a "magic flute" and remarked that the city had "pricked up its ears every night, for some time past, listening to the wildest—sweetest flute tones that ever were heard!" Despite the praise (he was "an original genius . . . [with] astonishing facility in execution . . . [and a] peculiar and pleasing" tone), the paper was sure to note that Carey was "an oddity of a mulatto."[124]

Many years later, when Sol Smith (the theatrical manager who accused Carey of stealing his pocket-watch in Natchez) wrote the first of his professional memoirs, he claimed to have met the virtuosic flutist a second time in St. Louis. Smith claimed that he helped devise a new persona for Carey during the 1840s and had invented the name "Okah Tubbee" when the musician was preparing to perform at his local theater. The concert was a benefit for one of the theatrical employees who complained that it did not "seem exactly proper for a *negro* to appear on the stage." So Smith suggested that Carey perform as an Indian instead. He cast about for something to inspire a stage name and exclaimed, " 'There is an oak tub; let the Indian's name be Oakah Tubbee!'—and Oakah Tubbee it has been ever since."[125]

While Smith's account is amusing, it may not be true. It is entirely possible, however, that he met the pied piper, who had come so far since his boyhood imitating animal sounds for coins in the streets of Natchez. And Carey may have even performed at Smith's theater, providing musical interludes between dramatic or comedic pieces, as he would later do in performance halls elsewhere. What is certain is that by the start of 1846, Carey was known from New Orleans to St. Louis as a gifted musician, who also happened to be a "negro" or mulatto. In time, this notoriety would be his undoing.

• • •

From a slave in rags to a renowned musician, the child born Warner McCary crafted a new life for himself as the acclaimed "natural" musician William Carey or McCary. His later recollections suggest that his only joy during youth came from brief and perhaps imagined encounters with Indians. His had been a peculiarly unjust experience within a notoriously unjust regime. Becoming an entertainer provided him with a means of income, a sense of self, and a ticket out of Mississippi. It also taught him to shift his identity according to circumstances, a skill that he would hone for the rest of his life.

CHAPTER TWO

Growing Up among the Mormons

. . . .

Lucy Stanton's Remarkable Youth

In the fall of 1830, shortly after Choctaw leaders signed a removal treaty, a small expedition of ambitious missionaries set off from central New York to visit the western Indian lands. The men believed that it was their divine calling to seek out the Lamanites, as they called American Indians, and bring them word of a new religion that would come to be known as Mormonism. Their trek began in a region later called the "burnt over district" in reference to the rapid succession of religious revivals and reform movements in the area that had "burned" through the minds of the people there, spawning tremendous excitement and intense skepticism. Traveling west through Buffalo, they stopped briefly to preach to members of the Seneca Nation at Cattaraugus and then continued along the southern shore of Lake Erie, stopping again in Geauga County, Ohio, in an area known as the Western Reserve.[1]

There they found not Indians, but fellow religious enthusiasts—a little community "who had formed themselves into a common-stock society" and according to observers, "had become considerably fanatical . . . daily looking for some wonderful event to take place in the world."[2] Among the participants in this community were the Stantons, including fourteen-year-old Lucy. They were followers of a popular Reformed Baptist preacher named Sidney Rigdon, described by some as a "Campbellite" in reference to his affiliation with Alexander Campbell, leader of a new church called "Disciples of Christ." Rigdon, Campbell, and their Mormon visitors (Oliver Cowdery, Parley P. Pratt, Peter Whitmer, and Ziba Peterson) all sought a "restoration of ancient Christianity," though they would soon disagree on how to attain it.[3]

One important point on which these restorationists disagreed was the role that American Indians would play in their emergent doctrines. This key feature of early Mormonism would, in turn, have a profound impact on the life of young Lucy Stanton, who came to believe she had a special connection to the poor Lamanites.

...

The religious ferment of the late Second Great Awakening (1820s–1840s) was characterized by a profusion of prophets; new, revived, and "restored" doctrines; revelations; and sectarian innovations.[4] All across the United States, preachers and followers were congregating, disbanding, and re-grouping, often on the basis of their unique understandings of Christianity. Methodists held ecstatic camp meetings; Baptists redeemed and reformed; Millerites prepared for Christ's second coming; Campbellites "restored"; and Shakers shook. Mormons, or "Mormonites," as they were sometimes called, were unique—perhaps "peculiar"—in many of their beliefs and practices, but they were nevertheless engaged in a nationwide phenomenon of seeking and receiving divine communications to help them navigate a rapidly changing society.[5] Indeed, many early Mormon converts were former followers of one or more of the other brands of popular sectarianism, each competing to deliver the right message through the right combination of messengers at just the right time.[6]

One such messenger was Joseph Smith Jr., who experienced a vision in 1823, when he was eighteen years old. An angel appeared to the poor farmer and occasional treasure hunter and told him of mysterious golden plates buried near his central New York hometown of Manchester. Over the next five years, following the divine instructions he received regarding the plates, he recovered them and translated their "reformed Egyptian" script. He accomplished this feat through the use of a "seer stone" that he placed in the bottom of a hat and then placed over his face. The resulting text was called the Book of Mormon. By March 1830, it had been printed and made available for sale, making Joseph Smith a "minor national figure." Reactions to his claims were swift, with more than one observer concluding that Smith was a religious impostor and his holy book "the greatest fraud of our time."[7]

According to Smith, the original text was crafted by a fourth-century American prophet named Mormon, who had himself transcribed the histories of ancient American civilizations, contained in other sets of plates.[8] These ancient civilizations had grown from a diaspora that arrived in the Americas from the ancient Middle East after the fall of Babel. Most prominent were the fratricidal factions of Nephi and Laman, named for two sons of Lehi, whose family had fled Jerusalem around 600 BCE. A millennium later, the Lamanites managed to destroy the Nephites, only to have their own civilization fall to ruin. According to the Book of Mormon, those Lamanites who survived were among the ancestors of American Indians. Although they were a degraded race, their skin darkened by their transgressions, the Lamanites held a special place in the prophetic vision offered by the Mormon testament. A prophecy held that they would one day have the "scales fall from their eyes," and by acknowledging the truth of Christianity would become lighter and "delightsome" (2 Nephi 30:6).[9]

Mormonism's early and urgent missionary efforts among Native Americans had several sources. These included the Book of Mormon itself ("impart the word of God to their brethren, the Lamanites," Mosiah 28:1), the initiative of the new religion's earliest followers to spread the word of God to "the Lamanites, residing in the west,"[10] and Joseph Smith's early revelations: "And now, behold, I say unto you that you shall go unto the Lamanites and preach my gospel unto them; and inasmuch as they receive thy teachings thou shalt cause my church to be established among them" (Doctrine and Covenants 28:8). The impulse to evangelize the Indians, although shared among many Protestant denominations, took on a distinct connotation for early Mormonism because Native peoples of the Americas were seen as an essential part of the faith's millenarian promise. Smith himself emphasized the centrality of American Indians to Mormonism, asserting that "The Book of Mormon is a record of the forefathers of our western Tribes of Indians" and that contemporary Indians would be key to building the New Jerusalem.[11] One modern scholar has gone so far as to describe the Book of Mormon as not merely a "record of the 'Lamanite' or Native American people," but a "manifesto of their destiny."[12] In addition to the special place accorded the Lamanites and their descendants within Mormon theology, Native Americans were also considered a sort of "spiritual kin" by some early Mormons, who often thought of themselves as diasporic and persecuted peoples.[13]

Shortly after establishing his new religion, Smith sent newly minted church elders on a mission to the western Indians. According to their covenant of cooperation, the missionaries promised to proceed to "the Lamanites to proclaim glad tidings of great joy" having been "commanded of the Lord God" to do so.[14] Their first stop had been among the Senecas in western New York, but finding the Indians there in a state of surprising advancement and generally unenthusiastic about yet another group of white men eager to help them, the missionaries only stayed for a few hours.

For good measure, they left behind several freshly printed copies of the Book of Mormon before making their way into Ohio.[15]

The Mormons were not the only American religious sect fascinated, if not obsessed, with Indians. The effort to Christianize the indigenous people of North America had occupied Spanish, French, and English colonizers in varying degrees for generations. But in the two decades prior to Smith's first revelations, a new enthusiasm had emerged for bringing American Indians into the fold. Methodists, Baptists, Moravians, and Presbyterians competed to establish missions among the Indians, with an emphasis on tribes in New York, the old Northwest, and the southern states. These proselytizers often met a lukewarm response, but that hardly dampened their enthusiasm.

In addition to these efforts to establish churches among the Indians, other groups and individuals advanced their own unique agendas. For example, in the 1820s, a New York City newspaper editor and sometime politician named Mordecai Manuel Noah proclaimed himself "Judge of Israel and Messiah of the Jews." When he had garnered enough support for his visionary project of establishing a Jewish homeland on an island in the Niagara River, Noah held a ceremony to bless the site. Since he subscribed to an increasingly popular American view that Indians were "in all probability descendants of the lost ten tribes of Israel," and thus were central to his movement, he arranged for the famous Seneca leader Red Jacket to attend the event.[16]

Like Noah and many others, Joseph Smith and the early Mormon converts accepted the general idea that Native North Americans were the descendants of one of the Lost Tribes of Israel. This belief gained momentum during the antebellum period and particularly during the era of Indian removal because it answered both the theological question of why the Bible had not accounted for this seemingly unique and isolated population and the political question of whether Native Americans were truly indigenous to the continent and thus had a prior right to the soil. As such, the theory of Hebraic origins distanced Mormons and other adherents from complicity in the dispossession of American Indians, while reassuring them that their beliefs did not contravene the biblical account of a single divine creation, referred to as monogenesis.[17]

Thus, though Joseph Smith's prophetic new faith was unique in some of its claims about the history and millenarian purpose of American Indians, it was nevertheless not the only movement of its kind during this era of widespread "sectarian invention."[18] In addition to the revivals and reform movements that swept through established Protestant denominations, numerous more radical leaders emerged in this era, including not only Noah, Campbell, and Smith, but also William Miller, founder of the millennialist Seventh-day Adventist Church, and the eccentric self-proclaimed prophet Matthias, who devised a bizarre scheme to end the social and religious influence of northeastern "evangelical businessmen."[19]

These spiritual innovations must be examined in the context of the social and cultural environment in which they emerged. In the 1820s–1840s, the transformations of the market revolution produced new opportunities for a burgeoning middle class and for the production of wealth, but many people were left out or newly marginalized as the new economic reality reshaped American society. Smith and his fellow homegrown prophets generally fell into this latter group and capitalized on the discontent of their peers. Indeed, the early Mormon movement welcomed the equal participation of men, women, and people of color, rich or poor, as did many other popular sects during the late Second Great Awakening. As one nineteenth-century observer put it, "It was a season of revivals, and the spirit that was moving the theologians was felt in the lowest stratum of home and rural life."[20] The participation of "the lowest stratum" in such sects reflected their attempts to access spiritual power and authority in the context of a social and economic transformation that increasingly denied them financial security and political legitimacy. But, as Smith would quickly learn, organizing a church (as opposed to just gathering followers) was awfully difficult when everyone felt they had an equal claim to power and authority. Indeed, the contradictory impulses toward equality and hierarchical authority embedded in the nascent Mormon faith reflected the tremendous social upheaval that was under way.[21]

Among the seekers who found themselves drawn to the promise of early Mormonism were the members of the "Big Family," an experimental commune on the farm of Isaac Morley near Kirtland, Geauga County, Ohio. When the first Mormon missionaries arrived there in 1830, the community included the family of Daniel Stanton, whose daughter Lucy would emerge as a memorable figure in the new faith, as well as ten other households.[22] They were devout Christians who sought to live according to "God's teachings as they understood them" and tried to establish a principal of common ownership and interest, working cooperatively in agricultural, domestic, and mechanical ventures. It was a diverse group, with men and women of all ages and several people of color, including one notable African American figure named "Black Pete," who believed so staunchly in the "community of goods" that he was known to dress in others' clothes whenever the mood struck him.[23]

It took less than a month after the arrival of the Mormon missionaries in Ohio for patriarch Daniel Stanton to convert; he was baptized on November 3, 1830. Before long, he was ordained a teacher and was instructing others in the faith.[24] Stanton's wife, Clarinda, was baptized at the end of November, and their five daughters also became active in the early "Mormonite" movement that was blossoming along the shores of Lake Erie.[25] Still several years from establishing anything like orthodoxy, early Mormon believers in Ohio experimented with a variety of methods for experiencing and expressing their faith, including exuberant and even ecstatic exclamations of feeling, speaking in tongues, and trancelike states of possession.

Other Protestant denominations also practiced bodily modes of religious expression, their churches and prayer meetings afflicted with "'the falling,' 'the jerking,' 'the rolling,' and the 'the dancing,'" that characterized the late Second Great Awakening in the United States.[26] The Methodists were the group most closely associated with inspirational witnessing of divine power, or what denominational forefather John Wesley referred to as "real Christian experience." During the early decades of the nineteenth century, the democratic and emancipatory potential of Methodist camp meetings inspired the enthusiastic physical participation of individuals whose salvation had been ignored or circumscribed by other denominations, namely women and people of color. Growing elite disdain for the "shouting Methodists" reflected suspicions about their vehement bodily demonstrations of God's power, but also signaled concern about a startlingly egalitarian system of worship that threatened the social hierarchies of the nation.[27]

Although the Mormon Church would later come to rely on an "ethos of fixed social relations and paternal power," the early Mormons in Kirtland trumpeted their egalitarianism and had a penchant for physical enactments of spiritual experience with women and people of color leading the way.[28] For instance, former slave "Black Pete" emerged as a charismatic preacher and a self-proclaimed "revelator," briefly leading his own prophetic movement among the early Mormon converts.[29] And local women like Ann Whitney, Printha Abbott, and the Stanton girls distinguished themselves by "getting the power" during prayer meetings. In fact, teenager Lucy Stanton was regarded as "a leader in the power business," sometimes practicing spontaneous tongue-speaking and other forms of enthusiastic worship.[30] According to observer Reuben P. Harmon, the Stanton sisters and other young women were known to "scream hello 'Glory!' and clap their hands, and finally apparently become unconscious," practices that were also common in Methodist camp meetings. He recalled of the Mormon gatherings that "order was observed until they got the power and began to talk in unknown tongues. Some called it talking Injun."[31]

Although a variety of sects and denominations practiced tongue-speaking and ecstatic spiritual expression, two things that characterized the early Mormon converts in Ohio were the prominent roles of women and the centrality of Indians to their thinking.[32] On the latter, one historian asserts that "new converts were open to Indian and slave observances under the rubric of manifestations of the Spirit," and they experienced visions and spiritual possessions that "often centered on the Indians that were then the focus of the New York missionaries' distant labors."[33] Another labelled these activities "frontier revivalism" and noted that speaking in supposed "Indian dialects" was a key feature.[34] Native Americans were not only considered a sort of "spiritual kin" by Mormon believers, they were also the most recent inhabitants of the Western Reserve prior to the settlement of the Big Family, their names and histories still very much alive. In this environment, Indians held a mystical, if not magical, power in the imagination of the early Mormon converts. Mormons, like other nonindigenous Americans, were fascinated with Native peoples, but they also accorded them special status within their religion and hung their hopes on Indian millenarianism, even as they participated in the displacement of these peoples from their homelands.[35]

The Stanton girls were not the only ones who lost themselves in ecstatic religious experience and babbled in Indian tongues. Men and especially women experimented with bodily spiritual practices that included fervent prayer, states of unconsciousness, leaping and falling, and mimicking Indians (or what they thought Indians did).[36] Whether or not these early converts had experienced much interaction with living Native Americans, they freely borrowed from popular representations of them. One observer recalled,

> They claimed to have the gift of tongues and talked with all sorts of gibberish. They claimed to have a special mission to the Indians, and they went through all sorts of Indian performances. . . . I have seen

them, in pantomine [*sic*] tomahawk and scalp each other, and rip open the bowels and tear out the entrails. At one meeting at which I was present three of them, one a Negro, were impelled by the Spirit to go out and preach to the Indians. They left the meeting house on the run, went up a steep hillside, mounted stumps, and began holding forth in gibberish to an imaginary audience.[37]

Fascinated by and perhaps inspired by the popular representation of Indian violence, these ecstatic expressions also foregrounded the practices of tongue-speaking (glossolalia) and speaking in previously unlearned tongues (xenoglossia). The "gibberish" was described by non-Mormons as "regular Indian dialects" that were heretofore unknown to the speakers.[38] Their spontaneous ability to speak or sing in Indian tongues reflected not only manifestations of divine spirit, but also signaled a sense of deep affinity between early Mormon converts and the Indians of their imagination.

Beyond simply imitating Native language and "customs," the call to missionize to the western tribes was a deeply held spiritual belief among those who converted to Mormonism in Kirtland. Indeed, the three missionaries who first brought the Book of Mormon to Geauga County were, as noted, actually on their way further west to the "borders of the Lamanites" to spread the new gospel to them. Among those who remained in Ohio after their brief visit in the fall of 1830, ecstatic religious experiences focusing on Indians assumed even greater importance. Some congregants would apparently "fall prostrate on the floor or writhe about on the ground like a serpent which they called 'sailing in the boat to the Lamanites,'" while others claimed to have visions in which they were "'carried away in the spirit to the Lamanites, the natives of this country, which are our Western Indians . . . [saying] they can see the Indians on the banks of the streams at the West waiting to be baptized; and they can hear them sing and see them perform many of the Indian manoeuvres, which they try to imitate."[39]

These sights and sounds had a powerful effect on young Lucy Stanton. Although she had been born in central New York (December 28, 1816), by her third birthday her family had moved to northern Ohio.[40] The reason for the Stanton family's move is unclear, but there were many that made similar treks.[41] Lucy's father, Daniel, was a farmer and a veteran of the War of 1812, and he may have received a grant of land in recognition of his service. The Ohio lands were among those that had made up the Northwest Territory, and although the far western reaches were home to significant numbers of indigenous people, by the time the Stantons arrived, many if not most had been displaced.[42]

During Lucy Stanton's youth, Ohio was rapidly expelling the remainder of its Native inhabitants. Indeed, between 1817 and 1825, twenty-five treaties separated tribes from their lands, including those belonging to Shawnee, Wyandotte, Potawatomi, Ottawa, Ojibwe, Seneca, and Delaware peoples. Most of these groups, including the Delaware Nation from whom Laah Ceil would later claim maternal descent, were already refugees from earlier episodes of violence and dispossession, steadily encouraged or forced westward from their original homelands. The Delaware, or Lenape, people were an extreme example of removal policies in action, having been dispossessed and relocated no fewer than seven times over the eighteenth and nineteenth centuries.[43] In their absence, American migrants poured into the Ohio country, clustering on the shores of Lake Erie and along the Ohio River. As canals were improved and steamboat travel gained momentum, the region was settled even more thickly by aspirational westering migrants, following in the footsteps of recently removed Indians.

Little more is known about Lucy Stanton's childhood beyond what can be ascertained from the brief background material included in Okah Tubbee's later autobiography, much of which is convoluted. She obfuscated the precise day and year of her birth (claiming to have been born a year later than she was), adjusted her hometown westward from its actual location in central New York, and claimed that her Anglo-American parents were actually Mohawk and Delaware.[44]

Nevertheless, some formative aspects of her youth can be gleaned from the text. She was a deeply devout child who was "the subject of religious impressions," but had no "knowledge of God" prior to having a visionary dream at age two, she claimed. In this dream, she was visited by a messenger who told her that she had a father in heaven, to which she replied, "'How can I have two fathers?'"[45] Her childlike concern with having multiple fathers mirrored the section of Okah Tubbee's biography in which he claimed he was passed from an Indian father to a white man and "began to understand that I could have but one father."[46] Her insistence that she experienced divine revelation also reflected the importance of such visionary practices among early Mormons, many of whom received otherworldly communications and manifestations of the spirit, some of which were deemed dangerous to the individual, the church, or both.[47]

In her extraordinary dream, young Lucy's celestial messenger told her that she was "given to a fallen people to do them good."[48] Her vision is imbued with Latter-day Saint theology, drawing on the Book of Mormon's characterization of American Indians as descendants of the Lamanites, a fallen people who had destroyed their kinsmen but would one day be redeemed. This brief statement also contains a veiled reference to a deeply held belief among early Mormons, especially those at Kirtland—the imperative to be of service to American Indians. It was this calling that had inspired the early missionaries to leave New York in the first place, putting the Stantons directly in their path. But the perceived connections between Mormons and Indians ran deeper still. Missionary Oliver Cowdery went so far as to assert that a Lamanite prophet would rise to prominence and inaugurate the new millennium, and Smith promised elders who would missionize the Indians that they would intermarry with the Native women, making the "red man's posterity 'white, delightsome, and just.'"[49]

Although Lucy Stanton maintained that she was an Indian in the later autobiography, her recollections often seem to externalize the Indianness she claimed. That she could hope to help "a fallen people" without acknowledging her own apparent position among them demonstrates the point. Despite these inconsistencies, her faith was clearly central to her sense of self.

She was a serious and zealous child, refusing to play and instead spending her time "conversing" on the visions she received. Because her heavenly visitor had instructed her to read the Bible to be saved, she pressured her parents for an education and recalled, "I made rapid progress in learning, and before I was eight years old, I had read the Bible through by course." These brief details reveal a sense of both her calling and her ambition and reflect the profoundly generative spiritual environment at Kirtland.[50]

Young Lucy's angelic visitor bestowed one additional blessing upon her—a patriarchal blessing. Although it shares some similarities with other forms of Christian shared prayer, the patriarchal blessing is a central part of Mormon religious practice. But in describing it, she took pains to characterize it as an *Indian* practice by including a separate section titled, "Patriarchal Custom of Blessing Children, Observed by the Indians." Even as she honored her upbringing, she worked to disguise Mormon practices as "Indian customs." In her own blessing ceremony, she recalled that the angel "put his hand on my head, blessed me, and taught me to pray. He told me that if I continue to do this, which I promised to do, that my Heavenly Father would give me whatever I wanted . . . [and] I should go and dwell with him in a neverending eternity."[51]

A key element of the Latter-day Saint patriarchal blessing is the recitation of one's lineage and ancestry, so it is perhaps unsurprising that in her effort to reinvent her identity, Laah Ceil would have invoked a form of patriarchal blessing within the later autobiography. Although the content of specific patriarchal blessings is sometimes withheld from researchers, evidence nevertheless indicates that several such blessings were given to women in Kirtland, promising them the opportunity to teach the "daughters of the Lamanites" and revealing that Lucy Stanton was not the only Mormon woman who received an Indian-inspired spiritual directive in Ohio.[52]

The physical manner of bestowing such blessings also reflects an important feature of early Mormonism—the power to bless and to heal through the laying on of hands. Indeed, in his earliest visit to Kirtland, rumors swirled about Joseph Smith's healing abilities. One eyewitness recounted Smith's claim that he could bring a deceased child back to life, only to discover after hours of waiting that the feat could not be accomplished.[53] Despite some notable failures, occasional successes confirmed Smith's holiness among believers and strengthened their faith in the ritual laying of healing hands on ailing bodies. Like other women in her community, Lucy Stanton probably witnessed some of these events and experimented with her own ability to exercise such powers. In fact, while other avenues of authority within the Mormon faith would increasingly be restricted to men of the church, attitudes about ritual healing remained more egalitarian.[54] When questioned about whether such practices should be confined to the priesthood of men, Smith endorsed the women's role, saying that "the sisters would come in possession of the privileges, blessings and gifts of the priesthood" by signs "such as healing the sick."[55]

Another aspect of the religious fervor in Kirtland also proved instructive in Lucy Stanton's life. As a young lady, she was among several white women who were briefly captivated by the man known as "Black Pete" and would reportedly "chase him about." An enthusiastic participant in the Big Family at Morley's farm, Pete was one of the first, if not *the* first, person of African descent to convert to Mormonism.[56] He had been born a slave in western Virginia and had worked as a blacksmith and a farmer before being manumitted around age twenty-nine. After settling in Geauga County, he joined in the religious ferment there and became a notable folk preacher, influenced by the same frontier Methodist evangelism that had taken hold in communities across the Middle West. As previously noted, he was already a member of the experimental religious community in

Kirtland when the Mormon missionaries arrived from New York and while it is unclear to what degree he accepted and was accepted by leading figures in the early church (there is some evidence he was admitted to the priesthood), he was certainly influential in the same circles. One historian asserts that Pete could apparently "offer something few others in the region had" as one of only six free blacks in the county, and most of the Mormon converts came from areas in New England where their contact with African American religious practices was minimal. In particular, Pete was a leading figure in grafting "the slave shout," a particular form of enthusiastic Methodist worship, onto the early practices of the Mormonites.[57]

When the Mormon missionaries arrived in Geauga County, Pete was front and center, his popularity reflecting in part the spread of African American Protestant enthusiasm and its attractiveness to white congregants. The Methodist practices of shouting and ecstatic bodily expression were notable among worshippers of African descent in the United States who were seeking both spiritual relief from their oppression and a conduit for expressing the distinct cultural influences that shaped their worldviews. But other aspects of his behavior were cause for concern. Among other peculiarities attributed to the charismatic visionary, it was widely reported that Pete could speak in tongues and had magical powers. He easily convinced a handful of followers, but was plagued with doubters too. He said he could not be touched by flames, but when skeptics made him sit upon a fire, his pants burned right off. He was known to run about grasping unseen pages from a sacred text that were falling in showers from the sky, once sailing off an Ohio rooftop and into the Chagrin River in pursuit of an invisible letter.[58] Still, he was not the only Kirtland worshipper who engaged in such behavior, and though he seemed to have a magnetic power to convince others of his talents, he was not initially regarded as dangerous.

Within a few months, however, Pete ran afoul of racial boundaries that even the egalitarian Mormons felt must be maintained. His behavior became even more alarming when he began to accumulate a disproportionate number of white female followers, some of whom were quite passionate about his "pretensions." When rumors began to circulate that white women were sharing not only his holy visions, but also his bed, he was widely criticized if not threatened.[59] Despite the rhetoric of racial harmony, the Mormons had their limits.

Lucy Stanton never mentioned these events in her autobiographical sketch, but debates about religion and sex in Kirtland must have influenced her. And she was not untouched by other local controversies. From 1831 onward, the Mormons under Joseph Smith's direction began to purchase tracts of land and to expand their property in and around Kirtland. Disagreements about the nature and ownership of these properties, as well as the failure of a church venture in banking, ultimately led to widespread discontent among and toward the Mormons. But their financial investments and the growing pains that accompanied them were not entirely attributable to the expansion of the church alone. Indeed, this period was one of development (though uneven) and commercial growth in the region as a whole. As new roads and canals were opened and old ones improved in the 1830s, thousands more migrants arrived from the East seeking a future in lands recently ceded by Native nations, like the Potawatomis, Miamis, and Delawares.[60]

In Kirtland, the Mormons distinguished themselves from other newcomers by building a temple, "the first superstructure erected by command of God."[61] It was the first of several planned Mormon houses of worship to be built, but Lucy Stanton missed the groundbreaking in June 1833. By that time, she had migrated along with a Mormon vanguard to western Missouri, near Independence, where Smith had prophesied that they would establish their Zion along the borders of the Lamanites. Although shrouded in misdirection designed to amplify claims about her father's Indian identity, she nevertheless alluded to this migration in the later autobiography, noting, "My father removed to Missouri."[62]

Their journey to the West was motivated by several revelations Smith received in Ohio during 1831 and 1832. These revelations provided for the ordination of numerous men, including Daniel Stanton, into the evolving priesthood structure. The newly ordained were then appointed by further revelation to pursue various means of maintaining and expanding the church. Stanton was among those who were directed to "journey into the regions westward, unto the land of Missouri, unto the borders of the Lamanites" (Doctrine and Covenants 54:8).[63] They were instructed to "not tarry" and to "obtain places for your families, inasmuch as your brethren are willing to open their hearts," whether sent east, west, north, or south. Smith's keenest interest, however, was for the Mormons to settle to the west, alongside or among the Lamanites whose destiny was intertwined with that of the church.[64]

Missouri shared its western border with the unorganized territories that were home to numerous established Indian nations and rapidly filling with the removed portions of others. In addition to Indians' theological centrality, many Mormons were influenced by the moralistic, political, and humanitarian concerns of other northern and eastern Protestants opposed to Indian removal. As such, they may have felt sympathy for the disappearing and presumably degraded people who had faded from their daily lives but appeared ever more prominently in their imaginations.[65] But the Mormons were not categorically opposed to Indian removal. Latter-day Saint newspaper editor W. W. Phelps remarked, for example, that the federal government's removal policies were a fulfillment of prophecies regarding the gathering of Indians in preparation for the end of days. For the early church, the Indians of the West, whether long resident or forcibly resettled, were now key to the creation of a New Jerusalem, a boundless Zion where red and white believers would ultimately flourish together.[66]

Important as it was, the Mormon migration to Missouri was not the only significant event in Lucy Stanton's life during 1833. That same year, she married Oliver Harmon Bassett, ten years her senior. Bassett had come to Ohio with his parents, but his father perished during a river crossing as they entered Geauga County. He and his brother Heman were largely on their own when their mother remarried and were quickly swept up in the excitement around the early Mormon movement in Kirtland. Heman, in particular, took to the faith with enthusiasm, emerging as an eager if inventive proselytizer who often teamed up with Black Pete to "harangue" the local population.[67]

Because Lucy Stanton Bassett's perspective on this period is veiled in her later autobiographical sketch, the circumstances of her courtship and marriage at age seventeen are somewhat mysterious. Nevertheless, it took place during a time of considerable excitement among the Mormons. In Kirtland, where Joseph Smith had remained with the bulk of the church members, work on the temple was well under way and various church-related financial schemes still occupied the attention of the citizenry. Meanwhile, a large group of Mormon migrants, including the Stantons and the newlywed Bassetts, had arrived in Missouri to reinforce the struggling brethren sent there earlier to minister to the Lamanites. Smith's call for his people to found a new Zion in Missouri would ultimately become one of the most important of his revelations, but realizing it was both difficult and dangerous.

Sudden and violent anti-Mormon sentiment emerged among Missourians in Jackson County who feared that their new neighbors harbored abolitionist sentiments, an intention to unite with the Indians on their borders, and a plan for political control. These radical new settlers declared their intention to righteously overspread the land that they believed God provided for them, and they did little to conceal their belief that Independence was the New Jerusalem. Non-Mormon Missourians contended that the new "sect of 'pretended Christians' had a corrupting influence on slaves, offered free blacks a share in their Zion, and boasted of their imminent possession of the county," and likewise charged them with "Indian tampering." They tarred and feathered local Mormon leaders and destroyed the recently installed Mormon printing press.[68] Objections to the Mormon newcomers from Ohio ranged from complaints about their sheer numbers to condemnations of their business practices. From the perspective of many non-Mormon inhabitants, however, many of the most distressing aspects of early Mormonism were theological, rather than social or political. Their practices of glossolalia and xenoglossia, in particular, disturbed their non-Mormon neighbors. Observers frequently identified this feature of the faith as the most impressive to gullible followers and the most ridiculous to critics.[69]

By mid-1833, anti-Mormonism, once limited to scurrilous editorials and obscure pamphlets, exploded into full-blown vigilante violence. Newly settled Mormon families in Missouri, including the Stantons and the Bassetts, were targeted in the ensuing attacks. Many fled to Clay County where they hoped to find refuge. Not unlike Indians who were being removed from their homes and sequestered in territories where they could ostensibly be "protected" from those who threatened them, the Mormon exodus had been endorsed by many in the region as a solution based on the logic of separation and containment. Recognizing the need to either insulate or isolate the Mormons from the non-Mormons in the state, the Missouri legislature then organized an "Indian-style reservation" in Caldwell County for their resettlement. The borders of the new counties proved entirely inadequate to protect the Mormons and the anti-Mormons from one another, however, just as they were proving useless in protecting the newly resettled American Indians from the onslaught of squatters and speculators who quickly pressed into Indian Territory.[70]

In this atmosphere of violence, persecution, and displacement, Oliver and Lucy Stanton Bassett welcomed their first child, a son named Solon, in 1834.[71] They had little in the way of property and may have been living with other church members because of their poverty. When their daughter Seraphine Ann was born two years later, Oliver Bassett paid only the county poll tax, suggesting that he still had little other taxable property to his name.[72] His payment of this tax, however, reflected the continuing Mormon determination to participate in local electoral politics, whether or not they possessed other means of influence. Nearly all the Mormon men in Clay County paid the poll tax and voted in large numbers, exciting the ire of their neighbors.

Beneath this turmoil, the Missouri Mormons were also experiencing internal controversies that shaped Lucy Stanton Bassett's relationship to the church. Just as the Missouri troubles began to worsen, her father Daniel Stanton was called to testify about the Hulet branch, a subset of the Clay County Mormons accused of having "imbibed certain principles concerning the gifts that are not thought to be correct."[73] The problem was not a new one.

When Joseph Smith had arrived among the early Mormon enthusiasts in Ohio, he had been surprised and alarmed by the widespread practices of ecstatic worship, receiving visions, and tongue-speaking. Almost immediately, he received revelations regarding the proper functioning of the church and restricting who could receive the "gifts."[74] But these irregular activities continued in Missouri, complicating the Mormon efforts to establish their Zion. Although the church had been largely egalitarian in its early days, with "public claims for authority . . . made largely on the basis of religious experience and charisma," by the mid-1830s, there was an increasing emphasis on organization along hierarchical lines.[75] Defining and enforcing an emergent doctrine was both important and difficult, particularly in the face of real and imagined persecution.

The problem in the Hulet branch was with Sister Sally Crandall. She and several other church members received spiritual "gifts" or revelations, quite apart from Smith's earlier directives. Some suspected that these activities were encouraged by a Methodist interloper named Samuel Brown. Others implied that Crandall herself was the mastermind. The resulting controversy revealed that similar problems were apparent in other branches, and the ruptures were causing "a split and disunion in the Church." An investigation into the members of the Hulet branch uncovered their belief that they "received the word of the Lord by the gift of tongues." Even more distressing, they apparently "would not proceed to their temporal business without receiving the word of the Lord . . . [and]

would not receive the teachings of the ordained members, even Brother Joseph Smith, Junr., himself, unless it agreed with their gifts."[76]

The Crandall family had long been at the center of the "power business." Years earlier, one observer recalled, more than thirty men and women had felt the power during a prayer meeting at Mr. Crandall's log cabin in Ohio. Among other antics, women fainted and fell scandalously across the laps of the men.[77] Suggestions of impropriety (whether sexual or spiritual) abounded later in Missouri, when Sally Crandall claimed that she alone could interpret Sylvester Hulet's spontaneous tongue-speaking and see into "men's hearts." Both she and Hulet were vigorously chastised, their activities deemed to be emanating from the devil.[78]

The controversy reflected two serious problems in early Mormonism, both relevant to Lucy Stanton Bassett's position within the church. These problems were central to emergent church doctrines and Smith struggled to resolve or contain them without alienating his followers. The first of these was the Book of Mormon's clear insistence on the power and necessity of personal religious revelation, an emphasis that nevertheless stood in stark contrast to Smith's own increasingly apparent beliefs that the pluralism and individualism of the era were a threat to the traditional patriarchal order his church hoped to restore. His efforts to retain control over the activities of church members may have been rooted in broader anxieties that emerged from the increasingly secular and superficially egalitarian social order that accompanied the Jacksonian period. Smith frequently cautioned other Mormons about tongue-speaking and receiving revelations, warning, "Do not indulge too much in the exercise of the gift of tongues, or the devil will take advantage of the innocent and unwary."[79] The Doctrine and Covenants, a collected statement of Smith's revelations and a central text in the Mormon liturgy, contains repeated references to early congregants and leaders who were reprimanded or even cast out for defying his authority and theocratic control.[80]

Although it is unclear whether Lucy Stanton Bassett continued to "speak Injun" or engage in bodily expressions of ecstatic faith as she had in her youth, in Missouri both practices were increasingly pushed to the margins of acceptable Mormon behavior because they endangered Smith's authority from within and brought unwanted attention from without.

The second problem also related to the question of authority, but centered more specifically on the proper role of women within the church and its rituals. In Ohio, women had been central to Mormon religious meetings and emerged as influential interpreters of both the Book of Mormon and their own spiritual experiences, in the form of visions, revelations, and healing. Suffice it to say that while healing continued as an accepted (even honored) sphere of female influence, the ecstatic religious experiences of women like Sally Crandall, the Stanton girls, and Laura Hubbell (a self-proclaimed "prophetess") were increasingly seen as a direct threat to the patriarchal authority that Smith, as well as other early church leaders (all male), intended to cement.[81] "Consolidation of authority" was "an early and persistent goal of the Mormon leadership," and defining and enforcing the appropriate roles women should play in the church was key to this effort.[82] As a female visionary, tongue-speaker, and ecstatic worshipper, Lucy Stanton Bassett may have existed at the extremities of emergent doctrinal Mormon practices, her activities viewed in terms of foolishness, defiance, or apostasy.

Although the Hulet episode and related controversies ebbed, anti-Mormonism did not. Back in Kirtland, church members who had continued building their bustling Ohio settlement were driven from the state by opponents in 1838.[83] And in Missouri the seething hostility of antagonistic non-Mormons was again bubbling to the surface. In the summer of that year, twenty-two year old Lucy Stanton Bassett gave birth to her third child, Semira La Celestine, in a covered wagon while "it was feared the Mob would attack the camp."[84] And attack they did.

In August, armed anti-Mormons tried to prevent Mormon men from casting their votes, fearing that their great numbers would unduly influence the outcome of the elections, as they had in Jackson County, where Mormon residents had settled densely—to better "control the elections," their opponents feared—and constituted a full third of the populace.[85] The fighting that erupted from the standoff at the polls began the Missouri Mormon War in earnest.[86]

The battles that characterized the conflict were fought mostly between Missouri militiamen and Mormons who had armed themselves following their expulsion from Independence. The presence of a number of Mormon men among the local militias complicated the situation further. Although anti-Mormon Missourians claimed that the Saints sought to bring on the millennium by combining with and inciting the vengeance of American Indians on the border, Mormon men had turned out in droves for militia service when an Indian attack was suspected, ready to defend against the "barbarous savages."[87] As a result, when these militias were called out to take action against the Mormons, confusion reigned. There were deaths

FIGURE 3 The Missouri Mormon War. The Missouri militia attacked Mormon families settled at Haun's Mill and elsewhere in Caldwell County, Missouri, in October 1838 following Governor Lilburn W. Boggs's "Extermination Order." The event is of singular importance in LDS church lore. Image appears in T. B. H. Stenhouse, *The Rocky Mountain Saints* (New York: D. Appleton, 1873), 97. (Courtesy Utah State Historical Society, Salt Lake City, Utah)

and casualties on both sides and a great deal of Mormon property was destroyed, including nearly all of their dwellings. Mormon and anti-Mormon forces took turns being the aggressor; in late October, Missouri governor Lilburn Boggs issued an order calling on state citizens to force the Mormons from their borders or kill them on sight.[88] (See Fig. 3.)

Mormons and anti-Mormon Missourians waged pitched battles, and the prophet, Joseph Smith Jr., was himself was thrown into the conflict. As militia detachments converged on the settlement of Far West, the Mormons were overwhelmed, and Smith was put in jail in Liberty, Missouri. The rest of his followers embarked on an eastward exodus toward the Mississippi River under the direction of thirty-seven-year-old Brigham Young.

Bundling their children into wagons and carts, at least 10,000 Missouri Mormons endured a forced migration into western Illinois during the winter of 1838–39. The surviving narratives of their exodus resonate with contemporaneous accounts of Indian removal.[89] The most well known of these episodes, the Cherokee Trail of Tears, took place that same bitter winter, as 15,000 Cherokee men, women, and children were marched from their homelands in the East to Indian Territory west of the Mississippi River. Both the Mormons and the Cherokees were accused of political presumption. Both saw their leaders unjustly jailed and had their printing presses destroyed. Both unsuccessfully petitioned federal leaders to intervene on their behalf.

As Native peoples marched west, the Mormons marched east, crossing the same great river in the same season and enduring conditions that were, at least superficially, strikingly similar.[90] Given their obsessive interest in the fate of the Indian "remnant"—an interest that had contributed to their own persecution at the hands of anti-Mormon Missourians—the Mormon refugees surely recognized the resemblance. Even though the Mormons were among the beneficiaries of Native dispossession—living on land recently emptied of its indigenous inhabitants—accounts of the Mormon exodus resonated with stories of Indian removal, down to the ubiquitous image of bloody footprints left in the snow.[91]

Lucy Stanton Bassett made no direct reference to this period in her later autobiographical recollections. In fact, she skipped over this era altogether as she recounted her life before meeting Okah Tubbee. Although she included a reference to her three children, she was careful to imply that they were Tubbee's children, mentioning their births within two sentences of remarking on her marriage to the flute-playing Indian. But the way she characterized her relationship to the children in the passage is revealing, to say the least. She confessed, "I have watched over my heart with a careful eye, lest I should place them between me and my duty, and the Father should take them to himself."[92] Her mission to the "fallen people" described in her childhood vision seemed to take some precedence over her relationship to the children. To please God, and by extension to preserve and protect her children, her focus on Indian salvation could not waver. But it is unclear to what degree or by what means she pursued this goal during her first marriage to Oliver Harmon Bassett. Like other Mormon faithful swept eastward during the Missouri debacle, her focus may have been less on millenarian prophecies and more on day-to-day survival.

Of the Mormons who successfully evacuated from Missouri in 1838–39, most gathered along the east bank of the Mississippi River about 150 miles north of St. Louis.[93] Situated in Adams County, Illinois, the city of Quincy became a refuge for many Latter-day Saints who arrived in a "suffering condition" but were "kindly treated" by local citizens.[94] Indeed, the memory of Quincy as a Mormon place of shelter remains an important part of Latter-day Saints (LDS) church history and lore. Ultimately, Joseph Smith would move the church to Commerce, establishing a new city called Nauvoo, based on his interpretation of a Hebrew word meaning "comely place" or "beautiful site." But in the meantime, the bustling city of Quincy with its excellent ferry facility proved a convenient gathering spot.[95] Lucy and Oliver Bassett arrived there in April 1839 with their three children and settled alongside Lucy's extended family.[96]

Although it seems likely that Oliver Bassett, like other displaced Mormon men, sought a temporary job in Quincy, it is difficult to determine what sort of work he pursued.[97] During the Missouri troubles, he sold all his carpentry tools for a team of oxen to carry his frightened family out of the state. Perhaps he pooled resources with his brother, Heman, who ultimately settled further east in Sangamon County with his wife and two young children. For his part, Lucy's father, Daniel Stanton, sold some land he'd acquired in Missouri to pay for his family's exodus and worked to establish himself within the church hierarchy once the family arrived in Illinois.[98] By 1840, he had been named stake president in Quincy, a position of some authority as it allowed him to oversee a number of Mormon congregations. But when Joseph Smith and church leaders settled upriver and selected that site for the new holy city, other Mormons followed, reducing Stanton's stake to a mere branch and effectively demoting him.[99]

During their time in Illinois, the scattered Mormons put the pieces of their community back together. They worked to increase their membership, expand missions abroad, and revise their organizational structure. During the Nauvoo era (1839–46), the Quorum of the Twelve Apostles, originally conceived as a sort of traveling Mormon high council that would handle church issues in the absence of organized stakes, increased in importance, and apostle Brigham Young distinguished himself as a talented administrator. Work began on a magnificent Mormon temple and roles and responsibilities within both church and city operations were defined. In many ways, Nauvoo was truly a place of Mormon innovation.

One such new creation was the Nauvoo Female Relief Society, founded in 1842 as a women's cooperative organization dedicated to healing the sick and helping the needy. Women's roles within healing rituals had increased since Kirtland and their participation in such rites, like washing and anointing, was authorized and defended by Smith himself. Although it was preferable for male elders to administer to the sick or injured through the laying on of hands, women were more commonly the doctors in antebellum families. From the beginning of the Mormon Church, women engaged in formal and informal healing rituals, making use of their considerable practical experience, often with great success—and Lucy Stanton Bassett was among them.[100]

During their first difficult year in Illinois, the Bassetts' fifteen-month-old daughter, Semira, suffered a terrible fall from which she was not expected to recover. Her injuries were severe; Lucy sent for Joseph Smith, but worked to heal the little girl herself until he arrived. They then prayed over the child together, and after the prophet "anointed and administered" to her, she was ultimately revived.[101] Although this was probably not Lucy Stanton Bassett's first experience with healing through the laying on of hands, this seminal moment helped determine her own later course as a professional healer, affirming the power of her faith as well as of her natural talents. That it took place alongside the formal recognition and institutionalization of women's roles as healers in Nauvoo highlighted healing as a way of accessing spiritual and perhaps social power.[102]

Despite the florescence of the Mormon Church during these years on the Mississippi, it was in many ways a detour for many of the faithful who still sought their New Jerusalem farther west. Nevertheless, it was a momentous period in Lucy Stanton Bassett's personal life. Though she may have felt empowered by changes that were under way in the church, she was stranded downriver in Quincy, rather than in Nauvoo, the real center of the action. In addition, she had three small children, her "little charge" as she called them, and her household was troubled.

Youngest daughter Semira later recalled that her father Oliver "had so little faith in Mormonism [that] he wished to return to Ohio . . . and take his 3 children with him." He initiated divorce proceedings on September 6, 1843, and four witnesses, including notorious revelator and Hulet branch agitator Sally Crandall, were subpoenaed. Although it is unclear whether they were ever legally divorced because the subpoenas were mysteriously withdrawn, the Bassetts were nevertheless separated by the end of 1843.[103] Lucy's perspective on the split remains unknown, but her daughter's suggestion that religious differences underlay the rift is an intriguing one. The involvement of Sally Crandall in the case also suggests that disputes about religious expression may have unnerved her less zealous partner. Perhaps to protect the children from abduction by their father, they were sent to live with Lucy's parents, Daniel and Clarinda Stanton, who had recently moved to Lima, in the Iowa Territory.[104]

Around 1845, somewhere between Quincy and Lima, Lucy first set eyes on the man then known as William McCary. She later recalled, "Casting an eye into the street, I saw an Indian whom I knew must be a stranger. Although I had no thought of ever seeing him again, yet I called my sisters, saying 'do you see that Indian brave? I never saw or heard of him before, but I *shall* know him well, for he will be my husband.'"[105] Although she claimed that this comment was a joke on her part, she was nevertheless deeply affected by their first conversation. After the chance meeting, the "brave" appeared before the Stanton family and immediately asked Lucy to marry him. When she coyly replied, "O yes," the assembled family shared a good laugh. Drawing forth a flute, he played a tune for them. He then played another on the "sauce-panana," an instrument he had invented after having a dream about its construction. In the dream, he was commanded by a mysterious voice to create an instrument from a sauce pan and use it to unite scattered flocks of sheep, whom he interpreted to be the Indians, "driven by the pale-faces." According to the later autobiography, he surmised from the dream, "If I could visit them with some simple instruments of music, the harmony might melt the savage heart, and unite the broken and wasting tribes."[106]

Upon hearing his visionary dream, the divorced mother of three reportedly confessed, "I was now willing to become his sheperdess in a cause which had engrossed the most of my attention through life, and was still dearer to me than all things else," including, possibly, her children. After their first encounter, she considered what had transpired. Although she still thought McCary's proposal might be "all a joke," she was intrigued. When the mysterious Indian returned the next day, he told her that he had foreseen their union in a dream. He said he had been travelling in search of her and insisted that his request to marry her was no jest. As she listened eagerly, he told her, "'The Lord had provided me a help meet in you, to teach [the Indians] the truths of religion, by precept and example.' . . . by uniting our destinies, [we can] do a good work for our poor people."[107]

Curiously, the Indian stranger insisted that the nuptials must take place immediately. Although Lucy had already determined to accept his proposal, she recoiled at the pace. McCary told her it was now or likely never, though it is hard to say precisely what motivated his sense of urgency. But the union of an Indian convert and a white Mormon was not unheard of. In addition to Smith's prophetic promise that Mormon elders would be united with Native women in Zion, there was the example of Louis (Lewis) Dana, an Oneida man from New York. Dana had been baptized in Illinois in 1840 and was charged with overseeing the Lamanite missions. He became a member of the Council of Fifty and was sealed to a white woman, "the first such mixed marriage so solemnized."[108] He apparently "styled himself 'an Interpreter of six tribes'" and planned to use his linguistic talents to convert other Indians. If Lucy's visionary Indian suitor needed a role model for gaining ground with the Mormons, he did not have to look very far.

Since the establishment of Nauvoo, the Mormons had frequently hosted other Indian visitors who no doubt contributed to views on the role of Lamanite converts in the church's future. In addition to Dana and a Shawnee convert named Joseph Herring, who was also confirmed in the priesthood in Nauvoo, a delegation of Sauk and Fox Indians led by Keokuk was received in the city in 1840. Over one hundred strong, they appeared in "full dress" and made quite an impression not only on Joseph Smith, who was busy devising a series of secret Lamanite missions, but also on the Mormon populace. Keokuk evinced a familiarity with the Book of Mormon and promised to follow Smith's instructions for right and good behavior.

Just a few years later, a deputation of Potawatomi Indians similarly appeared in Nauvoo, with more than mere formalities in mind. They complained of their treatment at the hands of the U.S. government, stressed that they had been unjustly driven from their homes, and appealed to Smith for help in uniting a confederacy of tribes in the Indian Territory. While Smith and his closest advisors secretly tried to capitalize on such meetings and observers accused the Mormons of more "Indian tampering," the appearance of these delegations made a strong impression on the faithful. Few went further than Jonathan Dunham, who was Smith's confidante and deputized liaison among the Potawatomi, Brothertown, Stockbridge, Oneida, and Delaware peoples, and known to some in Nauvoo as "Black Hawk," a moniker that signaled his opposition to U.S. Indian policies by referencing Keokuk's old anti-American foe. The provocateur even signed his letters "J Dunham Lamanite," suggesting his participation in Mormon appropriations of Indianness that had begun in Kirtland a decade before.[109]

When William McCary appeared on the scene, the Mormons may have called these predecessors to mind. For her part, Lucy Stanton saw in him the chance to fulfill the heavenly commandment she had received as a small child. By uniting with this Lamanite visionary, she could finally "do good" to the fallen people who were not only prophesied to help bring about the new millennium, but who were also actively seeking the assistance of the Mormons to unite their "scattered tribes" and resist further dispos-session. She agonized over his insistence that they marry so quickly, later recalling, "I gave him my hand to say adieu; my heart failed me. I asked myself if it could thus set aside an opportunity of realizing its long cher-ished hopes, if it could thus allow perhaps a false modesty to step between it and duty." And while she knew her parents "did not fully understand his plan," she confessed, "it seemed so beautiful to me."[110] Maybe she believed or wanted others to believe that he was *the* Lamanite prophet whose com-ing Oliver Cowdery had foretold in 1831.

Whether members of the church accepted him as such, Apostle Orson Hyde's willingness to baptize McCary and marry the pair apparently rested on his perception of the stranger as an Indian. Others reported that Hyde regarded McCary as a "Lamanite prophet" who, like Louis (Lewis) Dana, would carry the Latter-day Saints' mission to the western tribes.[111] After cryptically promising Lucy's parents that he would not take her to the South, the pair received their blessing.[112] In February 1846, amid the threat of another anti-Mormon mob attack, Lucy Stanton and William McCary were sealed (or married for all eternity) in Nauvoo.[113]

Being an Indian was thus McCary's entrée into both the Mormon world and Lucy Stanton's life. It was an identity that had already inspired the fascination of many early converts and a tool for demonstrating his use-fulness to the church.[114] He may have also hoped that it deflected suspi-cions of African American ancestry and any association with his past as a slave. For Lucy Stanton, channeling Indianness had also been founda-tional in her experience of Mormonism. Being married to a converted Indian provided her a practical way to fulfill her mission of doing good to the "fallen" Lamanites.[115] And becoming the wife of a charismatic mis-sionary could also bring her esteem and influence, offering a form of social redemption following the collapse of her first marriage and a means of accessing power increasingly restricted within the church.[116]

Like many other Mormons, Lucy Stanton McCary clearly felt a deep sympathy and affinity toward American Indians, or at least the Indians of her imagination. This affection and even identification was rooted not only in her understanding of the Book of Mormon and Smith's revelations concerning the Lamanites, but also in her personal visions and sense of divine purpose. By her own account, she was so intensely invested in this mission that she purposefully guarded against allowing her maternal affections to threaten it. Although she confessed that her "little ones still needed a mother's care," she was nevertheless willing to do what was necessary to see her "fondest hopes realized."[117] In addition, her experience of persecution and injustice at the hands of professedly Christian Americans and her subsequent flight from the Mormon promised land in Missouri resonated with the contemporaneous removal of thousands of American Indians from their homelands. Finally, her position as a divorced woman with a history of irregular spiritual practices placed her on the margins of Mormon acceptability. Marrying an Indian might have been more than a way to meet her personal and spiritual needs. It might also have demonstrated her particular commitment to what she believed was the original mission of the church at a tumultuous time when many were clamoring for the right to define its future course. Thinking herself Indian may have seemed like a logical next step. Picturing, mimicking, seeking, and saving American Indians—whether imagined or real—was key to how Lucy Stanton McCary (and many others in the early Mormon Church) understood and expressed their religion.

• • •

Indianness was not an alternative to Mormonness, but a register for experiencing and expressing it. Because it came through the laying on of hands in a patriarchal blessing, Lucy's particular Indian calling was also rooted in two aspects of early Mormonism that would suffuse her later life: a faith in the power of healing touch and an uneasy compromise between the authority of men and the gifts of women.

Appropriating an Indian identity could also have more practical immediate benefits for Lucy. Although the Mormons on the Mississippi may have accepted both William McCary's Indianness and the apparent marriage of a white woman to an Indian man (and there is evidence to suggest some accepted neither), their interracial union would most certainly face scrutiny among non-Mormons. Far more than merely a spiritual or intellectual project, performing Indianness would become an exercise in survival.

CHAPTER THREE

Building a Following in the West

• •

The McCarys Reinvent Themselves

In the spring of 1846, a St. Louis newspaper mentioned an interesting performance held at the Martha Washington society meeting in Quincy, Illinois. The "Martha Washingtons" were popular ladies' temperance societies that sprang up around the United States in the 1840s and frequently hosted entertainment events to raise money and awareness for their cause.[1] The Quincy meeting was of particular interest to the reading public in St. Louis because the featured performer was one "Mr. Carey, the celebrated Indian Flutist." The paper pointed out that he was a "worthy of some celebrity in St. Louis," but in a thinly veiled reference to his perceived African American ancestry, suggested dryly that he "belong[ed] to a pretty widely distributed tribe." An announcement for the event invoked pity for the removed Indians, while valorizing their communal ethic, asking the public to attend and "divid[e] with the poor, as the Red Man will do, that is now on his way to the far distant west."[2]

"Mr. Carey" (aka William McCary) and his new bride, the former Lucy Stanton Bassett, may have hoped that local audiences would "divide" their dollars and fund their journey out of Illinois. Having been sealed in eternal matrimony just a few months earlier, they were among the mass of Mormons who left the region in the face of growing anti-Mormon persecution that had already led to the murder of Joseph Smith in 1844.[3] In rhetoric evocative of Indian removal, Mormon opponents declared—at point of bayonet—that they "desire[d] the removal of the Mormons . . . [to be] effected peaceably, and with all possible despatch."[4] Lucy's daughters had already migrated into the Iowa Territory with their grandparents and most of the Nauvoo Mormons fled to adjacent unorganized territory west of Missouri. The newly married pair chose a different path.

The next two years were a tremendously generative period for the Mc-
Carys, who were busy fashioning new identities for themselves. It is unclear whether they collected many donations for their cause in Quincy. But
the fact that they did not head straight for the temporary western Mormon
encampments known as Winter Quarters suggests that they were either
still short on cash, or had another agenda, or both.

. . .

When the McCarys resurfaced, it was along the Ohio River in Cincinnati.
By October 1846, they had established themselves at the corner of Race
and Centre Streets, less than a mile from the bustling port that peered
across at slave-state Kentucky. One wonders why they chose to travel to
Cincinnati. Perhaps William McCary thought of the city with some fondness because he had received his freedom there, Robert McCary having
appointed local attorney Almon Baldwin for the purpose of "manumitting
liberating and setting free from slavery forever" his half-brother.[5] Or perhaps the locale offered inviting prospects for his newly Indianized musical stage show.

In either case, the nature of the McCarys' activities in Ohio reveals that
they were experimenting with new identities and practices that probably would not have met with the approval of Mormon leaders, who were
otherwise preoccupied trying to restore order to the church and move its
headquarters further west. Since Joseph Smith's death at the hands of an
angry Illinois mob two years earlier, the Mormons had been in considerable disarray. Although the threat of violence persisted and the Illinois
state government put increasing pressure on the Mormons to abandon
Nauvoo, it was a succession crisis within the church that generated the
greatest sense of anxiety. Former Campbellite preacher and prominent
Kirtland figure Sidney Rigdon was one contender hoping to follow in
Smith's footsteps, and several others also came forward to claim the authority of church guardian or president. Among them was James Strang,
a self-styled monarch and prophet who led a group of supporters called
"Strangites" into Wisconsin and Michigan. Ultimately, church authority
was determined to rest with the Quorum of the Twelve under the leadership of Brigham Young, who dismissed other claimants. Nevertheless, it
was a time of contention, confusion, and defection, as some Mormons lost
faith and left the church.[6] As one contemporary put it, "There has been a
great falling off on account of aspiring men that wish to set themselves up
for something when they are nothing."[7]

Although he was not directly involved in the succession crisis and the Mormon flight from Nauvoo, McCary's role in the church became a point of contention during these debates. A Strangite newspaper in Wisconsin went so far as to accuse Orson Hyde, another contender for church leadership who had recently baptized McCary, of maliciously endorsing him as a Lamanite prophet in a perverted effort to "to destroy the churches which he cannot rule."[8] Although this opinion was probably not widely held, it suggests that in spite of McCary's status as a newcomer among the Mormons, he was a magnet for controversy.

His departure to Cincinnati did not end speculation about his possible role as a schismatic pretender. There were already a handful of Strangites in Cincinnati, including noted African American convert Elijah Abel, priest Frederick Merryweather, and Charles Thompson, who knew and briefly worked with the McCarys.[9] At the same time, there were at least a handful of other Mormons in the city working to uphold Young's claims to the presidency. So it is unclear whether the McCarys were Strangites, Brighamites, Rigdonites, or perhaps simply McCaryites.

Regardless of what brought them to Cincinnati, the McCarys did not go unnoticed. In late October 1846, a local newspaper reported, "We are informed of a new fanatical sect in this city, now numbering about 60, more than half females, following a big burley half Indian, half negro, formerly a Mormon, who has proclaimed himself Jesus Christ! He showed his disciples one day last week, the scars of wounds in his hands and limbs received on the Cross! He does miracles with a golden rod and professes that he was the cause of the destruction of Natchez by whirlwind." Given that Warner McCary was reported to stand five feet four inches in 1843, when he appeared before the Natchez Police Court, the Ohio paper's description of him as "big" and "burley" is curious. Perhaps it referred more to his charisma than his stature; he was larger than life.[10]

The McCarys established a headquarters in the city and began organizing their followers into different stations, or positions, within the new church. One account claimed that the "Pretended Lamite Prophet" was teaching transmigration as a means to apostolic restoration. That is, he claimed the ability to inhabit and to appoint others to inhabit the identity of deceased apostles. He said he was Jesus Christ and then appointed other men of his little church to assume other identities. For instance, the apostle Paul was reported to have been "restored" in the person of Charles Thompson, although he later denied it.[11] Beyond the controversial nature of these practices within emergent Mormon doctrine (to say nothing of wider Protestant views), McCary's assertion of his ability to shift identities so boldly is striking. In addition, his performance in Cincinnati was a doubled one; even as he claimed to be Jesus Christ restored, he was simultaneously claiming to be an Indian prophet. This insistence on the flexibility of his identity had already become a hallmark of his performative career.

In addition to concerns about racial and spiritual imposture, the Cincinnati press also warned about the potential for sexual transgression among the McCarys' followers. Their pretensions, editors claimed, were "well calculated to deceive people who are void of stable principles, and would rather be led away than otherwise. Look out for more sensuality in open daylight, in your families, and almost before your eyes, all under the cloak of sanctity."[12] Indeed, fears about the allure of charismatic pretenders, prophets, mesmerizers, and spiritualists—and the particular vulnerability of women to their charms—were widespread in this era. Salacious stories and cautionary tales appeared in newspapers across the country, reflecting a widespread anxiety about the decline of traditional patriarchal authority and women's foolish embrace of philosophies that challenged it.[13] Owing to their perceived sentimentality and weak intellect, American women were considered easily manipulable, in danger of being seduced away from their fathers and husbands by dangerous, if faintly ridiculous, impostors who upset the social order to satisfy their own base desires. Joseph Smith himself had been widely vilified as a seducer and defiler of innocent women, and Mormon marital practices would continue to come under such scrutiny for decades.[14] In a similar vein, one observer in Cincinnati specifically accused the McCarys of having "abolished marriage" and "practiced many evils" among their followers.[15]

Although the couple's activities in Cincinnati may appear distinct, if not bizarre, the local newspapers recognized the relationship between the McCarys' "new religion" and both Mormonism and Millerism (William Miller's nascent Seventh-day Adventist Church), couching the McCarys' little movement within the broader wave of sectarian innovation still rolling across the nation in the late 1840s. Described as an "Indian flu[t] est," McCary was sketched as a unique sort of pied piper, leading followers to ruin and relieving them of their dollars. Nevertheless, he was also understood as one of many such pretenders plaguing the nation with their schemes.[16]

One month later, the *Cincinnati Commercial* updated the public on the "big Indian Mormon." He had traveled alone to Louisville, where he claimed he had trouble raising money for the return trip to Cincinnati.[17] His followers across the Ohio River took up a collection and paid his way, after which he dispensed blessings written on white paper with an iron pen, or keel, like those used to mark sheep. The newspaper claimed to have obtained an "exact copy" of the blessing, which it guessed the pair was selling rather than giving to their followers. The "very secret" and "highly prized" blessing was presented as an Indian custom, but it was distinctly Mormon in origin. It read, "Accept this blessing in the name of the Son, Jesus Christ, Mary the mother, God our Father, our Lord, AMEN. It will preserve yours, yourself, your dead, your family, through this life into celestial Kingdom, for your name is written in the Lamb's Book of Life. AMEN." Only the mention of "Mary the mother" departs from the typical form of contemporaneous Mormon patriarchal blessings. Despite their early success through this and other means, however, by November 1846, their followers numbered only thirty.[18]

Given her longer experience in Mormon liturgy, Lucy McCary may have taken responsibility for crafting their rituals and practices in Cincinnati. She was also busy creating a new identity for herself. During this brief period, she adopted an Indian persona using the name "Luceil Bsuba." Although she had exhibited an interest in Indians since childhood, the Cincinnati paper provides the earliest evidence of Lucy performing Indianness outside the Mormon context, describing her as the "big Indian" prophet's "Delaware wife."[19] She may have chosen the Delawares as her fictive tribe because of the success the first Mormon missionaries claimed they had among the tribe in 1831. Maybe she had also been influenced by stories about a buried Delaware ancient text, the *Walum Olum*, that bore a strong resemble to Joseph Smith's golden plates.[20] Or perhaps the historical importance of prophecy to Delawares and other Algonquians, like the Shawnees, who had given the world revolutionary prophets Neolin and Tenskwatawa, inspired her own prophetic aspirations.[21]

Regardless of her motivation for claiming Delaware ancestry specifically, thinking Indian had been a central part of her experience of Mormonism. Indianness was thus a mode of spiritual expression. But fears of anti-Mormonism may also have encouraged her to become Indian as a way to mask her involvement in the Mormon Church, for which she and her family had been cruelly persecuted, and channel her ambitions into devising a new life that she found spiritually, socially, and financially more fulfilling.

By transforming themselves into enterprising spiritual leaders and experimenting with various means of attracting followers, William and

Lucy McCary were also honing their performative techniques and learning about the desires of urban antebellum audiences. He brought his experience as a mimic and entertainer. She brought her firsthand knowledge on how to build a church out of charisma and nerve. In these early days, religion was their stage, and Indians were characters they played for protection and for profit. But the pragmatic aspects of their strategy do not preclude the possibility that their spiritual imperatives were genuine and deeply felt. Even prophets have to eat.

In their public performances of Indianness, the McCarys were hardly alone. In the era following Indian removal, the practice of playing Indian had been expanded and transformed. Whereas earlier fraternal organizations such as the Tammany Society (named for seventeenth-century Delaware leader Tamanend) paid little attention to the accuracy of their representations, new groups launched in the 1840s were increasingly concerned with Indian disappearance and were thus more invested in salvaging what could be saved from the vanishing tribes. Authenticity was the name of the game. For example, Lewis Henry Morgan's New Iroquois Confederacy, a fraternal organization whose membership peaked in 1846, went beyond the activities of earlier societies that had simply appropriated Indian names and images for political and social activities largely unrelated to Native people. Instead, Morgan's group claimed descent from the Iroquois and made extensive use of both costuming and ethnographic props to perform what they referred to as Indian rites and rituals. The quest for genuine Indianness, ironically couched in a form of impersonation, marked the birth of salvage ethnography, an effort to capture, document, and preserve authentic cultures believed to be fading away.[22]

In addition to fraternal societies, Indian figures were also common on the antebellum stage, as orators and activists, dancers, musicians, and as characters in tragedies and comedies.[23] At the same time that McCary and his "Delaware wife" were launching their professional Indian act in Cincinnati, Anishinaabe orator, activist, and performer George Copway (Kah-ge-ga-gah-bowh) was on a lecture tour through the northeastern United States. He sought to bring attention to his people's acceptance of "civilization" in order to secure a permanent territory for them and was also active in the temperance cause. As one contemporary observer put it, "Indian lecturers" such as Copway and his mentor, Peter Jones, had the ability "to touch the nerves of the great sensorium of philanthropy," even if they were not particularly eloquent.[24] In addition to advocating for certain policies, professional Indians also capitalized on antebellum audiences' desire for trivia on the vanishing race, such as "Indian traits and customs" lore largely calculated to highlight Indian otherness, while mourning their inevitable decline.[25] Topics included "Romantic Life of the Indians" and "How Indians Get Their Names" and were found both on the stage and in popular literature, including the composite autobiography the McCarys would later produce.[26] Professional Indians used such ethnographic details to perform their authenticity for primarily white audiences, particularly in the Northeast where narratives of Indian extinction were obsessively rehearsed in pageants, memorials, and town histories.[27]

In effect, the displacement of thousands of American Indians from the eastern United States encouraged a growth in certain kinds of Indian performance as a form of "guilt-cleansing" entertainment.[28] As a consequence of such "imperialist nostalgia," recently removed Native peoples—like the Choctaws and Delawares—emerged as popular objects of both pity and charity.[29] In Cincinnati, the McCarys capitalized on this increasingly popular mode of thinking about Indians, even as they were also defining a religious movement. Performing Indianness could provide them with both an audience for their spiritual message and a source of income. In fact, the temperance event in Quincy may have been a kind of test run. A civilized Christian Indian couple, presented in "bold relief to the mind of the philanthropist," could solicit contributions to help relieve the "melancholy" plight of their red brethren.[30] And, of course, claiming Indian personae might have also deflected attention away from their interracial marriage.

Although the McCarys had early success in Cincinnati, detractors began to put a strain on their "new fanaticism."[31] The little church was falling apart. As one observer put it: "The Black Indian has blown out, and all his followers here are ashamed."[32] By the beginning of 1847, the McCarys had a choice to make.

The pair decided to join the rest of the Mormons out west and by the end of February they were in Winter Quarters, a sprawling collection of encampments situated along the Missouri River and concentrated near present-day Florence, Nebraska. (See Fig. 4.) This vast camp was the gathering place for church members preparing for the overland trek further west.[33] It was surrounded by a variety of smaller settlements across the river in Iowa that altogether boasted a population of nearly twelve thousand, despite the departure of the large Mormon Battalion sent to fight in the Mexican War. By the time the McCarys arrived there, Winter Quarters had several hundred dwellings, and while some were hardly more than

FIGURE 4 Mormon settlement near Winter Quarters. One of many vast
temporary encampments erected along the Missouri River in Iowa and Nebraska,
following the expulsion of the Mormons from Nauvoo, Illinois. Conditions at these
settlements varied. Some were barely more than a few mud dugouts in the river
bluffs, but others had streets, shops, and even a dancing school. Image appears
in *Harper's Monthly*, April 1853. (Courtesy Utah State Historical Society,
Salt Lake City, Utah)

lean-tos and dugouts, there was nevertheless a dancing school, a store, and
a council house.[34]

Despite her brief effort to adopt a Delaware identity in Cincinnati, Luceil Bsuba returned to being known as Lucy Stanton McCary. She did not
present herself as Indian to her family, her Mormon neighbors, or to the
Indians who surrounded them at Winter Quarters. Though the Mormons
had been busy building houses and planting acres and acres of crops
from Kanesville southward along the Missouri River, they were sometimes squatting on Indian land. Indeed, in addition to the many Mormon
refugees, the area was home to a jumble of resident and removed Native
groups, including Potawatomi, Sauk and Fox, Wyandotte, Illinois, Omaha,
Stockbridge, and Delaware people.[35]

While the McCarys had been, as they later put it, visiting "the principal towns in Missouri, Kentucky, Indiana, and Ohio," Lucy's "little charge"
had remained with their grandparents at Kanesville (present-day Council
Bluffs), one of the outlying settlements. The girls spent most of their time

farming, spinning, and weaving, much as the Indians on their borders had been instructed to do under the federal "civilization" plan.[36] Rather than settling down with her parents and children, however, Lucy and William McCary went to work.

In February 1847, newly installed church president Brigham Young was treated to an unusual concert by "Mr. McCarey," who demonstrated his talents on a flute, fife, whistle, and saucepan. Alternately regarded as "the Indian musician," "a professed Spaniard," "a half-blooded Indian," "the Choctaw Indian," and "the nigger Indian," his musical entertainments were well-attended.[37] It was a welcome diversion for the sprawling community that had suffered great hardship over the winter and seen many of their number perish from disease and malnutrition.[38] Perhaps the Mormon audiences had been primed by the performances of the Nauvoo Brass Band, whose remnants had also made their way to the Missouri River.[39]

"McGarry . . . a half blooded Indian," as Mormon diarist John D. Lee called him, impressed Brigham Young, who concluded that he could be of use and amusement to the emigrant companies, provided he would listen to counsel. Young declared, "His skill on the flute cannot be surpassed by any musician that I have ever heard," and instructed the church leaders to "use the man with respect."[40] Although Lucy McCary could not keep up her Delaware persona in Winter Quarters, she soon distinguished herself as a person of influence too, largely through the claims of her entertaining and enigmatic Indian spouse.[41]

At the same time, William McCary was refining his performance of Indianness. Once, while visiting Young's home, he became annoyed with noisy children nearby. He wondered aloud, "'How people could talk easy when others were talking & playing in same room,'" and asserted that "amongst Indians[,] 'children were not allowed to talk or make any noise, you may be amongst 100 Indians from 1 year old to 10, or from 10 to 15, or from 15 to 20, & you will not hear a word, neither any noise. But you may hear a Cambric Needle drop on the ground.'"[42] The statement probably reflected McCary's legitimate irritation at the dissonance, but it also resembled the sort of "traits and customs" trivia that his listeners might have both expected and desired of Indians. And it makes clear that McCary was practicing his Indian identity both on and off stage, seizing even informal opportunities to convince the Mormons of his authentic Indianness.

Meanwhile, visits by Native men and women, particularly Omaha people on whose land some Mormons had settled illegally, were fairly common. Like the Choctaws who came to Natchez during McCary's youth, the Omahas and other Native peoples came selling moccasins and other beaded items, but were also accused of begging, pilfering, stealing livestock, and generally making a nuisance of themselves. However, some observers also recorded their communal ethic—a value deeply shared by many of the Mormons, some of whom had been original members of the "Big Family" experiment in Kirtland. Robert Campbell noted in his journal that "when any of them got any Johnycake they would divide with each other all the time. A Bro: said of the Indians, that although it was only one potatoe they would divide it all round."[43] That this observation was recorded at all reflects the sort of ethnographic impulse that underlay the popularity of "traits and customs" lore evident in other aspects of antebellum popular culture.

The McCarys might have had contact with the Native people who frequented the Winter Quarters area, perhaps even acquiring clothing and props they would incorporate into their later performances. And they probably took note of the admiring comments made by Mormon women who pronounced one visiting Potawatomi man "stately looking" and declared the Shoshones the "best looking" Indians when decked out in their "costumes of skins, ornamented with beads."[44] In other words, Mormon attitudes about Indians may have been as instructive as observing Native people themselves.

On February 26, 1847, the McCarys had their first formal meeting with church leaders. According to church secretary and future editor of the *Deseret News*, Willard Richards, the pair was introduced as "Mr. McCarry— a professed Spaniard—with Lucy his wife formerly Lucy Stanton, & a Stranger." During this meeting, the McCarys reported news from Columbia, Missouri. On their way through the area, they heard that "the 'Mormons' were gone to California last fall, & some who had stayed behind had been in battle, & were all killed off by the Indians." This information was probably a reference to the activities of the Mormon Battalion then still in the far West, and the McCarys may have brought word simply because current news was hard to come by at Winter Quarters. But it is difficult to determine what else they meant to convey by presenting such a message to church leaders. Perhaps they hoped that by bringing news of Indian violence, they could highlight the difference between savage Indians and McCary himself, a temperate, trustworthy, and Christian Indian. In any case, delivering this purportedly urgent message secured them an audience with the Quorum of the Twelve, the emergent center of church power. Although the alleged Indian attacks seemed to garner little notice, Richards did take care to report that "the Council separated about 9 many going to hear the Nigger Indian play on his Flute," his choice of descriptors revealing an early ambivalence about the newly arrived musician's race.[45]

Soon the McCarys attracted more serious attention. A little more than a week after their report on Indian depredations, Richards recorded this note: "Heard report that the Nigger Indian McCarry was holding private meetings over the River. first entering into a Covt. of Secresy."[46] Perhaps it was an effort to revive their Cincinnati congregation, and they had resurrected their secret covenant. Just as in Ohio, they quickly inspired both followers and detractors. There were early rumors about irregularities involving "Mr. McCarey a Choctaw Indian married to a white woman named Lucy Stanton, a sister," but church leaders had their hands full with the many unauthorized "kinds of religion" going on in Winter Quarters.[47]

In fact, there were a number of controversial meetings and schismatic sects in Winter Quarters that spring and summer as the Mormons prepared for the arduous transcontinental trek. As one diarist wrote, "There was as much dissension now as ever I saw in or at any other period of Church history." In March, the Quorum of the Twelve delivered a "warning [to] the people against those who may rise up and try to lead off parties."[48] Such fractures had multiplied in the years after Joseph Smith's death. Even though Brigham Young was largely confirmed as the "rightful" successor to Smith, other claimants to the position of church president lingered, and a number of powerful factions and schismatic experiments were in operation. Some of these groups sought immediate fulfillment of Joseph Smith's revelation to convert the Lamanites and tried with varying degrees of success to unite with area Indian nations in order to realize that mission. For instance, both Lyman Wight and Alpheus Cutler were invested in drawing the church closer to American Indians and split off with cohorts of supporters in 1845 and 1847, respectively. George Miller, a follower of Wight, also left with a group of adherents to missionize the Delawares and Oneidas living in the vicinity. Regardless of the minor successes they had among the Indians, such schismatic activities were viewed with extreme concern by church leaders.[49]

Thus, when Richards reported on "the Nigger Indian McCarry" and his divisive activities, the implications were serious.[50] The McCarys, like others vying for some measure of power and authority, took advantage of widespread confusion and despair at Winter Quarters in launching their own little movement. Because of his claims to be a Lamanite prophet, some observers associated McCary with the "Lamanite redemption doctrine" of both Wight and Miller.[51] The McCarys' movement may have been of particular concern, however, not only because it undermined emergent church authority, but also because it appeared to transgress both racial and sexual boundaries.

From his first appearance in Winter Quarters, there had been widespread disagreement about William McCary's race. And his marriage to Lucy Stanton, consistently identified as "a white woman," did not pass without notice.[52] While interracial sex between white women and black or Indian men was not uniformly condemned in the United States, popular antebellum attitudes toward such pairings nevertheless reflected anxiety and sometimes hysteria.[53] Interracial marriage was especially problematic. At the time that William McCary and Lucy Stanton were sealed in Nauvoo, for example, Illinois state law held that marriage between blacks and whites was punishable by fines, whipping, and prison.[54] Despite an initially tolerant attitude toward the (limited) participation of African-descended people in the church and the marriage of Oneida convert Louis Dana to a white woman, the Mormons at Winter Quarters shared some of these broader antebellum antipathies towards interracial pairings. In the context of both schismatic threats and transgressive relationships, the McCarys' Mormon neighbors began to turn against them.

One observer recalled that William McCary "had converted a good many to his kind of religion" but also noted that he was "in favor of holding his meetings of the men and women separately." It appeared that "his teaching to the men and to the women was entirely different," implying spiritual—and perhaps sexual—indecency.[55] When the McCarys were called to appear before Brigham Young and the apostles in March 1847 to answer for their actions, they deflected any suggestion of apostasy and sexual misbehavior by accusing their Mormon neighbors of gross racism and disrespect. In other words, they relied on a classic performative technique—misdirection.

William McCary addressed himself to the assembly as "a brother" and told them bluntly that he was being abused in Winter Quarters. He complained that church leaders had counseled his neighbors not to allow him into their "wigwams" and said that when he walked by, he often heard them say, "There go the old nigger & his White Wife." He wanted to know who had sanctioned such contempt. If he had erred, he wanted to learn to "walk right." But he was more interested in pointing out the prejudice he faced in Winter Quarters than answering for his sins. Referring to biblical stories of the curse of Ham and mark of Cain that provided scriptural justification for white supremacy in American Protestantism broadly and the Mormon faith specifically, he asked, "We were all white once, why [have] I the stain now?"[56]

With his wife at his side, McCary then waded further into the murky question of his origins and focused the assembly's attention on his identity.[57] First, he said, "I came in as a red man & want to go out as a red man," suggesting that despite skepticism about his religious pretensions, he was determined not to surrender his Indianness. But suppose he was *not* Indian, he proposed, still "dont these backbiters think that I [have] feeling [even] if I was a nigger [?]"[58] His fixation on the injustice of epithets and falsely ascribed racial labels recalls the time he assaulted a Natchez teenager who also called him "nigger," but his statements also hint at his faith in the flexibility of his identity.[59] Although McCary's tone before the assembly was mostly humble and contrite ("I have got baptism I am thankful for it," "if I am wrong I want to walk right"), he was nevertheless critical of his white Mormon neighbors and attributed their disrespect to racist and unchristian behavior.[60]

As he continued his oration, McCary asserted that the Mormons at Winter Quarters recognized little difference between blacks and Indians. He declared, "I'd as like to be as a nigger as [an] Indian as many think they are as [one]," suggesting that many Mormon believers thought similarly of the two races.[61] Although Mormon liturgy provided frequently idealized references to American Indians and both missionaries and schismatic leaders were actively working in Native communities, the Mormons in and around Winter Quarters were nevertheless squatting on Indian land and *actual* Native people had become something of a problem. For instance, in addition to fears of thieving Indians "lurking about" Winter Quarters, a group of Potawatomis tried to kidnap one Mormon girl and succeeded in kidnapping another near present-day Council Bluffs around the same time.[62] Mormon fantasies of Lamanite redemption met a hard reality when Native people resisted the intrusion of trespassers or otherwise acted in ways incongruent with romantic ideas about them. Perhaps, like other antebellum Americans, the Mormons at Winter Quarters "desired Indianness, not Indians."[63] Such ambivalence had already provided McCary the opportunity to perform a brand of Indianness that capitalized on

Mormon desires, while distancing him from an association with Native violence. Now he used it to hint that white supremacy was at the core of the faith.

Turning from his racial to his spiritual identity, William McCary then addressed the counselors on the topic of transmigration. Between Cincinnati and Winter Quarters, he had claimed to be "Adam, Ancient of days, Jesus, and the Lamanite prophet," in addition to giving a variety of more prosaic aliases.[64] Initially, these claims may have raised the most concern among the Quorum of the Twelve, given the context of fractious assaults on church authority. McCary offered to change his ways, but only if they agreed to help him determine his true identity.[65] He told them: "I am come here for my Salvns. sake & providing I get this feeling from you I will walk the rit. road. some say I am as Adam, some as the Indian Prophet."[66]

He then apparently began to speak in non sequiturs that included jokes, stage asides, rants against Mormons, and frequent, if not obsessive, references to his body.

> If I am Adam. & we was to say here comes a head jumping along with a head white as wool. they wod. say where is your body?—oh Ive left that home (laugh) I wish to cleanse my self my heart, my manners c [&] I want to love you if I am black sheep. I am speaking of 4 leg sheep now. to see the head come along c [&] sa[y] I am ancient of days c [&] leave body at home is two things—provided ancient of days comes he must bring his body along—provided I was Adam what wod. the ppl do—why theyd be as the dog was with the hot dumpling—if old [Jos. Fatr.] was to come—I want to know how many Fatrs. c [&] mors. to save ppl.—we must [av] far. c [&] mor. [Fathers & Mothers] to save ppl in some wa[y].[67]

In both the reference to Adam and the image of the disembodied head (and presumably, a disembodied voice), McCary may have been acknowledging the accusation that he had, "by his ventriloquism made [some] believe that God spoke unto him" or through him in the figure of Adam.[68] McCary was apparently drawing on skills that he had developed as a performer in Natchez and elsewhere. For example, his claims of apostolic restoration, first evident in Cincinnati and seemingly continued at Winter Quarters, required a set of extraordinary techniques, including xenoglossia, mimicry, and throwing his voice, not to mention considerable audacity.

As he continued, McCary increasingly focused the attention of the assembly on his body itself. Indeed, his fixation on his physical characteristics and others' perceptions of them dominated much of his testimony.

I av [have] got as strait hair as any other prson—look at it there is no sight in left eye—no hearing in left ear—I want to understand among the 12 wher. I am protected if I do right. if there is so much fuss about it that I have a lost rib you give it up there can be no stuffing, one man confesses to be Adam. and. the ancient of Days.

He then undressed, chiding the Mormon leaders for their "mock modesty," and saying, "you can see c [&] examine . . . my body, see all . . . ex. for yourself." He donned his "red skin . . . costume," which apparently left his abdomen exposed, and invited the counselors to examine him, noting that he was missing a rib. Willard Richards touched McCary's flesh, reporting, "I don't discover any thing novel." McCary pointed to his wife, Lucy, and remarked that there sat the odd rib, making a humorous reference to Eve having been created from Adam's rib.[69]

Besides his claims to transmigration, McCary was apparently keen to convince the Twelve that he was not of African descent, using his "strait" hair as evidence. Although he willingly submitted to, and in fact insisted upon, their physical inspection, the scene of powerful white men touching and inspecting his partially nude form nevertheless resonates with contemporaneous images of both slave auctions and the "scientific" examination of racialized bodies.[70] McCary emphasized his awareness that the body was both the subject of and the very site of debates about race and identity, not only among the Mormons, but beyond them as well. And he offered his own figure as proof of his claims.

Finally, McCary came to what he believed was the heart of the matter—his marriage to a white woman. This, he contended, was the central objection to his presence in Winter Quarters. He declared, "so long as a White woman is so much in the way, good God why dont they give me a red woman . . . as my Wife is not ashamed I dont think you will be ashamed."[71] It is unclear whether he hoped to add a plural wife (a practice increasingly apparent at Winter Quarters) or exchange his white wife, Lucy, for a "red woman." But these statements, along with his earlier reference to nasty comments about the "nigger and his white wife" imply that his marriage to Lucy Stanton was the principal complaint against him. Although such disapproving attitudes were readily apparent, McCary was also emphasizing this particular controversy to distract the Quorum away from concerns about his spiritual pretensions.

After getting dressed, McCary returned to a focus on the bodily aspects of his presumed race. He pressed Young to clarify his status in the church, saying, "I am not a Prest., or an leader of the ppl but a common bror.—because I am a little shade darker," suggesting that he lacked the priesthood because of his skin color and perceptions about his identity. Young cut him off, saying, "Your body is not what is your mission" and later averring, "we dont care about the color." Despite his protestations, Young's response implied that he was indeed concerned with race and its place in Mormon thinking. For instance, on the question of McCary's identity, Young asserted, "its nothing to do with the blood for of one blood has God made all flesh, we have to repent c [&] regain what we av lost—we av one of the best Elders an African in Lowell—a barber," referring to Q. Walker Lewis, a free black man recently ordained into the priesthood in Massachusetts. Interestingly, Lewis's son had also married a white woman. Despite assertions of tolerance, both Lewis's ordination and his son's interracial marriage provoked condemnation from various members of the church.[72]

Young's decision to compare McCary to Lewis is thus particularly revealing. Ultimately, both men inspired controversies about the position of African-descended people within Mormonism. The statement also implied that Young thought McCary was clearly of African ancestry, despite his claims to the contrary. Mentioning Lewis's profession as a barber, the antebellum vocation so closely associated with free black men that one observer called it their "birthright," further revealed that Young thought of the two men in similar ways.[73] Although he claimed their race was of no consequence with respect to their position in the church, he could not help but point it out anyway.

Nevertheless, Young assured McCary that his race (whatever it might actually be) was no impediment to participation in the church. Still not satisfied, McCary pressed the assembly further, asking "do I hear that from all [?]," and receiving an "aye" from the brethren. Heber C. Kimball asked him, "Dont you feel a good spirit—here bro William [?]" Sighing in relief, McCary replied, "Yes—thank God—there r 2 or 3 men at the end of the Camp who want to kill me."[74] Although church leaders may have been chiefly concerned with McCary's spiritual pretensions in the midst of a schismatic crisis, the "Lamanite prophet" still insisted that local Mormon attitudes toward him were grounded in presumptions about his identity and his marriage to a white woman—ideas that were more or less confirmed by Young's effort to compare him to Lewis.[75]

For her part, Lucy Stanton McCary took a different approach to deflecting criticism. In the midst of the meeting, she defiantly asked Young and the Twelve whether they truly believed the Bible. She stated that while some of it had been fulfilled, some "was not translated right," suggesting a pluralistic view of the Bible and its relation to Mormon theology that had emerged in the succession debates. Young responded that the Twelve believed in the Bible, the Book of Mormon, and the Doctrine and Covenants, as well as the redemptive power of baptism, but Mrs. McCary's reaction to his answer is not recorded. It must have been a tense moment. William McCary tried to lighten the mood by joking, "If we dont be bel the bible, we r in a poor fix for [Stumpers]," humorously lumping the Mormons together with revivalist stump preachers. But he also took the opportunity to again foreground his identity claims by mentioning his Choctaw ancestry and his intention to take his wife to meet his tribe. Against the backdrop of an ongoing debate about Mormon theology, he worked to gain control of the conversation once more, and refocused attention on his identity.[76]

As the meeting came to a close, William McCary declared his intention to travel to the Rocky Mountains along with the rest of the Mormons. He pointedly joked, "That is if you dont pick up the road c [&] put it in your pocket (laugh)." And then, as if by instinct or compulsion, he once more played on his identity and quipped, "I am a Frenchman by trade, but never practice it—(laugh)." After a quick reference to his ability to speak Choctaw and other languages, one of the Twelve spoke to him in Dutch, to which he apparently replied in Dutch (by Dutch, they may have meant German), before taking out his "little thirty six cents flute" and playing a tune. Turning the meeting into a kind of showcase, he followed the impromptu concert with another series of jokes (including a story of the bullfrog who says, "'knee deep,' 'knee deep', & 'deeper' 'wants more bacon,' 'more bacon,' 'fried bacon' & then when they r going to apostatize they sing out 'more rum, more rum.'") These humorous asides were evidently part of his stage repertoire and were repeated in the later autobiography. But they also riffed on the anxiety of apostasy that simmered in Winter Quarters. Concluding his show, he once more reminded the assembly of their promise to protect him and then proposed a (mock) toast. To "the trouser loon gang," he pretended to drink, that they may never be overcome by the "petticoat loon" gang, or that women never prevail over men, a sentiment he may have believed the all-male church leaders shared.[77]

The appearance before the Twelve was an electric and pivotal moment for the McCarys. But since the church leaders were in the thick of planning their westward migration, dealing with fragmentation and factionalism, and handling conflicts with neighboring Indians, it might not have felt as momentous to them. Brigham Young recorded his memories of this meeting: "At sundown, I met the brethren of the Twelve, and others, also William McCarey, the Indian negro, and his wife at the office. McCarey made a rambling statement, claiming to be Adam, the ancient of days, and exhibited himself in Indian costume; he also claimed to have an odd rib which he discovered in his wife. He played on his thirty-six cent flute, being a natural musician and gave several illustrations of his ability as a mimic."[78]

Despite Young's apparently cavalier attitude, just two days after the meeting, the Quorum delivered an oration against false leaders like McCary.[79] More than debates about the doctrine of transmigration or even the pitiful condition of many Winter Quarters inhabitants, Young worried about the defection of believers from the church. Although he and the Twelve may have meant to sanction the McCarys for their schismatic activities, the pair took the counselors' guarded assurances of spiritual equality to mean that they could continue building their own little movement.

By April, they had established a headquarters on the east side of the Missouri River at a place called Mosquito Creek. According to an observer, McCary had "induced some to follow him," by telling them that he was "a prophet the ancient of days whose hair was as wool" a reference to visions revealed in the Book of Daniel (Daniel 7:9) that could be interpreted as referring to Adam. McCary's apparent insistence on his own embodiment of the first man and his interest in transmigration reflect topics of "warm" discussion along the Missouri River during the Mormon sojourn at Winter Quarters.[80] His claims may have also reflected the considerable involvement of his wife who, it will be recalled, claimed to have read the entire Bible by age eight. She may have been mobilizing her own interpretation of the scriptures, contrary to emergent Mormon doctrine, while also working to shape her husband's image in terms that would be legible to his Mormon audience. Despite a scathing condemnation of such schismatic sects delivered by Apostle Orson Hyde, who had been credited with baptizing and sealing the "Lamanite prophet" just a year before, the McCarys' movement was hardly slowed by the rebuke.[81] But William McCary's emphasis on performing an alternate persona that drew attention to the texture of his hair suggests that questions about the physical evidence of race continued to vex him.

By October 1847, the vanguard of Mormon pioneers returned east from the Rockies to find considerable confusion at Mosquito Creek. Despite mounting opposition, the McCarys' following was growing. They had built their own "kind of religion" among the people of the Springville branch situated at Mosquito Creek, exploiting frustration among Mormons temporarily settled there while catering to their fascination with Indianness.

Nelson Whipple, a member of the Quorum of Twelve who had witnessed McCary's "rambling speech" earlier in the year, was sent to assist the Springville branch president, whose ailing health prevented him from keeping control of the situation. Whipple recalled, "[McCary's] talk and pretensions were of the most absurd character, and it would appear that no rational being would adhere to it for a moment, but many did." Whipple had no respect for McCary's "pretensions," religious or racial, calling him "a mulatto or quarterrun who professed to be some great one, and had converted a good many. . . . It appeared that he understood the slight of hand, the black art or that he was a magician or something of the kind, and had fooled some of the ignorant in that way."[82]

What drew the McCarys' followers to them at Winter Quarters? In addition to the possible lure of interacting with a comparatively "civilized" Indian, some followers might have simply been seduced by his considerable performative talents. In light of recent battles for control of church authority and the lingering desire among some adherents to experiment with unauthorized demonstrations of ecstatic faith and revelation, his xenoglossia and ventriloquism were probably thrilling. Perhaps being accompanied and assisted by his white wife, a woman once distinguished for her own prominent role in "the power business," underscored his claims to spiritual authority in the eyes of congregants, while elevating her status from a divorcée to the wife of a prophet.

Indeed, Lucy McCary's presence and participation must not be overlooked. She was at McCary's musical performances and may have even arranged them, acting as manager and agent, as she would later do in the East. She had been at both meetings with the Twelve, even interrogating church leaders about their faith. Clearly, she was willing to speak her mind and determined to be heard. She was probably also instrumental in the development of her husband's prophetic movement, shaping his claims according to her interpretations of Mormon theology and possibly her own ambitions.

Despite the rising tide of concern at Mosquito Creek, the McCarys put their unique religious principles into practice by formulating their own rituals. Most alarming to Whipple was that the McCarys had devised their own sealing ceremony, which they were apparently using to experiment with a form of plural marriage.

"Celestial," or plural, marriage had first been introduced when Joseph Smith revealed its importance to the faith in 1843. He had a revelation that men and women "could be 'sealed' together for eternity in the temple," a union distinct from "carnal" marriage, but he also asserted that men could take multiple wives, a "return to the practice of Old Testament patriarchs."[83] Former Mormon Joseph H. Jackson explained, "A spiritual wife is a woman who, by revelation, is bound up to a man, in body, parts, and passions, both for this life and for all eternity; whereas the union of a carnal wife and her husband ceases at death." In this way, Smith differentiated between "carnal" marriage, in which a man was forbidden to take more than one wife, and "spiritual" marriage; he often quoted from the Hebraic scriptures "to prove his position."[84] Reaction among the Mormons was mixed, with at least some evincing a "great reluctance" to participate in plural marriage. Shortly thereafter, the fire of anti-Mormonism was fueled by lurid rumors, newspaper exposés, and salacious pamphlets about Mormon sexual depravity and abuse of marriage, partly necessitating their flight to the West.[85] Concerns about plural marriage were also evident at Winter Quarters, where it was being practiced more openly than ever before.[86] But the "problem" of polygamy exceeded debates about Mormon practices alone. It also signaled broader antebellum American anxieties about marriage specifically and gender roles more broadly.[87]

Among the charges that anti-Mormon writers leveled at the practice of plural marriage was that it provided church leaders with a "multitiered system of wives and concubines at [their] disposal."[88] Jackson asserted that Smith himself explained the system with a certain fiendish glee, boasting that he had "seduced four hundred women." According to Jackson, Smith told him that he had a number of older women in his employ called "Mothers in Israel."

> If Joe wished to make a spiritual wife of a certain young lady, he
> would send one of these women to her. The old woman would tell the
> young lady that she had had a vision, in which it was revealed to her
> that she was to be sealed up to Joe (or his friend, as the case may be)
> as a spiritual wife, to be his in time and eternity. This would astonish
> the young innocent; but Scripture would soon be resorted to, to prove
> the correctness of the doctrine, and that it was proper in the sight of

the Lord. Soon after this, Joe would appear, and tell the lady that the Lord had revealed to him that Mrs. So-and-so had had a vision concerning her, and had been to see her. Not suspecting any collusion, the young lady would be astonished, and being strong in the faith, she could have no doubt but that Joe spoke by the authority of God.[89]

Jackson was a hardly an objective source, and there is little evidence that Smith ever engaged in such lascivious discussions or activities.[90] But the process Jackson described—of proposing via visions and messengers—is nevertheless striking because it bears a strong resemblance to the McCarys' courtship, as described in the autobiography. Like Jackson alleged of Smith, William McCary had approached the astonished Lucy Stanton and informed her of a vision that they were to be united immediately by divine will. Such an approach may have also formed the basis for the McCarys' experimentation with unorthodox marital practices in Cincinnati and resurfaced in their Winter Quarters sect.

Upon investigation of the Mosquito Creek movement, Whipple concluded that William McCary was engaged in large-scale deception and seduction of Mormon women, with the help of his white wife. He contended, "[McCary] had a number of women sealed to him in his way which was as follows; He had a house in which this ordnance was performed. His wife Lucy Stanton was in the room at the time of the performance, no others were admitted. The form of sealing was for the women to bed with him, in the daytime as I am informed three different times by which they were sealed to the fullest extent."[91]

Perhaps Lucy was leading the women to her husband the way the "Mothers of Israel" allegedly provided partners for Joseph Smith. If so, it is unclear whether she did so of her own accord, following her own understanding of celestial marriage, or reluctantly obeyed her husband's commands, deferring to his authority. Whipple's description of the practice suggests not only a form of plural marriage but also group sex, or at least a shared sexual experience, that certainly exceeded Smith's revelations but was frequently alleged in anti-Mormon diatribes. Although Lucy McCary's feelings about the matter are unknown, she was nevertheless an active participant.[92]

In recounting the experience of one Mrs. Howard "who revolted and ran when she found what the sealing ordnance really was," Whipple claimed that "Mrs. McCarry tried her best to prevent her escape from the house." As a consequence of Howard's flight, the secret of the McCarys' ceremony was revealed. Mrs. Howard confessed her involvement to her husband and told him "who they were that had been sealed in that way to the old darkey." Mr. Howard then approached Sisson Chase, another follower of "the nigger prophet," who was unaware that his own wife had been through the sexual sealing ceremony. When Chase confronted his wife, a woman "upwards of sixty years of age," she confirmed his suspicions. According to Whipple, Chase "was very much astonished at the idea and it is said that he did not speak a loud word for about three weeks that anyone knew of."[93]

When Whipple wrote his account of this affair, he was reflecting on an event that took place some sixteen years before. He named names, not to "bring disgrace upon them," but simply "for posterity." Among the men he counted, "Daniel Stanton, Sr., Sylvanus Colkins, John Atchison, Sisson A. Chase,——Eldredge, Jonathan Haywood," and among the women, "Widow Pulsipher and daughter, Meriah Atcheson, Harriet Stanton, Caroline Stanton, Constanza Stanton, Mrs. Sisson A. Chase." Three of these women, Harriet (age 19), Caroline (18), and Constanza Stanton (16), were Lucy's younger sisters. Whipple called patriarch Daniel Stanton "a full believer," who, despite his later denials, "allowed [McCary's] meetings to be held in his house and his family to attend them and his daughter to marry him." Interestingly, Lucy's mother, Clarinda, was not named among the deluded followers.

Once news began to spread about their sexual ceremonies and unorthodox beliefs, the McCarys' neighbors became openly hostile. Toward the end of October, William McCary fled to Missouri "on a fast trot." Their erstwhile followers were disgraced and cut off from the church, though all but one would later be rebaptized. McCary bore the brunt of local anger; at least one Mormon father declared his intention to "shoot him if he could find him for having tried to kiss his girls."[94] Add to this anger the death threats that he had received earlier in the year, and his immediate motivation for leaving town is clear.

Church leaders were also in the midst of reenvisioning the relationship between race and status within Mormonism. Although intermarriages between whites and Indians were deemed permissible, Young and the Twelve left little room for black-white couples. Since reactions to the Mosquito Creek scandal revealed that few Mormons had continued to accept William McCary's Indian identity, the McCarys' union was increasingly problematic. By the end of 1847, church leaders had taken steps toward a ban on men of African descent in the Mormon priesthood that would be publicly proclaimed in 1852 and not rescinded until 1978.[95] The role of interracial marriage—and by extension the McCarys' union—in the emergence of the priesthood ban appears significant.

When William McCary left for Missouri, Lucy stayed behind. She may have wished to stay closer to her children (ages thirteen, eleven, and nine) living across the river at Council Bluffs with their grandparents. Or she may have stayed behind to take care of their affairs, which raises the question of their income. Although it is possible that their Mormon followers were sustaining them through donations, as was implied about their Cincinnati church, the extraordinary poverty of many people settled in and near Winter Quarters makes this source of income seem unlikely. Other Mormons had been engaged in forms of wage labor for neighboring non-Mormon communities, but there is no evidence that the McCarys were earning money that way. The autobiography offers little in the way of explanation, but local legal records provide a useful clue.

In the fall of 1847, local merchant William Waddell paid William McCary one hundred dollars to cure his wife's epilepsy.[96] According to Waddell, the Indian "doctor" (now using the name William McChubby) had "craftily and subtly deceived" him and had "wholly neglected and omitted and entirely failed to perfect a cure." Waddell told the court that his wife was still quite sick, and he initiated a suit to recover his money from Dr. McChubby.[97]

• • •

Even as he was developing his identity as a Lamanite prophet, Adam, the "ancient of days," and an Indian musician, William McCary was also experimenting with new skills and personae. It is difficult to determine precisely how much he relied on claims of medical expertise to support himself during this period, but the Waddell case suggests a burgeoning strategy that also resonates with Lucy McCary's long-standing interest in healing. Although she was not named in the case, one wonders whether she had advised her husband on the language of healing.

When some of the McCarys' property was attached to pay the alleged debt, William McCary (aka McChubby) claimed that he never owed Waddell a dime. On the contrary, he maintained that he was the one being swindled. To be sure, one hundred dollars was a considerable sum for such a cure and raises the question of Waddell's gullibility or culpability. Had Waddell invented the charge to falsely obtain the McCarys' property?[98] The records yield few further clues.

Shortly after he fled Winter Quarters, William McCary (or McChubby) sent for his wife.[99] Leaving her children and her parents behind, Lucy joined her husband, and they departed almost immediately for the eastern United States. William Waddell's $100 may have paid their way.

CHAPTER FOUR

Becoming Professional Indians

. . . .

The Eastern Debut of Okah Tubbee and Laah Ceil

The end of the 1840s was a time of tremendous contrasts for the couple born Warner McCary and Lucy Stanton. Their highs and lows mirrored a tumultuous and polarizing time across the nation. At the close of the war with Mexico, the United States extended its territorial claims over expansive western lands and thousands of Mexican nationals, whose inclusion within the boundaries of the nation spawned vigorous debates about race and "manifest destiny." Within the McCarys' lifetimes, the territory of the United States tripled in size to include millions of acres of Indian land, much of which had never been ceded or sold. This rapid expansion had already resulted in the dispossession and removal of thousands of eastern Native people, while enabling the extension of slavery into newly "emptied" lands. Mormons sought Zion, and others sought gold in the West, as popular revolutions in Europe displaced thousands of refugees who sought a new beginning in the United States. Debates about race, sex, citizenship, and authenticity abounded, and as the nation grew larger, sectional differences also became more pronounced.

Amid this tumult, the McCarys saw opportunity. Departing from Missouri in September 1847, they made their way east, leaving behind the controversies of Winter Quarters but still constantly endeavoring "to interest the citizens in behalf of the Indians." They publicly advocated that "the present home of the civilized tribes should be a permanent location," a plan almost identical to the one George Copway submitted to Congress the following year.[1] As they traveled from west to east, William McCary or McChubby, the entertaining "Lamanite prophet" and sometime doctor, became "Mr. Chubbee," the long-lost flute-playing son of a Choctaw chief.[2] Lucy Stanton Bassett McCary resumed her Native guise, but now claimed a Mohawk identity instead of and sometimes in addition to a Delaware one.

"The Indian musical genius . . . Mr. Chubbee" made his eastern debut at Carusi's Saloon in Washington, D.C., during the week of Thanksgiving 1847. For twenty-five cents, the audience could hear him play a variety of airs on his "thirty-seven and a half cent" flute (either he had upgraded to a better instrument, or its value had appreciated over the course of the year, since he had told Brigham Young in March that it was a thirty-*six* cent flute).[3] One reviewer claimed that "the air warbled, as it were, above his fantastically caparisoned head," suggesting not only his ability to mesmerize audiences with his music, but also his stage presence and costuming.[4] He may have chosen to wear a sort of turban, reminiscent of the popular portraits of Southeastern Indian men that hung in the Office of Indian Affairs at the time. Or perhaps he wore the tight-fitting beaded cap that became a staple of his outfit in later years. Such ethnographic detail added authenticity to his costume, even as it offered a pragmatic solution to the problem of his hair. His phenotype might have been an especially dangerous liability in antebellum Maryland, which had the largest free black population of any state and frequent demonstrations of antiblack violence.[5] Even though Chubbee (McCary) had been free since at least 1843, his professed Indianness might have spared him some of the scrutiny to which he would otherwise have been subjected.

An advertisement for his first eastern show provided necessary details concerning his origins and background and addressed the question of his race matter-of-factly.

> The celebrated Indian Flutist, Mr. CHUBBEE, will present himself before the citizens of Washington THIS EVENING, in a CONCERT, at Carusi's Saloon. His history is interesting, as one who has been long lost, and is now about to be restored to his friends, and placed in his proper position in the Chubbee family of the Choctaw nation, having been recognized by an old Indian Chief whom he has met in his travels. Thus, after having been torn from his tribe when a boy, he has now been able to trace his origin as the descendant of one of its Chiefs.[6]

This announcement marks Chubbee's first public attempt to claim kinship to Mushulatubbee, still unnamed here, but soon to be identified as the Choctaw chief in question. Perhaps he had been inspired by the claims of Eleazer Williams, a Mohawk Episcopal minister who convinced himself and a few others that he was the Lost Dauphin, the long-missing child of Louis XVI and Marie Antoinette, or the still resonant tales of Ibrahima, the Fulbe prince discovered in his own hometown of Natchez.[7] Whether or not his audience members fully believed this newly crafted backstory, they would have recognized its heroic outlines. And in any case, his music never failed to impress. At least one account claimed that he was wildly successful; his music "threw the audience into raptures" as he played the flute and the sauce-panana. He used his powers of imitation to create the sounds of the flageolet, the clarinet, and the bagpipes, and then astonished the crowd as he played the flute with one hand while accompanying himself with castanets in the other.[8]

Somewhere between Winter Quarters and Washington, D.C., the husband and wife had refined their act and added new details. Ohio River steamboats and hotel barrooms along the stagecoach line between Philadelphia and Baltimore would have provided ample audiences along the way. Although Chubbee's music was at the center of the act, his very presence on stage was part of the allure. Advertisements emphasized that he would appear in his "real" or "original" Indian costume, and one wonders whether it was the same one he donned for Brigham Young and the Quorum of the Twelve.[9] When he took the stage at Carusi's, the Choctaw musician confidently presented himself, not as a Lamanite prophet or Adam, ancient of days, but as "Mr. William Chubbee, the celebrated Indian Flutist," who had only recently and quite coincidentally become aware of his elite Indian lineage.[10] Claiming Choctaw ancestry enabled him to market himself to eastern antebellum audiences captivated by "vanishing" Indians, particularly a tribe that had furnished such renowned figures as Pushmataha and Mushulatubbee. Meanwhile, his costume might have helped suppress suspicions of African descent that would associate him with slavery and amplify concerns about his marriage.

In developing their skilled performance of Indianness, the couple drew on the example of Native performers themselves. In addition to George Copway and Eleazer Williams, they had many other professional Indian role models to choose from, such as Ojibwe minister and activist Peter Jones; Jones's half-brother, Maungwudaus, who managed his own dance and performance troupe; as well as Pequot author William Apess and Cherokee missionary and journalist Elias Boudinot, who had traveled the same circuit in previous decades.[11] "Literary entrepreneur" and "self-invented" celebrity Copway, whose autobiography had as its frontispiece a feather-and-buckskin-clad Indian warrior standing nobly on a rock, may have had the greatest influence on them. He would soon share both an agent and a stage with the Chubbees.[12]

In addition to these Native performers, all published authors who used the three-pronged strategy of antebellum ethnic performance (publish, lecture, republish), the Chubbees would have also been influenced by the proliferation of Indian dramas. Although by the end of the decade, Indian farces were becoming more common than serious dramas, the 1830s and 1840s were the high-water years of the genre and audiences had considerable familiarity with noble but doomed Indian characters. Like the centrality of Native peoples to sectarian movements such as Mormonism and the popularity of playing Indian, the rise of secular Indian dramas coincided with the era of Indian removal. As Indians were being actively expelled from their homelands in the East, the figure of the Indian became "sufficiently remote" from audiences' everyday life to "permit the dramatist to spread the aura of romance around him," while remaining familiar enough "to be rendered convincingly."[13] Northeastern audiences, in particular, were long since blind to the "remnant" Native people in their midst, preferring instead the romanticized and heroic Indians of the West or the past.[14]

The wildly popular Pocahontas theme captured the romanticism of the era. The first successful Pocahontas play was James Nelson Barker's *The Indian Princess; or, La Belle Sauvage* (1808), and other playwrights continued to reproduce dramatic or melodramatic versions well into the 1860s. But the most successful Indian play of the era was *Metamora; or the Last of the Wampanoags*, first performed in 1829 and long associated with actor Edwin Forrest, its successful original male lead. *Metamora* and derivative Indian plays typically portrayed Native protagonists as noble savages, courageous yet kind, with an "indomitable will," fine figure, and vanishing footstep. Metrical romances of Indian life also frequented the stage during this era, with a similar emphasis on heroic and often historical but ultimately doomed central characters, such as Pocahontas, Tecumseh, and Black Hawk.[15]

Another common register of popular Indian performance was the "Indian dance." At first, Indian dances were associated only with frontier settings and perhaps the occasional visit to Washington, D.C., by an Indian delegation.[16] But the throngs of eager spectators at such events ensured that they would quickly make their way into the theaters and meeting halls of eastern cities where audiences hoped to catch a glimpse of the "vanishing" Indians and their curious customs, even as Native people were still being actively removed from their homelands. The patina of authenticity in these shows was the draw.[17] Consider the Philadelphia handbill for a "grand exhibition" at Peale's Museum, which promised, "A company of real Indian warriors and their squaws" or Maungwudaus's claim that his traveling troupe's performances would present "an accurate picture of real Indian Life."[18]

By the late 1840s, however, both the intense romanticism of the Indian dramas and the proliferation of "real" Indian performances spawned farce and parody. *Metamora* was caricatured in *Metaroarer*, which poked fun at Forrest's intensely loud stage voice, and a satire called *Metamora; or the Last of the Pollywogs*. Such parodies "produced a lusty, gay and savage humor, full of barbs flung at the current scene, full of native extravagance." Their central theme was the "false romanticism of American sentiment for the Indian."[19] More "authentic" performances were similarly lampooned. The *St. Louis Weekly Reveille* announced that an upcoming "Grand Exhibition," would include "A Grand War Dance, by Han-Ka-Tan-Ka-Wan-Ka, the Only Surviving Squaw of the Sap Head Chief," as well as a "Duett—On a B flat Gridiron, with See-Saw Accompaniment," and a glimpse of the P. T. Barnum's "Feejee Mermaid!"—all organized by stage manager "James Crackcorn."[20] In such an environment, the very idea of the real was stretched to its limit.

The public appetite for satire suggests both the popularity of Indian-themed entertainment and the potential over-saturation of the market at the moment the Chubbees entered it. That audiences were receptive to these parodies made it all the more important for them to strike the right chord. They needed to be unique but also familiar, entertaining and even amusing, but not ridiculous. They could not risk being associated with the bawdy humor of the popular blackface minstrels shows that toured eastern theaters in the same era, nor did they want to become fodder for caricature or satire.[21] And yet, within a year, Choctaw chief William Chubbee would appear at Barnum's museum, playing a saucepan and other curious instruments alongside Tom Thumb and a giant boa constrictor. Nor were the Chubbees averse to using the bold language of theatrical advertising to solicit support for their shows.

When the "Indian flutist" appeared in Baltimore in December 1847, the concerts were heralded with grandiose advertisements. One read:

GRAND MUSICAL ENTERTAINMENT.

Wm. Chubbee, the celebrated INDIAN NATURAL FLUTIST, will give some of his Musical Entertainments at the University Buildings, Lexington street, on TUESDAY EVENING, Dec. 21, 1847. He will perform, in his original and peculiar style, upon the ONE-KEYED FLUTE AND THE SAUCEPANIANNA. This instrument was discovered by Mr. CHUBBEE through the singular instrumentality of a dream, while he was in search of his home, and for melodious sweetness of tone, is unsurpassed by any musical instrument.

He will be assisted by Mrs. CHUBBEE of the Mohawk Tribe.

He will appear in his Original Costume, and will perform a great variety of MARCHES, WALTZES, COTILLIONS, &c.

Doors open at half past 6 and performance to commence at half past 7 o'clock.[22]

The word "natural" in this advertisement operated on two levels. First, it signaled that he was "self-taught in every respect," rather than a trained concert musician. Second, it underscored his claim that he was an untutored Indian, which made his extraordinary skill that much more impressive.[23] The advertisement also emphasized the uniqueness of his homemade instrument and its origins in a visionary dream, "while he was in search of his home." As in earlier advertisements, the reference to his own mysterious background, reflected an effort to build credulity in his newfound Indian heritage, broadcasting it alongside his distinctive musical talent. Noticeably, Mrs. Chubbee's Native identity was not couched in terms of recent revelation but was instead stated simply as a matter of fact.

"Mrs. Chubbee of the Mohawk Tribe" was a key part of her husband's performance of Indianness. For him to be accepted as an Indian, she had to be an Indian too; her presence helped to legitimate his identity claims. The Winter Quarters episode had proven that even among a relatively tolerant population, the marriage of a white woman and a man suspected of possessing African blood could be an endless source of questioning, if not ostracism and persecution. Because Lucy Stanton's whiteness had been so much "in the way" there, perhaps making her into a "red" woman was the answer. In her first eastern appearance and for many years afterwards, she faced little or no scrutiny regarding her background or her claims of Indian ancestry.

As a white woman, Mrs. Chubbee's race was comparatively unmarked. Over time, her whiteness effectively enabled her to "pass" as Indian more successfully than her husband, whose phenotype subjected him to more suspicion. Although we do not know precisely what she looked like, we might presume that she was "tawny" enough in her features to conjure up a something like the popular antebellum images of Pocahontas, the

Algonquian heroine whose baptismal scene hung in the U.S. Capitol rotunda and whose name and (imagined) likeness was plastered on a vast array of commercial products. Popular Pocahontas plays in which white women exclusively played the role of the Indian maiden-turned-missionary probably also encouraged theatergoers to accept a dark-haired white woman as an Indian. These female Native characters—on stage and in writing—were frequently complimented, not questioned, for their relative whiteness, with their non-Indian traits highlighted and praised. Consider, for example, the following description of "The Fawn of Pascagoula," from a story of the same name that ran in the *Brooklyn Daily Eagle*:

> Among the Choctaw Gipsies who visited Mobile in the winter
> of 1846, was one of unusual beauty and attractiveness. Although
> scarcely developed into womanhood . . . she was yet tall, round
> limbed, straight and graceful—a very model of feminine form—Her
> features more prominent and regular than is usual with her tribe,
> were delicately sculptured, and the erect attitude of her head, with
> her large fawn like eyes, and abundant coal black hair always neatly
> plaited in massive folds, gave to her appearance an air of superiority
> such as youthful Pocahontas is said to have possessed. Her dress
> was extremely neat, checkered with a large number of silver and
> wampum ornaments, and her small feet, which any of the fair
> promenaders en Dauphin might have envied, were invariably
> dressed in moccasins ornamented in the most fanciful style, with
> many colored beads.[24]

Pocahontas and comparable Indian maidens, like the Fawn of Pascagoula, were idealized as loyal friends to white colonizers and sexually available to white men.[25] Although Mrs. Chubbee—by virtue of her marriage, if nothing else—probably did not read precisely as an Indian princess for eastern audiences, she nevertheless capitalized on the popularity of such figures in crafting her own performance.

What was harder to accept, though perhaps no less interesting to these audiences, was the puzzle of the Indian man who looked curiously like a black man. As one scholar has put it, passing, or the ability to choose one's race, has been "dependent on obscuring the non-choice of race."[26] Mrs. Chubbee's unmarked whiteness meant she could choose to act Indian or not, but Mr. Chubbee invariably faced more scrutiny in his claims to Native ancestry, which caused him to make constant references to his body as exhibiting evidence of his Indianness.

In the dominant racial logic of the antebellum period, Indians could be part-white, and some of the most popular Indian characters—historical and fictional—of the era were either of mixed ancestry or perceived as having been "whitened" through acculturation, like Pocahontas. But people of African descent, whether part-white or part-Indian, were increasingly perceived as black, no matter what other ancestors they had. This assumption was ultimately made abundantly clear by the Mormons at Winter Quarters, though they were largely reflecting rather than inventing the notion of African ancestry as a "stain." In the antebellum period and arguably into the present, "skepticism surrounding claims of 'Indianness'" was "dictated not by the color of the 'Indian blood' but of the mixed 'other' blood."[27] In their performances, advertisements, and later writing, the Chubbees did not so much repudiate the logic of biological race as try to work within it, countering accusations of African blood with "certain evidence" of Indian blood and trying to balance black-Indianness with white-Indianness.

Interestingly, the Chubbees' appearance in Baltimore coincided with the first public procession in that city of the Independent Order of Red Men, a fraternal organization that also reified essentialized notions of Indianness. Not unlike the Freemasons and other secret societies and men's associations, the IORM was composed of primarily middle-class (or aspiring middle-class) white men who were inducted into local or regional divisions, called "wigwams," and assumed Indianized names and titles. Related to Tammany societies that had first emerged in the urban Northeast around 1800, these new organizations tended to emphasize the participation of mechanics and artisans—a Jacksonian-era revision of the earlier patriotic and fraternal societies that had appropriated Indianness to their own purposes since before the American Revolution.[28] Such organizations flourished in the East, especially after 1830. As eastern American Indians were "pushed back beyond the boundaries of most daily interactions with Easterners, . . . destined to be 'loved to death,'" non-Indians aggressively tried to assume their place in civic and popular culture.[29]

Like the Martha Washingtons, the IORM appealed to the emergent middle class—and they were fascinated with Indians. But instead of merely sympathizing with Native people or raising funds for their moral improvement, fraternities such as the IORM actively participated in Indian play. That they were becoming active in Baltimore at the very moment Chubbee and his wife launched their eastern careers as professional Indians is particularly notable. On the one hand, such organizations were invested in custodial history, the idea that since the *real* Indians were vanishing, it was incumbent upon the IORM and others to salvage and protect the nation's aboriginal heritage. As one "Red Man" explained, the members "seek not merely to imitate, but to preserve. When the time comes that the Indian race is extinct, our Order will occupy a place original and unique."[30] On the other hand, the presence of such societies also suggests that easterners were amenable to the idea of Indian impersonation, and perhaps, the broader principle that individuals could adopt (and perhaps discard) alternative identities. But the liberating possibilities of such racial masquerade were limited during the antebellum period, particularly if a person showed "evidence" of African ancestry. The fluidity of identity and the utility of Indianness reached its outer limit at the threshold of blackness.

Still, William Chubbee was no ordinary performer. Despite potential questions about his appearance, he seems to have been successful at charming many audiences into believing his claims. For his stage performances, he drew from many sources; his repertoire reflected his long experience as an entertainer. His skills as a mimic and ventriloquist, learned on the streets of Natchez and most recently deployed in Winter Quarters, served him well. His years as a militia musician taught him all the patriotic standards, and he knew scores of popular dancing songs from his time as a musician-for-hire playing balls and cotillions. And Chubbee was adept at learning new tunes that had local appeal as he and his wife moved from place to place. His musical influences may have also included indigenous American as well as African-descended musicians he knew in the South and West and were undoubtedly shaped by his interaction with the lively entertainment scene on steamboats and in port cities.

Despite performing as an "Indian flutist," his early concerts were not advertised in terms of Indian music. Rather, seeing an "unbettered Indian" expertly play "La Marseillaise" was a central part of the shows' appeal. Calling himself a "natural flutist" rather than "science musician," he was regarded as a "virtuoso" whose talents were a gift of native genius.[31] But if the Chubbees hoped to prevent their performances from being associated with farces, curiosities, or freak shows, they were quickly disappointed. Performing at "museums" in particular ensured that they could not remain above the rabble. Although museums would later come to stand as "leading pillars of bourgeois self-definition," in the 1840s and 1850s they were "socially inclusive institutions driven by profit," where dockworkers rubbed elbows with bankers—each having paid the same twenty-five cents for the privilege of ogling the oddities.[32]

On Christmas Eve, 1847, the Baltimore Museum offered the comedy "Yankee Land," to be followed by "the celebrated Indian fluitist [*sic*], Mr. Chubbee [who] will, in company with his wife, give one of their interesting concerts." Also appearing at the museum that night was nine-year-old Tom Thumb, the diminutive performer who worked under the management of P. T. Barnum. The venue had been recently renovated and was said to seat 1,600 people, with three tiers of boxes supported by ionic columns and embellished with elaborate papier mache decorations. The Chubbees' concert was sandwiched between two farces, but how far they had come from the rude conditions in Winter Quarters just six months before! A sign at the theater read: "No Colored Persons Allowed."[33]

On December 28, the Chubbees were again sidelining at this same "fashionable place of amusement" where another farce called "Beauty and the Beast" was received with shouts of laughter by a crowded audience.[34] They performed several concerts in conjunction with this popular "serio-comic" play on several nights, though it remains a matter of speculation whether the actors or audiences drew any parallels between its title characters and the Chubbees. Finally, the museum held a benefit for the "Indian Flutist."[35] Such shows typically benefitted performers themselves, allowing them to earn a share of the ticket sales, as opposed to their usual flat fee per show. Although benefits were considered a measure of the local public's appreciation for a performer's efforts—the more popular a performer, the more s/he might earn in a benefit—they could also be a sign of the performer's state of financial need (sometimes openly referenced in advertisements).[36]

After the New Year, Mr. and Mrs. Chubbee went back to Washington, D.C., for several more performances in their "native costume." Perhaps in an effort to authenticate their new identities, or perhaps to capitalize on their recent stage success, the Chubbees then followed in the footsteps of other professional Indians by writing a book. Sometime during the previous fall, "Mrs. Chubbee of the Mohawk Tribe" had begun writing biographical letters to Rev. L. L. Allen, a former Methodist preacher and army chaplain who was touring on the temperance circuit with George Copway. It was Allen, a minor travel writer himself, who would publish the first edition of the Chubbees' composite autobiography, *A Thrilling Sketch of the Life of the Distinguished Chief Okah Tubbee, Alias Wm. Chubbee, Son of the Head Chief, Mosholeh Tubbee, of the Choctaw Nation of Indians*, in the spring of 1848.[37] The work opens with "An Essay upon the Indian Character," filled with material recycled from popular writings on "Indian

Traits" with a few specific elements highlighted to explain Tubbee's (formerly Chubbee's) Choctaw origins. For instance, the prefatory essay contains an example of "How Indians Get Their Names" lore, defining Okah Tubbee as "Big Chief, not only referring to a great and enlarged mind but to a powerful tribe, a Chief of the Choctaw nation," and Laah Ceil Manatoi Elaah as "the Great Spirit's gift, a Princess of the Mohawk tribe."[38] This passing reference is the only place in the first edition of the autobiography in which Mrs. Tubbee (aka Mrs. Chubbee), identified as a Mohawk woman, is mentioned. Her new Indian name incorporated a mangled version of the Algonquian spiritual term "manitou," reflecting precisely the sort of "vaguely Algonkianized/Iroquioianized" image that had become predominant in popular representations of American Indians by the late 1840s.[39]

The rest of the essay constructs an Indian type that is made manifest in the "Biography," essentially providing readers with instructions on how to situate the subject of the narrative that follows. In this way and many others, the text shares characteristics found in other ethnic autobiographies, including not only those written by professional Indians, but also those written by fugitive or freed slaves. In such works, the subject was frequently understood to be telling the story, not merely of himself or herself, but of an entire people.[40]

Like popular Indian-themed fiction and drama of the preceding decade, the "Essay upon the Indian Character" is explicitly nostalgic in tone.[41] The opening lines make apparent the belief that American Indians were rapidly becoming people of the past:

> In contemplating the Indian character, there is an interest thrown around it, which cannot fail to impress the mind of every inquiring person, although the Indian race is fading away; their palmy days being gone; yet there is a charm thrown around their past history, and the most lively emotions are created in the mind of the Patriot and Philanthropist in contemplating their past and present history, and are led to look upon the high and lofty bearing of the red man, with the most intense admiration.[42]

The introduction thus informs readers why the subsequent account should interest them ("Nation after nation, and tribe after tribe, are passing away") and reassures them that they could safely feel admiration for the noble savage, now that "the red man's tomahawk" was no longer "wreaking in the blood of its victim."[43]

The opening section also invokes the recent episodes of forced removal by sketching a scene that not only referenced the expulsion of American Indians from their homelands to territories further west, but also resonated with the flight of Mormon refugees.

> Behold a mother bidding a final farewell to the place of her nativity . . . view her standing upon the last green hill pressing her little one to her bosom, covering its little face with her burning tears; she moves on a few steps, and then for the last time bids her long and much loved home farewell forever, and often in her migrations to the far west, does scenes of the past crowd upon her memory.[44]

Every effort is expended to render the Indian worthy of interest or pity, a noble child of the forest—with a reputation for stubbornness but a benevolent streak too—admirable but doomed to disappear. For over a decade, the popular character of Metamora, among many others, had embodied this trope nightly for theatergoers.

The overarching purpose of the Tubbees' autobiography was propagandistic—to convince readers that Okah Tubbee was an Indian, and not just any Indian, but a chief, endowed at birth with remarkable talent and chosen for divine purposes. And yet, like many other ethnic autobiographies of the mid-nineteenth century, the text is extraordinarily complex in its layering of interests and influences.[45] It contains outright lies. But it is also remarkably accurate. It includes not only lofty accounts of historical moments, but also excerpts from of their stage performances, like the humorous tale of the bullfrog Tubbee had included in his testimony before Brigham Young just a year before.[46]

In addition, the text contains a "Covenant" between the Choctaws and the Six Nations of Iroquois, possibly a tribal analogue for the partnership of Okah Tubbee and Laah Ceil, as representatives of their respective tribes. This section alludes to the covenant chain imagery of historic Six Nations diplomacy, but also evokes the pair's secret covenants in Cincinnati and Winter Quarters.

An ethnographic section containing a description of the history and condition of the Choctaws then living in the Arkansas Territory was included to "show that the Indian is not the degraded being that some would have him to be, but that he has been endowed with a mind as susceptible of improvement as the pale face."[47] American Indian autobiographical writing frequently contained stories of conversion to Christianity, progress in education, and evidence of civilization and argued implicitly that the writers of such texts—and their people more broadly—were worthy of consideration, as well as inclusion, in the "imagined community" of the United States.[48]

George Copway's autobiography exemplifies this approach and may have also provided a model for the Tubbees' text. His was the first self-narrative written by an American Indian raised within his own culture and followed a similar construction, with autobiographical statements, speeches, and pseudoethnographic essays. Likewise, the Anishinaabe orator's stated goal was to raise money for converting, settling, and sobering the Indians, and his combination of authorship with live performance was virtually de rigueur for professional Indians of the day.[49] Despite the emphasis on Indian improvement in such texts, the public appearances of Copway, the Tubbees, and others hinged on the apparent irony of "untutored" Indians managing to wax philosophic or perform civilized music. Indeed, the cognitively dissonant experience of hearing an unlearned Indian playing marches and airs while his surprisingly articulate wife lectured audiences on the perils of Indian intemperance and their hopes for converting the "poor red man" was openly touted in advertisements. In other words, such professional Indians were often popular because they were presumed to be exceptional, even as they were thought to represent a type.

A narrative of Okah Tubbee's life follows the autobiography's opening essays and asserts that it was "drawn up from his own lips in a simple, touching and beautiful style, which may be relied upon as true."[50] The details are already familiar—his early memories of a kind but vanished Indian father, his placement in "the slave woman's" household, his altercation with a local boy, his first efforts as a performer, his experiences on steamboats and with the militia, and most importantly, the various evidences of his genuine Indian identity, mostly based on the logic of racial recognition—a belief that his "Indian nature" was intrinsic and visible.

Although this first edition of the autobiography contains no biographical information about Laah Ceil except for the definition of her name, the text was a work of composite authorship, a common practice among ethnic autobiographies. While the book told Okah Tubbee's story and was based on letters written by his wife, Allen received credit as the author, and a statement at the close of the work promised, "This thrilling and deeply interesting sketch will be continued in forthcoming numbers," suggesting that like other literary entrepreneurs of the day, they intended to continue publishing new and enlarged editions. Other elements of the text likewise mirror contemporaneous fugitive slave narratives and Indian autobiographies, particularly in their emphasis on establishing credulity and credibility through references and testimonies by white benefactors.

While Laah Ceil was writing the letters that comprised the autobiography, she and her husband had continued on their eastern tour. They spent January 1848 in the nation's capital with several weeks of shows at Apollo Hall and Odd Fellows' Hall, while Copway (and possibly Allen) appeared in Baltimore. Perhaps public interest in Baltimore could only sustain one celebrated Indian at a time, so the Tubbees had departed for Washington following the benefit show. News of Copway's lecture in Baltimore shared the page with an IORM notice announcing a meeting of the "Uncas Tribe" to be held at their "Wigwam, on the 5th sleep in the 1st 7 suns of the snow moon."[51] Audiences in Washington, D.C., were likely the same mix of curious elites and middle-class types that jostled one another in the Baltimore public houses and popular urban associations, promoting temperance, fraternity, and charity. The Tubbees would later claim that they even performed for President James K. Polk and "his lady" during their engagement in the capital city.[52]

By the end of the month, they were in Philadelphia where they appeared at the Chinese Saloon, a theater and museum that housed artifacts and oddities on the first floor and offered a performance space on the second.[53] Tubbee took the stage "rigged out completely in savage toggery" and made quite an impression on the audience. One later account described his appearance in the following manner: "His face was printed in fancy style, from his nose was suspended a huge silver ring, his head was surmounted by a wig and feathers, his body was encased in buckskin shirt and leggings trimmed Indian fashion with fringe, while his feet were stuck into a pair of gaudy moccasins. In addition to all, he was loaded down with little bells and tinkling gewgaws, and as he came upon the stage they rattled and jingled to the great delight of the more juvenile part of the audience."[54]

That the star performer wore a wig hints at his ongoing effort to keep his hair covered and the sheer quantity of accessories whispers of desperation. Interestingly, news of this "musical curiosity" was carried as far away as Natchez, where the Choctaw flutist was referred to as "War-ne-wis ke-ho-ke Chubbee," either a garbled version of his new moniker or a knowing play on his old (Warner) and new (Okah Chubbee) names.[55]

Following their Philadelphia shows, including an appearance at Peale's Museum, recently purchased by P. T. Barnum, Mr. and Mrs. Tubbee traveled to New York City, where they appeared alongside George Copway at the Tabernacle.[56] By summertime, they were firmly ensconced in the

FIGURE 5 Performance hall at Castle Garden. Located on an island off the tip of Manhattan, Castle Garden was a theater and park that offered concerts, plays, and other amusements. The Tubbees gave several concerts there in the summer of 1848. This lithograph shows Jenny Lind making her American debut at Castle Garden in 1850. Like the Tubbees, Lind worked briefly under the management of P. T. Barnum. N. Currier, 1850. (Courtesy Print Collection, Miriam and Ira D. Wallach Division of Art, Prints and Photographs, the New York Public Library, Astor, Lenox and Tilden Foundations)

New York entertainment scene, and Okah Tubbee (still frequently performing as Chubbee, despite the autobiography's contemporaneous use of Tubbee) made quite a spectacle walking down the street bedecked in "paint, rings, & feathers" with "forty street Arabs" following him about everywhere he went.[57] In July, they began a series of shows at the Castle Garden theater, a former army depot off the southern tip of Manhattan Island, where they performed in between seriocomic plays or comediettas.[58] (See Fig. 5.) As in Baltimore, the concerts included pieces on both the flute and sauce-panana, and though newspaper advertisements asserted that the Castle Garden shows were "elegant and refined," this language may have been more aspirational than descriptive. The *New York Herald* called the July 9 performance a "wild concert" of original music, suggesting that he was experimenting with his repertoire. He introduced his own arrangements and may have also added some improvisation to his standard fare of "marches, waltzes, and cotillions."[59]

The next appearance by "the eminently gifted son of the forest" was described in a more restrained fashion as a concert that "delighted the audience with several beautiful airs on the flute-solo, and also on his splendid instrument, the saucepaniana [sic]." His wife joined him onstage, demonstrating her linguistic talents by offering "a very beautiful translation of one of his songs in the Choctaw language," displaying "proficiency and talent" worthy of admiration.[60] While Tubbee claimed to be able to speak Choctaw, there is no evidence that Laah Ceil had learned the language. Thus, while it is possible that he genuinely sang in the Choctaw tongue, her translation was probably not original and possibly bore no resemblance to the song's lyrics. In either case, such demonstrations were rooted in both her teenage years "speaking Injun" and his xenoglossic talents. Their success at Castle Garden thus depended in part on the *absence* of Choctaw speakers in the audience, just as the broader American cultural practice of "playing Indian" depended upon the removal, erasure, or extinction of Native people.[61] The pair concluded their run at Castle Garden with a rather disappointing benefit on July 15, the dismal results of which left promoters complaining, "There is a singular lack of taste and kindness in the New York fashionable world, or else Castle Garden would be more visited, and poor Chubbee would have had a better benefit."[62]

Perhaps because of the lackluster benefit and the high cost of constant travel, the Tubbees signed on with P. T. Barnum for a grueling run at the notorious showman's American Museum, performing two shows a day. It seems likely that they had first met Barnum during their stint in Baltimore the previous fall, continued their connection in Philadelphia, and then secured a spot among the New York museum's well-attended attractions. Barnum's establishment was known for featuring amusements focused on race, including blackface minstrel acts and the display of racialized bodies, like that of Joice Heth, whom he represented as once having been the enslaved nursemaid of George Washington.[63]

The performances at the American Museum were at once a high point and a low point for the Tubbees. On the one hand, they probably received more exposure than ever before because of the sheer number of shows and the patrons who thronged them. On the other hand, they shared the bill with an "enormous Boa Constrictor, 30 feet long. The three Living Ourang-Outangs . . . the Highland Mammoth Boys, Giant Baby, Wax Scripture Statuary, [and] Madame Rockwell, the famous Fortune Teller."[64] This environment was precisely the sort that lent itself to caricature, if not ridicule. Although the advertisements for the appearances of Tubbee (aka Chubbee) at the American Museum did mention his flute playing, it seems unlikely that these were precisely the same kind of concerts he had presented further south in Philadelphia, Baltimore, and Washington, and less "refined" than those he and his wife had just concluded at Castle Garden. At least one American Museum advertisement referred to him simply as "Wm. Chubbee, the Chocktaw Chief," with no mention of his musical talents, implying that they were secondary to the experience of simply viewing a real live Indian, or perhaps someone humorously professing to be a real live Indian.[65]

Barnum's various entertainment schemes are a good example of the popular culture of pretense that had emerged in the antebellum period.[66] His shows were as much about voyeurism, imposture, and freakery as they were about talent, so it would have been understandable if the Tubbees felt somewhat degraded by their participation in them.[67] At the same time, however, they may have been exhilarated by the emancipatory possibilities of masquerade and self-invention (or reinvention), with which they had both been experimenting since youth. Such acts of "theatrical self-hood" were widely apparent in the antebellum period. Indeed, performers like the Tubbees and managers like Barnum were actively shaping a culture of exhibition that blurred the lines between public and private identities, between the real and the fake.[68]

By August, the pair had left New York for Boston, stopping in New Haven, Connecticut, along the way. They were traveling with Rev. Allen, and he may have once more (or still) been acting as their agent. The three of them took rooms at the Tontine Hotel, overlooking the Elm City's historic town green. The couple signed the hotel guest register as "Okah Tubbee" and "Mrs. Tubbee" from "Indian Territory, Missouri," suggesting that even when they were not on stage, they found it necessary or desirable to maintain their Indian personae.[69]

The New England shows that would occupy them during the fall and winter of 1848 were more closely aligned with the oratory of Anishinaabe activist Peter Jones than P. T. Barnum's visually stimulating museum shows. But even Jones was compelled to appear in his "odious Indian costume" during his fund-raising speeches, narrowing the distance between the two registers.[70]

The context of professional antebellum Indian performance influenced Laah Ceil's revision of the autobiography. In late 1848, when a second edition was printed in Springfield, Massachusetts, under her name, it was apparent that she had worked to make the narrative less exotic or "thrilling" and more respectable. The account included not only details of her life as the child of Mohawk and Delaware parents but also revelations about the Tubbees' divine calling to help their red brethren. Later, she even added parts of her personal journal (sadly lost to modern historians) in which she had recorded her impressions of New England. After the demanding summer performance schedule in New York, their brief respite in Connecticut had been a welcome change of pace. Laah Ceil relished the opportunity to rest and take in the scenery in New Haven.

> Oh! what a lovely spot! I can but conclude that some hundreds of beautiful country seats, or I might say American palaces, had agreed to take up their walks, parks, gardens, summer-houses and pleasure grounds, and called together here to luxuriate in the sea breeze, and withal to hold council under the old elms, which look to me like so many guardian angels stretching forth their giant arms in their defence. Again they once sheltered the councillors of the red men who assembled here in olden time—they must have loved them. Oh! children of the forest where hast thou fled.[71]

Laah Ceil's revision of the autobiography reflected her growing sense of herself as an author, and she strove to differentiate the text from the version published under Allen's name earlier in the year. Many of her emendations served to underscore the pathetic figure of the Indian, whose noble footsteps no longer echoed through the forests of the East.[72] This strategy allowed her to integrate her own words and sentiments while contributing to the potential appeal the book might have on sympathetic (and possibly philanthropic) readers. At the same time, Laah Ceil was participating in a broader literary convention of the era: creating uniquely American literature that linked "archaic Indians" with "successor Americans" by focusing on sentimental descriptions of experiencing de-Indianized landscapes.[73] That she was not only aware of but sought a voice among writers like James Fenimore Cooper and Lewis Henry Morgan hints at both her astute understanding of popular cultural Indian representations and her own personal ambitions.

In the fall of 1848, the Tubbees proceeded from New Haven to Massachusetts. In Boston, they resumed their musical performances and returned to the activism that had first garnered the attention of the St. Louis press in 1846—temperance. At the Tremont Temple, "Okah Tubbee, the Musical Indian Wonder, son of a Chief of the Choctaw nation" and his wife made their first highly anticipated appearance on November 11, 1848, "in their original Indian costume." The event was touted as an "extraordinary novelty," and they performed to packed houses alongside the Raymonds, a popular family musical group, for a full week.[74]

They also appeared with reformed alcoholic and orator John Gough and other local leading lights. But instead of presenting a concert, "The Choctaw prince [gave] a brief, graphic account of the Temperance cause among his people, said it had been the means of saving to the nation at least six hundred thousand dollars, which they had appropriated to education purposes!" Given Tubbee's history as a storyteller, one wonders what details he included in his "graphic" account. In any case, the pair made a notable impression on the audience, with one observer describing Laah Ceil as a "well educated daughter of a Mohawk Chief" and asserting that they were "both noble specimens of the elevating influence of Christian Missions."[75]

According to the account, the Tubbees had been traveling through the states and using their music to awaken "among the Christian portions of the 'pale faced nations,' such an interest in favor of their red brethren, of different Western tribes, as shall secure from 'their great Father' guarantee[s] to them 'while water runs or grass grows.'"[76] It appeared they were indeed working to fulfill the missions they had each described in the second edition of the autobiography, including Laah Ceil's childhood vision that she was to do "good to a fallen people" and Okah Tubbee's dream of using "simple instruments of music" to "unite the broken and wasting tribes." Combining their appearances and activism with the revised autobiography, Ceil had also included other heretofore undisclosed revelations, like her husband's sudden recollection that even though he "had always been temperate," his poor father "drank fire water," thus inspiring his crusade against drunkenness.[77]

The pair gave concerts in the Boston area for nearly the entire month of November before traveling to New Hampshire for a series of highly successful appearances in and around Concord. While performing at venues in the Granite State, they also made the acquaintance of some leading figures in the Masonic brotherhood. According to one account, "'Brother Okah Tubbee, an Indian of the Choctaw tribe,'" appeared in the New Hampshire lodge and "addressed the Grand Lodge . . . on the subject of establishing Masonic Lodges among the 'red men' of the various tribes, now located in the Indian territory."[78] At a special meeting in December 1848, he took "the first three degrees of Masonry under a dispensation for that purpose."[79] The occasion must have been an auspicious one.

On the most pragmatic level, Okah Tubbee may have sought out the Masons in New Hampshire to validate his identity claims by securing the endorsement of a well-known men's association with broad national influence. But there were also important links between the Masonic brotherhood, the Mormons, and notions of identity transformation. Early Mormonism shared many similarities with Freemasonry, including a legend about sacred words inscribed on a plate of gold; a strong emphasis on secrecy, oaths, and covenants; and highly ritualistic observances, including one involving the embodiment of Adam and Eve. Although the later Latter-day Saints Church would work to distance itself from both Freemasonry and its magical overtones, one scholar asserts that "both Indians and Masons had a central place in" Joseph Smith's "spiritual imagination."[80] It was even suggested that temperance societies among Mormon women mirrored the organizational structure of Freemasonry.[81]

The Masons also took their initiates through several levels of personal transformation that were attractive to a wide variety of individuals seeking to transcend their old lives and may have been exhilarating for a man on the make with a painful past. One way to think about these initiation rites is that they were ceremonies in which the audience was the Lodge, and the initiate did not merely "act" his new part, but fully became another person. This personal transformation was particularly evident during initiation into the Third or Hiramic degree that Okah Tubbee attained in New Hampshire.[82] The ritual drama of the Masonic orders mirrored the controversial doctrine of transmigration that contributed to the demise of the McCarys' schismatic sect in Cincinnati and later Winter Quarters, and may have had special significance for him personally. It is also possible, of course, that he did not respect the solemnity of either of these practices, instead merely using them to gain the respect and support (financial or otherwise) of powerful whites. Ironically, Tubbee's secret induction into a Masonic lodge would later contribute to his downfall.[83]

Okah Tubbee (now his preferred name, having been affixed to two separate editions of the autobiography and countless newspaper advertisements) made a few appearances in late 1848 and early 1849, as he and his wife made their way from New Hampshire south again to Massachusetts. They stopped in Lowell, where African American Mormon Q. Walker Lewis still owned the barbering business mentioned by Brigham Young in Winter Quarters.[84] Lewis, like Tubbee, was also a Freemason. Although it seems impossible that Lewis and Tubbee were unaware of each other, there's no evidence they had any contact. Because Lewis was an African American, a "militant abolitionist," and later revealed to have been assisting fugitive slaves, it stands to reason that Okah Tubbee would have avoided associating with him for fear of being perceived as black or pro-black, even if he supported the elder's efforts.[85]

The Tubbees went on to New Bedford where they stayed for just over four weeks, boarding with a local temperance activist, constable, and religious leader named Eliphalet Robbins, from whose home they operated a medical business. Robbins recalled that "the house was thronged from 6 A.M. to 9 P.M." and asserted that Tubbee "performed great cures," deserving far more credit than he received for his talents.[86] It is possible that the Tubbees had been engaged in healing practices of some kind since the episode with William Waddell a year before in Missouri, but testimonials from former patients, as well as Robbins's recollections, suggest that by March 1849, they were engaged in doctoring almost exclusively.[87]

Their New England appearances in early 1849 imply that, over the course of their tour, the Tubbees had attained a new level of confidence in their Indian personae and represented themselves ever more boldly. For instance, Okah Tubbee was referred to in two separate Massachusetts advertisements as "The celebrated Indian, Okah tubbee, the greatest natural musician in the known world, who has been received with the most unbounded applause in all the Southern Cities, by crowded houses." Such announcements didn't fail to mention "Mrs. Laah Ceil Tubbee, wife of Okah, of the Mohawk Tribe," who accompanied her husband in song.[88] A certain humorous incident that would become locally famous also took place during the pair's successful Yankee tour.

In one New England hall, the participatory audience was a bit too enthusiastic for Okah Tubbee's liking. As the papers described it, "Okah Tubbee the celebrated Indian musician . . . was annoyed by his audience keeping time with their feet during his performances. By particular request he commenced playing 'Hail Columbia,' and the musical prodigies in the different parts of the house began their usual accompaniment. The musician suddenly stopped, and addressing the foot performers, expressed the hope that they would not attempt to keep time with him; 'because,' said he, 'as I aint a science musician, I'm afraid I shall make a mistake, and put you out.'"[89] The quip was likely intended to and probably did elicit laughter from the assembled audience, but one cannot help but recall his request for silence from the rambunctious children crowded into Brigham Young's house back in Winter Quarters.

Despite such memorable performances, after March 1849, the eastern newspapers go curiously silent on the Choctaw musician and his Mohawk wife. But Laah Ceil herself provides us with an explanation, confessing that after visiting "the principal cities in the New England States . . . circumstances rendered me very anxious for a speedy return to the West."[90] She was going to have a baby.

Before the month was out, the Tubbees left New England and headed west toward family and property they had left in the Missouri River valley. From New York, they went to Philadelphia and then Harrisburg, where they took a canal boat to Pittsburg and were crammed in among "California Emigrants" rushing west with dreams of finding gold. Travel was difficult for Laah Ceil and made all the more uncomfortable by the loss of their baggage, which they were compelled to leave behind in the crush of westward-bound passengers. They stopped in St. Louis to await their delayed trunks only to find when they finally arrived that their valuables had been plundered.

On May 21, 1849, sequestered in St. Louis, some 200 miles east of the "small well-furnished farm," they claimed to have left in Lafayette County, Missouri, and at least 400 miles from her female relatives, Laah Ceil Manitoi Elaah Tubbee gave birth to her fourth child, a son they named Mosholeh, after his putative Choctaw grandfather.[91]

As with all births, the scene was dramatic. But Laah Ceil's autobiographical narration reveals particularly difficult circumstances. The catastrophic St. Louis fire of 1849 began just hours before little Mosholeh was born. Even worse, a massive cholera epidemic was "at work in every street."[92] Some citizens alleged that the disease had been brought by Mormon converts arriving from England and preparing to journey overland to the Rocky Mountains.[93] By mid-1849, there were reportedly some 3,000-4,000 Mormon faithful gathered in the city.[94] Through luck or extraordinary providence, the Tubbee family managed to avoid both these dangers, but the desperation with which they had headed west from New England suggests the urgency Laah Ceil felt to rejoin her family before her son's birth. Instead of laboring with women she knew, she had her baby in a boarding house, without even the comfort of her personal items. As soon as she and the baby were able to travel, they gathered what "thieves, fire, and expenses had not swallowed up" and departed once more for the West.[95]

During their absence from Lafayette County, Lexington resident William Waddell had lodged his complaint against "William McChubby" in the county circuit court. As a result, the little homestead they had left behind was attached for debt by the time they returned in the summer of 1849. On July 24th, the defendant appeared before the Justice of the Peace in Lafayette County and stated that he never owed Waddell any money nor was he even aware of the suit until returning to the area. Still apparently unable to read and write, he attested to his version of events by making his mark instead.[96] The defendant was then informed that, in accordance with the law, a notice of the charges against him and an invitation to rebut them had appeared in the local newspaper for four weeks during the autumn of 1848. Tubbee (McChubby) protested that he had not been the region since August 1847, a fact known to Waddell, and thus could not have known about the notices. He maintained that he was never indebted to the plaintiff or anyone else, but his countersuit failed.[97] Laah Ceil later summarized their ordeal, saying, "through false debts and sham sales, everything had passed into the hands of others."[98]

With a newborn child and no home, they made their way up the Missouri River. Since they were not performing publicly during this period, it is difficult to track their movements precisely. The autobiography further masks their activities by asserting that after the problems in Lafayette County during July, they had worked their way through various resettled Indian nations along the course of the Missouri River. Specific mention is made of "remnant" groups like the Munsees, Wyandottes, Delawares, and Mohicans, "generally supposed by many novel readers" to have become "extinct," but then suffering a marked need for temperance efforts.[99]

Indeed, a variety of removed Indian groups were living along the Missouri River from Fort Leavenworth northward to Council Bluffs, where Laah Ceil's family and other Mormon refugees were still busy tending cattle and sheep, cording cloth, raising flax, and building meeting houses.[100] The many Indian communities in the area were enduring a good deal of turmoil at that very moment. For example, the Mohicans, as well as the Stockbridge and Munsee Indians who had been removed from New York, Ohio, and Indiana, were then settled among the Delawares and complained that they were continually mistreated by the latter nation. The Delawares and Wyandottes regarded the smaller groups as merely tenants-at-will on their small parcel of land.[101] The new arrivals, who had once been known as "praying Indians," insisted that their Christianity and advancement in "civilization" entitled them to the sympathy and consideration of the federal government. Laah Ceil's autobiographical references to "a fearful misunderstanding" that had arisen among the tribes might have been a reflection of the western Indian situation, but her statement that their differences hinged on "vying how there could be so many different yet right ways to worship one God, all taken from the Bible" might have also been an allusion to ongoing schisms within the Mormon Church.[102]

After Brigham Young and the first party of Mormon migrants had left Winter Quarters in 1847 and reached the Salt Lake valley, they founded their holy city. Back east, the Mormons formed emigrant companies to join them, and some families embarked that very year. Many others remained behind to secure sufficient funds and provisions for the arduous overland trek, but confusion and sectarian strife persisted. To try and streamline the massive migration, between 1848 and the mid-1850s, certain outposts were designated for the gathering and outfitting of Mormons headed for Utah. One of these locales was Council Bluffs, Iowa, where Daniel and Clarinda Stanton were working and saving in preparation for the journey, while raising Laah Ceil's daughters from her first marriage: Ann (age 13) and Semira (11). Other Mormon villages were scattered along the border between Iowa and Missouri and as far south as Fort Leavenworth, but Mormon migrants tended to avoid the area around Jackson County and the town of Independence that had been the scene of considerable anti-Mormon violence fifteen years prior.[103]

In late 1849, Okah Tubbee and Laah Ceil rented a house in Weston, Missouri. It was just north and across the Missouri River from Fort Leavenworth, Kansas Territory, and about 150 miles south of her parents and daughters in Iowa. They took "much pains" to furnish the house, put in their "winter stores [and] filled it to overflowing." They did this, they claimed, in order to provide a model for nearby Indian tribes, "that they might see the comforts of an industrious sober life." But when they left their home and belongings to fetch the girls, they were again the victims of theft—this time perpetrated by the very "dissipated" Indians they were trying to reform.[104] A group of sympathetic Weston citizens petitioned the Indian agent at Fort Leavenworth to intervene on behalf of Okah Tubbee, who "represents himself as a Chactaw," and asserted that his property had been taken out and divided up "under a false plea of indebtedness to them." They further informed the agent that the perpetrators were Stockbridge Indians named John Hendricks and Levi Kunkapot and white men named John Smith and Mr. Woods (a discharged soldier).[105]

Okah Tubbee, or more probably Laah Ceil, wrote a letter directly to the Commissioner of Indian Affairs in Washington pleading for assistance. Among the items stolen were Tubbee's gun, his master Mason's suit, his "royal arch chapter badge," his Sons of Temperance regalia, and a set of "jewels" he planned to use to open a Masonic lodge among the Indians. The Tubbees claimed they were invited to settle among the Stockbridges and Delawares and had been endeavoring to teach them temperance. The pair alleged that the Indians were bribed into the thefts by greedy white men in the neighborhood. They concluded by confessing that they were completely destitute in Weston, without even a blanket, and stated that the thieves, "have caused us to suffer with cold."[106]

Around this time, Laah Ceil's daughters moved in with their mother, step-father, and half-brother. The family was in dire straits. Frustratingly, their pleas for intervention from the Indian agent went unheeded, and their situation remained difficult. As Laah Ceil put it, "We often met with what perhaps had been a present to us and now owned by another." Finally, they retreated from the site of their losses at the Kansas border and settled in Independence, where Mormons who might recognize them were probably scarce. Okah Tubbee again established himself as a doctor, a profession they had come to depend on "for a support."[107]

While he was setting up shop in Missouri, however, Tubbee's Indian facade was beginning to crack. In October 1849, an unnamed correspondent from Natchez wrote to the *Freemason's Monthly Magazine* on the subject of "Br. Okah Tubbee."

> The October number of your Magazine came to hand this morning, and I hasten to warn you against an impostor, "Br. Okah Tubbee, an Indian Chief of the Choctaw tribe," of whom you speak under your head of "Masonic Chit Chat." Okah Tubbee, alias Warner McCary, was born in the city of Natchez, and is a cross of the Scotch and negro, a mulatto. I have known him from childhood. His Brother Robert is an intelligent, industrious and sober man, is an excellent barber, and is much respected; but Warner was always a wild, haram scaram fellow, up to all kinds of devilry, never would work, but would discourse the finest music in the world, for a self taught boy; and when playing the fife for our military companies, his superiority on that instrument was wonderful. But I learned some time since, from Br. Boyd's paper, in New York, that he passed his like in advocating the cause of

temperance, and had spent his time in works of benevolence! The identity is undoubted.[108]

Although Tubbee's identity was "undoubted," the identity of this correspondent is uncertain. But the autobiography boasted of his association with a number of respectable men in Natchez, some of whom were Masons, so it seems a ghost from the past had caught up with him in Missouri.[109]

If Tubbee knew about this published letter, he must have been stung by the unfavorable comparison to his half-brother, Robert (Bob) McCary, as well as the matter-of-fact reference to him as simply "a mulatto." But evidence suggests that such accusations were beginning to plague him from several quarters. Just a few weeks after settling in Independence, "a noted gambler" visited the Tubbees and attempted to publicly reveal the doctor's "true" identity. The unnamed man made his first effort late one Saturday night, calling Dr. Tubbee out of bed to hurl insults at him from the street. On another occasion, the antagonist accosted Tubbee saying that he had "always known" him and that he was no physician. This "rich . . . liberal, genteel, drunken gambler" continued to harass the Tubbees for nearly a year.

Finally, in the spring of 1850, Okah Tubbee determined to leave. The Indian doctor claimed he "could not brook" the abuse of the Mississippi gambler, but he also found his medical practice hampered by accusations that he falsified testimonials and botched cures. Doctor Tubbee left town to escape the intensifying scrutiny. At least at first, Laah Ceil remained behind. On the occasion of their parting, she wrote a sentimental poem, which she claimed she was "induced" to share "by the urgent request" of her husband.

Then fare thee well, my lover,
I cannot bid thee stay,
For that thou must watch over
Calls thee from me away;

And I must be contented
To part from thee awhile,
Although my heart relenteth,
And tears my eyes do fill.

Oh! could I have but seen thee,
And pressed thy lips with mine,

And heard thee say, God bless thee,
In that fond way of thine;

Oh! I could have borne thy absence,
Without so much regret,
Having the sweet assurance,
That thou dost love me yet.

I know, on thy returning,
Thou wilt this lone one greet;
My heart's already burning,
I long my love to meet.
Although we're forced awhile to part,
We'll ever constant prove—
Each aspiration of the heart
Shall be in perfect love.

Oh! that the winds could bear me
Thy breath while thou art gone,
To comfort and to cheer me
While I am thus alone
Should misfortunes e'er o'ertake thee,
Oh! then remember me;
Should other friends forsake thee,
Thine own I still shall be.

Her husband's description of his departure was more prosaic: "I felt that I had rather seek friends elsewhere, and have since been travelling. . . . I sell medicines for cases, sell recipes, and hold musical entertainments, &c."[110] More of an abbreviated resume than a farewell speech, Tubbee's terse summary of the episode nevertheless explains his decision to leave Missouri. In addition to allegations about his business practices, questions about Dr. Tubbee's race probably also played a role in his decision. The Fugitive Slave Act of 1850 had made refugees of many free blacks, cast out from their homes in some states and subject to scrutiny, abuse, and kidnapping in others. The autobiographical depiction of a Mississippi gambler who haunted and harassed Okah Tubbee in Missouri might even be read as a personification of the insidious law and the policies it inculcated. Perhaps he felt he would face less persecution in the eastern states.

A Masonic magazine explained Tubbee's departure from the West somewhat differently. The author mentioned the news that a New Hampshire lodge had inducted Tubbee into several degrees of masonry, with a view to having him establish lodges among the Indians. Not only did the writer object that the majority of Indians were unchristian, immoral, and intemperate, thus making them unsuitable for inclusion among the Masons, he also took the opportunity to lampoon his eastern brethren for allowing themselves to be "so easily humbugged" that they had "failed to notice the *real* character of Brother Okah Tubbee." Reporting on conversations with unnamed "gentlemen in Mississippi who were well acquainted with Tubbee and his ancestors," the author revealed that "no one seemed inclined to award him credit for any *aboriginal* blood, but they all agreed in awarding to him the honor of being descended, in a pretty direct line from the *African* race, but whether from the royal line they could not say," a reference to the famous case of the Fulbe prince, Ibrahima, who had been enslaved for many years in Natchez before establishing the truth of his royal birth and returning to Africa, as well as copycat cases that proliferated throughout the 1830s–1840s.[111]

The Masonic writer cast the controversy in explicitly sectional terms, ascribing differential racial acuity to observers in the North, the South, the East, and the West, from which latter place the magazine was published. In light of the eastern lodge's gullibility, he confessed, "we are constrained to ask them, in fraternal kindness, to make no more of our citizens Masons" and insisted that "we have Lodges enough in the West and South to answer all merited demands . . . by leaving our citizens to apply *at home* for admission, the harmony and interest of the Craft will be promoted. Tubbee could not have been made a Mason at home."[112]

· · ·

Although Okah Tubbee may have departed Missouri in hopes of leaving such accusations behind him, the damage had been done. His southern past would continue to follow him in the North, while sectional debates unhinged fragile national compromises. Fleeing to the states where he had found comparative prosperity and perhaps more importantly, acceptance as an Indian, may have seemed like the only option. But it had meant breaking the family apart. When Laah Ceil finally left Independence to rejoin her husband, she and Mosholeh said goodbye to the girls, Ann and Semira, who moved back in with their grandparents in Iowa. She would not see them again for twenty years.

CHAPTER FIVE

Defending Their Indianness
• •

The Tubbees' Trials and Tribulations

In the spring of 1850, Natchez entrepreneur William Johnson picked up an interesting volume he referred to as the work of one "O. Ka. Chublee." A prominent free black businessman in Adams County, Johnson was a barber, a landlord, and a notorious gambler. He was also a prosperous slave owner and a close friend of Robert McCary, Okah Tubbee's putative half-brother and former owner. Johnson was born into slavery just two years before his neighbor Warner, but he was manumitted nearly twenty years before the younger man received his freedom. He would have certainly known the person described in the book and may have either worked alongside or employed Warner McCary as a shop hand or messenger. When he finished reading the autobiography, Johnson pronounced it "a tisue of Lies from beginning to Ending."[1]

Although it is difficult to know how widely the autobiography was read in Natchez and environs, by 1850 news of Okah Tubbee's pretensions had definitely reached the South and the West. An explosion in American print culture combined with the development of new transportation networks meant that the put-ons of a confidence man might catch up with him, particularly if he committed his lies to paper. One year earlier, when Okah Tubbee had been inducted into a New England Masonic lodge, a Natchez Mason who read the news hastened to warn his Yankee brethren of their error. Word of the induction and the subsequent southern reaction to it were both carried in the *Freemason's Monthly Magazine*, published in Boston but circulated nationwide.[2] When news of this event spread to St. Louis, readers recognized the description of a flute-playing virtuoso who had performed in their city. Perhaps the dogged New Orleans "gambler" who tormented Tubbee in Missouri had learned of his pretensions from similar stories.

These attempts to unmask Okah Tubbee must be understood in sectional terms, just as his performances of Indianness are best approached with an awareness of local contexts. By and large, the exposés that would effectively end the Tubbees' stage careers originated in the southern and western locales where McCary or Carey had become well known as "a negro" musician. Individuals in these regions mocked their gullible counterparts in the North and the East. Although often delivered in humorous tones, these criticisms resonated with those that slaveholders used to argue for their superior racial acuity. The logic of racial recognition helped justify the fugitive slave laws, which endangered people of African descent across the nation. What were once humorous jabs could have serious consequences.

In contrast to the public disclosures of Okah Tubbee's past, Laah Ceil managed to keep both her whiteness and her Mormon history a secret. The more scrutiny her husband faced for his claims, the less hers were examined. Still, she too faced a difficult shift in public opinion during the 1850s. While revelations plagued her husband, Laah Ceil maintained her Indian persona. But the terms of "Indianness" were shifting around her.

• • •

Before Okah Tubbee and Laah Ceil departed Missouri in the winter of 1850, they had been living near the town of Independence, Missouri, Joseph Smith's prophesied "New Jerusalem." They appeared among the "Free Inhabitants" of Blue Township, Jackson County, on the census taken that year, with thirty-nine-year-old Okah Tubbee described as a "physician."[3] Interestingly, the column that usually contained a description of inhabitants' race was left entirely blank on this page.

By spring 1851, the pair had resurfaced in Indiana, holding "musical entertainments" and hawking "real Indian medicine."[4] Although news of Tubbee's "negro past" had already been circulating for almost a year, it was not yet a complete liability for the pair. But doubts were beginning to emerge.

The *Daily Ohio Statesman* carried news of one appearance in Terre Haute, Indiana, and hinted in a pun-filled story that the musical physician was not what he seemed. The notice mentioned the Choctaw performer's "oak tub" origins, referencing theatrical manager Sol Smith's claim that he had devised the name and "[made] a savage out of him" so that the performance of a "mulatto" would not "give dissatisfaction." Smith took credit for investing Tubbee with the "romance of barbarism, and the glories of the

Choctaw nation," when, while casting about for a suitable stage name, his eyes rested on an oak tub, and Okah Tubbee was born. The paper's knowing allusion to the tale suggests that his pretensions were an open secret, but Indiana audiences were too dim to realize it.[5] Indeed, they were thrilled with the appearance of "Dr. Okah Tubbee," billed now for the first time as a musical physician. Combining his occupations as such may have reflected the Tubbees' decision to diversify their business strategy, given that the success of their stage shows was threatened by rumors and bad press.

The crowd that assembled in Terre Haute's Prairie House was called the "most discriminating and fashionable audience" ever seen in that city, even lining the aisles and hallways, all to catch a glimpse of the popular musician who not only astounded them with his skill as a flutist, but also gave an impressive performance on guitar.[6] One paper described Tubbee's show alongside a story about the genuine curiosity of 2,000 Terre Haute spectators crowded into an outdoor arena to watch an Oto delegation perform. The Native troupe displayed "singular and unique War and Marriage Dances, together with other manners and customs of Indian life," suggesting that locals were thrilled with Indian performances of all kinds. But an editorial comment that "the juveniles" of the city "were out in their strength" undermined the respectability of such events and implied that descriptions of the "discriminating" audience at Tubbee's show may have been more sarcastic than sincere.[7]

Nevertheless, Dr. Okah Tubbee made quite an impression on the Indiana crowds, whose desire "to be humbugged," a later observer put it, "was further satisfied by the circus, the barbecue, the camp-meeting, and last but not least, by patent medicines."[8] He performed in Franklin, Indianapolis, and several other locales, and by late spring, had reportedly "taken all of Hoosierdom by storm."[9] Despite reference to his medical credentials, his extraordinary skill on the flute, flageolet, and other wind instruments was still at the center of the performance, and his musical abilities were complimented in the highest terms. The Tubbees were also still articulating their desire to influence "the American people with a view to the ultimate admission of his people to the rights of citizenship in the United States." The Choctaw chief, his wife, "the Indian princess," and their young son, Mosholeh, presented themselves as examples of civilized Indianness, even as they capitalized on public fascination with exotic otherness. Following the apparent success of their midwestern performances, a southern newspaper editor confessed to being "much amused reading newspaper accounts" of Okah Tubbee's "progress."[10]

In addition to his remarkable musical talents, Dr. Tubbee's linguistic abilities were also in evidence during the spring of 1851. In Franklin, Indiana, a newspaper reported, "He speaks the English language with singular facility and appropriateness, when it is considered that he never learned letters' [*sic*] and, what is still more remarkable, can speak in fifteen living tongues, and claims considerable knowledge of three or four dead languages." Tubbee's philological talent was juxtaposed with his lack of formal education, his "natural" abilities giving evidence of his Native genius. Although the practices of glossolalia (especially apparent in the reference to "dead languages"), as well as xenoglossia, particularly with regard to indigenous languages, had shaped Laah Ceil's adolescence and played a significant role in the pair's prophetic movement just a few years earlier, the root of these linguistic claims was probably not apparent to the Tubbees' audiences.[11]

Fusing culture and biology to make a complex identity claim, Okah Tubbee had implied in the autobiography that he had not *learned* Choctaw, but he knew it innately because he *was* Choctaw. Tongue-speaking in "Injun" languages among the Mormons had held a similar significance for Laah Ceil, validating a sense of kinship between herself and the Lamanites she hoped to convert. Both Okah Tubbee and Laah Ceil continued to display their linguistic abilities as part of their stage performances, as evidence that their Indianness was authentic and "natural."[12]

Despite the continuance of earlier performative techniques, however, the Tubbees' Indiana appearances mark a turning point in their career. Driven out the West by debt and meddlers, they had made their way east presenting concerts and practicing medicine. They combined authenticating aspects from their previous appearances—a reliance on Indian costumes, an emphasis on Indian rights, and a demonstration of linguistic skill—with the wildly popular musical entertainments that had served them so well. But medicine was now no mere side job. It was central to their livelihood. As Indian physicians, the Tubbees worked, as they had done in so many other contexts, to capitalize on their audiences' needs, desires, and expectations. But they were entering a crowded field.

In the early 1850s, so-called Indian cures had been available to American consumers for over fifty years and were still widely sought after and used. Indigenous names, words, and images, as well as allusions to esoteric Native knowledge, filled advertising columns and medical recipe books. Customers could choose from a vast array of tonics, like Montague's Indian Lung Syrup, Wright's Indian Vegetable Pills, Dr. Kilmer's Indian

Cough Cure, E. Arnold & Co.'s Celebrated Indian Stomach Bitters, Louden's Indian Expectorant, Cherokee Remedy, and Clement's Genuine Osceola Indian Liniment, all of which claimed to cure an unbelievable variety of ailments. A common advertisement for Montague's syrup summarized the popularity of such salves: "This is truly an Indian medicine and probably the only real one in use amongst the white people, although there are so many in circulation called Indian medicines."[13] These substances, often referred to as patent medicines, were available via mail order by the middle of the nineteenth century and were frequently for sale at neighborhood druggists.[14]

In addition to the various nostrums, literate Americans could make use of an array of manuals, guides, and recipe books that claimed to illuminate the secrets of Indian medicine. *The Indian Guide to Health, or a Treatise on the Cure of Various Diseases* (1839), *The Indian Guide to Health, or Valuable Vegetable Medical Prescriptions for the Use of Families, or Young Practitioners* (1845), *The Indian Doctor's Family Physician, Comprising about two hundred receipts, for the cure of different diseases* (1849), *The House-Keeper's Guide, and Indian Doctor* (1856), and *Dr. R. Greene's Indianopathy, or, Science of Indian Medicine* (1858) were just a few popular titles available to physicians, druggists, and housewives during the antebellum period.[15] Some books contained elaborate authenticating statements about the author's personal experience among American Indians, while others simply affixed the word "Indian" to common folk cures and herbal medicines in order to profit from the association of Native people with effective botanic treatments. Many of these guides went through multiple editions, attesting to their continued popularity throughout the era. But the widespread use of botanic medicines and home medical guides also earned the ire of "professional" medical men, who increasingly referred to these cures and those who sold them as dangerous "quackery."[16] Although the Tubbees had faced an accusation of medical fraud before and thanks to such professional backlash they would again, in the summer of 1851, they had bigger problems.

On June 28, suspicions about Okah Tubbee's "real" identity resurfaced. His newfound fame in Indiana gained the attention of readers in Louisville who recognized the celebrated performer as "Carey, a negro, or rather mulatto, who lived in this city some ten or twelve years since." The *Louisville Courier* published a biting exposé that left few doubts about the performer's "true identity." According to the paper, "Carey has shown himself to be a worthy rival of Barnum in the humbugging line." It was certain, the editor asserted, that "Dr. Okah Tubbee" was none other than the popular former musician of the Old Louisville Guard militia company, recalling that when the company paraded, "he discoursed his music to the infinite delight of the crowds of urchins who 'followed the sogers!'" Remarkably, even in this effort to unmask him, the paper nevertheless confessed that "Carey . . . was an excellent performer on the fife, flute and other musical instruments." Although word of his charade might "amuse" knowing observers in Louisville, Tubbee's obvious musical talents still deserved considerable praise. The editor surmised that the Natchez native "thought it would prove more profitable to turn Indian," so he proclaimed himself an Indian chief.[17] Though largely benign, the story set off a chain reaction.

A few days later, a follow-up in the New Orleans *Daily Picayune* stated that "Carey . . . is about as well known in New Orleans as any where else." As in Louisville, his musical renown was obligingly acknowledged, "for we doubt whether any of our readers that resided here five years ago, have not heard him discourse just about as eloquent music as was ever blown into or out of a fife. On this instrument Carey was a genius—there is no use in denying it."[18] Indeed, as early as 1839, the *Daily Picayune* had made passing reference to Carey's delightful fife variations of the "Star Spangled Banner" and "Yankee Doodle" on the assumption that the talented performer needed no introduction to locals.[19] Now that news of his great success as "Dr. Okah Tubbee" had reached the Crescent City, readers could not fail to recognize the notable former resident.

Despite the willingness of southern newspaper editors to grant Tubbee's musical "genius," his claims of linguistic expertise, not to mention temperance, were quickly dismissed. The *Picayune* confessed that his ability to speak "fifteen living languages, and . . . three or four dead ones, is really news to us," and recalled, "Here he always passed as an easy, good-natured, fair-drinking sort of a chap, with no other claim to notoriety than an extraordinary talent as a performer on the fife, flageolet or octave flute."[20] Although such a revelation may have dismayed the Tubbees' allies within the temperance movement, it suggests little of the scathing condemnations that would soon follow. Indeed, this exposé, like the one that first appeared in Louisville, conveys a tone of amusement, treating the success of a "humbugging" mulatto as simply a sign of the times.

The New Orleans paper also included another revealing story, however. A pair of Louisiana gentlemen had apparently happened upon one of Tubbee's northern performances several years before. The show was advertised with a "flaming" poster that announced the appearance of "The

Great Choctaw Chief, Okah Tubbee, The Mighty Son of the Howling Forest!" During the course of the performance, the southern men recognized a familiar face, one of them saying to the other, "I know him through all that paint, and those Indian fixings." As the concert proceeded, one of the men suddenly declared, "I've heard that same identical music before." He called out from the audience, "Carey, by all the powers! Oh, I know you, Carey: you can't deceive me." The startled performer hit a wrong note, then hastily disappeared behind the curtain.[21]

The southern gentlemen's ability to recognize Okah Tubbee's "true" identity, through "all his paint, feathers and finery," while he duped foolish northern audiences implied their superior ability to discern race.[22] As had become evident in the Masonic "chit chat" a year earlier, southern and western observers claimed powers of racial recognition that they believed northerners and easterners lacked.[23] The same confident racial gaze underlay the Fugitive Slave Act of 1850 and found its expression in the writings of the American school of ethnology, which had their widest circulation in the South. Journals like the *Southern Quarterly Review* and *De Bow's Review* offered a wide swath of southern readers "scientific" evidence of the "natural, unalterable, and eternal inferiority" of blacks, whose race was easily discernible through their physical traits.[24] Likewise, whites in the South and the West tended to assert that they had more intimate and realistic knowledge of Native people than their sentimental northern and eastern counterparts, who hypocritically opposed Indian removal from other states even though they had "literally exterminated" the Indian nations in their own regions.[25]

Southern newspapers reinforced such claims by printing stories of racial misrecognition that could not have happened in the South. Even when race scientists were employed, they posited, a certain debility prevented northerners in particular from correctly discerning a person's race. The *Louisville Democrat* reported, for example, that a suspected fugitive slave, "a mulatto," was arrested in New York, but was deemed an Indian by "Doctors, phrenologists, physiologist, &c., &c., [who] were summoned to show that the mulatto was no part African, but an Indian. They swore very strongly upon the point." The Kentucky editor derisively asserted that the man arrested was undoubtedly a "mulatto," an obvious "half negro," and lamented that the opinion of northern "experts" would likely lead to the man's release from custody.[26]

An account published in the *Choctaw Intelligencer,* the national organ of the Choctaw Nation in Indian Territory, similarly emphasized the gullibility of northern audiences, with specific reference to Okah Tubbee. It offered clear evidence that his assertion of Choctaw ancestry was viewed with suspicion, if not contempt, by the very people from whom he claimed descent. Titled "How Free Negroes Succeed at the North," the story identified Tubbee as "Andrew Carey" and contended that he had been a "servant of respectable par[,] barring impudence" in 1813—when he would have been only three years old. Despite these inaccuracies, the core narrative is consistent with other accounts: a "mulatto fifer" had re-invented himself as a Choctaw Indian, married an Indian princess, and fooled audiences across the North. "By this means," the *Choctaw Intelligencer* concluded, "he has successfully imposed upon the credulity of the Northern people."[27] Okah Tubbee's Choctaw expositors neither elaborated on his enslaved past nor threatened a return to bondage, but they nevertheless communicated the same ideology apparent in other accounts: race, especially blackness, was undeniably visible, but you had to know what to look for. Northerners, they implied, were ridiculously, if not dangerously, color blind.

The exposés also revealed another important aspect of Tubbee's difficulties. Stories about the performer's "real" identity depended not only on purported visual evidence of race, but also on his notorious talents—his fame. In most stories, he was referenced as a familiar and gifted musician, well known in port cities across the South and the West. As word spread back to the Northeast, Tubbee's celebrity likewise ensured that the story would receive wide circulation. The *Daily Journal and Courier* in Lowell, Massachusetts, reprinted the original story from Louisville under the headline "Okah Tubbee Barnum," and blandly recalled that "Tubbee figured somewhat, 'on natural principles,' in Lowell, two or three years ago," a reference to his performances there the previous year. Other northern papers reprinted the Louisville story on the "celebrated Indian musician" without further comment, on the presumption that readers were already familiar with the memorable flutist.[28] Tubbee's fame was both the means of detecting him and the reason the story was newsworthy: a popular Indian musician who had traveled widely across the nation turned out to be a "negro" confidence man. His very success ensured he would face greater scrutiny.

Although accusations were mounting, the Tubbees went on with the show. In early August 1851, they appeared in Buffalo, New York, with an English tenor from the Seguin Opera Troupe named Frank Gardner. The pair might have met Gardner during their stint at Barnum's museum in

New York because the Seguin troupe also worked under the legendary showman's management. After making quite an impression during an appearance with world-renowned soprano Madame Anna Bishop, Okah Tubbee, the "celebrated Indian Chief of the Choctaw Tribe . . . the Greatest Natural Musician in the World . . . [and] Greatest Wonder of the Age" returned to the Buffalo stage with Gardner providing accompaniment and, apparently, management. An advertisement for the show included brief testimonials from Bishop and her lover, composer Nicholas-Charles Bochsa, also a flutist. Bochsa affirmed Tubbee's "astonishing" talent and offered this understatement: "He is indeed a very remarkable person." The performance consisted of pieces played on the flute, flageolet, and Tubbee's newly invented "musical walking cane." A brief editorial in the same paper observed, "The Indian, 'Okah Tubbee,' is stated to be a remarkable natural musician." Neither announcement acknowledged the recent gossip about his past.[29]

Only a few days after his first performance alongside Gardner, a laudatory and probably promotional account of Tubbee's concert appeared in another Buffalo paper. The writer begged leave to introduce Tubbee, "one of the most wonderful beings (not excepting Jenny Lind)," the wildly popular Swedish songstress who had been touring in the United States under P. T. Barnum's management. The endorsement indicated that the Choctaw performer would be "tarrying a short time in our midst." Of his most recent concert, the anonymous correspondent opined, "I listened to Okah Tubbee at Mr. Gardner's Concert, which I am sorry to say was very thinly attended, owing to the various other attractions in town, many of them of much less worth. Concert Hall should have been crowded from considerations alone of the rare talents of the performer, in connection with Mr. Gardner's own personal entertainment. Certainly, when we consider the object, which we learn from the Chief, is one of pecuniary devotion for the furtherance of the moral and intellectual culture of his tribe." The writer considered Tubbee's music, which was said to "fairly ravish the ear with delight," particularly impressive given that he was "an unbettered Indian." The account also mentioned his facility with five or six languages and innumerable imitations, skills he had acquired "unaided by the advantages even a common school education."[30] As before, part of Tubbee's ability to impress his audience hinged on popular ideas about American Indian intelligence, including access to the means of "improvement" through civilized education. His talents were deemed incredible because of his professed Indianness. Lacking betterment because of his race, the letter maintained, Tubbee nevertheless possessed "Real Native Genius" and was putting his natural talents into service as a means of financing the uplift of his people.

It seems likely that Laah Ceil, Frank Gardner, or another patron wrote the letter in an effort to stimulate interest in Tubbee's upcoming performances. Whether she authored the advertisement, a handbill for this August performance in Buffalo indicates that Mrs. Laah Ceil Tubbee was still assisting her husband on stage. Both appeared in their "Indian Costume," along with two-year-old Mosholeh "in full costume of the Brave." The program began with an "Address by Mrs. Laah Ceil Tubbee, Giving an Interesting Account of her People," the Mohawks of Canada West. In addition to the walking stick and the sauce-panana, Okah Tubbee played on the "musical tomahawk," one-keyed flute, flageolet, and fife, frequently accompanying himself on castanets. He played variations on popular tunes such as "Auld Lang Syne" and "La Marseillaise," a variety of Scottish hymns and folk songs, and "Okah Tubbee's Waltz" and other work of his own composition. The handbill stressed the "respectability of his person and performance," now more important than ever given recent revelations about his background.[31]

Indeed, in the context of swirling rumors about Okah Tubbee's race, he and and his wife may have felt ever more pressure to maintain their Indianness. Even as citizens in free states debated their obligation to enforce discriminatory legislation such as the Fugitive Slave Act, prospects for slaves, free blacks, and individuals of indeterminate race had worsened dramatically. Two weeks after the Tubbees' performance in Buffalo, authorities apprehended an alleged fugitive slave known as Daniel aboard a steamboat in that city. The city marshal delivered him to an agent of the fugitive's purported owner, George Moore of Louisville, Kentucky. Buffalo was in a tumult for some time afterward, as many citizens grudgingly lent support to enforcement of the unfortunate law, while free blacks protested the arrest, allegedly incited by "unprincipled white men." The resulting case came before a judge, where the owner's agent produced witnesses and documentation regarding Daniel's background, while the defense "proposed to introduce testimony to destroy the identity" ascribed to the defendant, asserting that he had lived in a free state longer than he had been a slave. But it was to no avail. Facing riot threats from the free black community and the "strongest prejudices against slavery" among some vocal whites in Buffalo, the judge nevertheless declared his intention to uphold the law.[32]

The case of Daniel became national news and could not have failed to impress the Tubbees with its import. Although it is clear that Okah Tubbee had been a free man since at least 1843, if not before, willful misrecognition and kidnappings were not uncommon. In this volatile environment, characterized by an increased public interest in naming and assigning race and combined with specific revelations about the fife-playing "Negro turned Indian," they had to tread carefully. Free blacks and their allies recognized the insidiousness of the new law; many gathered their things and left for Canada rather than risk enslavement.[33]

Even if they were not directly threatened by the specter of slavery, the Tubbee family could not escape the scrutinizing racial gaze that increasingly beheld them. Although popular culture was a realm in which ideas about race were often at their most unstable, as aspects of the wildly popular blackface minstrel shows suggest, there were limits to the elasticity and emancipatory potential of Indianness. Suspicions about Okah Tubbee's past had surfaced before, but the newly polarized national conversation about race, race science, and their relationship to slavery and national expansion raised the stakes for the former Natchez slave. In addition, despite the growth of the abolition movement and protests from some quarters of the North and the East about the disgraceful compromises that underlay the Fugitive Slave Act, there was considerable antiblack sentiment in many of the northern cities and towns the Tubbees frequented.[34] In this atmosphere, and with little Mosholeh to protect, the pair had to double-down on their Indian act. Escaping the stigma of blackness required them to rely ever more heavily on the narrow popular stereotypes of Indianness. Endangered, impeded, and annoyed, the couple sought refuge from one set of constricting racial ideas in another, which made Okah Tubbee's next move all the more extraordinary.

The day after the alleged fugitive Daniel was apprehended in Buffalo, Okah Tubbee took another wife. On Saturday, August 16, 1851, he wed a white woman named Sarah Marlett at Niagara Falls.[35] Within a few days, the news was all over the papers.

One early response came from "A Buffalonian," who wrote to a local paper that although much was said about women's rights, "I do not believe that one woman has a right to marry another woman's husband."[36] The *Spirit of the Times* from neighboring Batavia, New York, carried a short write-up on the marriage, not failing to emphasize that Tubbee had married a *white* woman, before calling him "an old *Tubb*-ee," a possible reference to the "oak tub" theory of his name's origins, and by extension, his putative African ancestry.[37] Neither of these early accounts of the marriage, however, directly mentioned Tubbee's alleged past, though it had been widely discussed in other locales since June.

By the end of the month, the *Daily Standard* in Syracuse had put most of the pieces together. The summary account encapsulated a number of the themes that would characterize newspaper coverage of the unfolding scandal, most notably that Tubbee was once a "negro barber."[38] An article the following week in the *Brooklyn Daily Eagle* repeated the "negro barber" tale, embellished with a fuller version from the *N.Y. Citizen* (Medina, New York), the hometown of his new bride. The earlier exposés penned by southern whites who professed to know "Carey" from his younger years consistently referred to him as a musician rather than a barber, but this feature of the story became a popular shorthand way for newspaper writers to affix blackness to Okah Tubbee, just as it had been for Brigham Young in Winter Quarters.

Despite the apparent belief that Okah Tubbee was actually black, not Indian, one paper also saw fit to compare his case to that of another professional Indian who had wed a white woman a few years before. The editor suggested that readers might recall traveling Anishinaabe Methodist orator Peter Jones, "an Indian Chief" who married "an English lady of moderate fortune and undoubted respectability." Others might have remembered another high-profile marriage between an Indian man and a white woman that had occurred some years earlier in New England when Cherokee student and later politician John Ridge married Sarah Bird Northrup. Although there was little backlash against Jones's marriage, the Ridge/Northrup nuptials, along with the contemporaneous union of Ridge's cousin Elias Boudinot to a local white woman, had resulted in an explosive controversy involving burned effigies and the closure of the Indian mission school the men attended.[39] In Tubbee's case, however, the courtship was more rapid, likened to the sudden onset of a matrimonial disease, and occurred outside the context of Christian missionizing that framed similar cases.[40]

Another local paper provided the outlines of Tubbee and Marlett's romantic affair. The story hyperbolically referred to Okah Tubbee as a Choctaw chief from Arkansas who could speak seventeen languages and play over one hundred musical instruments. Ms. Marlett had approached the dusky stranger on a canal boat, requesting a demonstration of his talents. She was reportedly so impressed with his performance that she refused to disembark upon reaching her destination. According to the account

Their mutual esteem had ripened with such amazing rapidity, that the lady, now fully given over to the fates, declared, in the most passionate language, that she loved the chief with unconquerable fondness, and gave proof of her sincerity in a flood of tears.

The Indian, in return, fell upon his knees and assured the trembling girl that her love was reciprocated. He told her that seven years ago that very day he had a dream, in which he saw a beautiful woman who was presented to him as his wife. Since then he had been wandering up and down the earth in search of her, but to no purpose, until this providential meeting had brought him face to face with the identical image whom he had seen in his dream.[41]

The similarity between this account and the one that appeared in the second edition of the autobiography is striking, although it is not clear whether Tubbee told Marlett this story or papers reproduced its outlines from the published text. In either case, the inexplicably rapid courtship, the instrumentality of a vision in bringing the lovers together, and the image of the wandering Indian all resonate with the autobiography's depiction of Okah Tubbee and Laah Ceil's romance.

The day after they'd met, Okah Tubbee and Sarah Marlett were united in matrimony at Niagara Falls (American side). Although they experienced a brief delay when the presiding clergyman "gazed wildly at the swarthy Choctaw, cast a hasty glance at the fair woman with a bridal wreath" and suddenly backed out, they quickly secured another officiator, whom the bride paid in cash on the spot.[42] After their nuptials, the pair parted ostensibly so that Okah Tubbee could travel to Europe with Mr. Gardner. Near exact versions of this story appeared in at least seventeen newspapers from Natchez, Mississippi, to Manchester, England, and summaries were carried in at least fifty others.[43] It was the most publicity Okah Tubbee had ever received.

Almost immediately after word of the union appeared, follow-up stories raised the issue of Tubbee's first wife. These references to Laah Ceil, though they rarely mention her by name, are interesting because they uniformly present her as an Indian woman and frequently depict her as an innocent victim of Tubbee's chicanery. In Utica, New York, a local paper reported that the new "Mrs. Tubbee" must soon realize that "a dusky sister, (or perhaps, half a-dozen of them,) has, or have rights precedent to her's [sic]," a reference to both Laah Ceil's presumed Indian identity and the possibility that Tubbee had more than one other spouse. Besides the problem of the original Mrs. Tubbee, the paper suggested that the Choctaw chief's newest bride, referred to as "a poor deluded girl," might have just become the stepmother of some "little straight-haired urchins," a choice of words that probably delighted Okah Tubbee given his preoccupation with the texture of his own hair. The account concluded, "This falling in love with an Indian, on a canal boat, beats anything that can be found in any 'cheap,' 'yellow-covered' book," both a reference to lurid popular fiction that catered to the masses and a sign of the declining respectability of Indian themes.[44]

A Buffalo paper similarly reported that Okah Tubbee acknowledged a previous wife, by whom he had three children.[45] The article continued, "This Squaw was at Buffalo at the time of his marriage. The Indian says that he was married to his first wife only for a term of years, according to the custom of his nation—that the time had expired, and he renounced her, as the laws of the Choctaws permitted him to do."[46] No longer the "Indian princess" or a "well educated daughter of a Mohawk chief," Laah Ceil was instead depicted as an ignorant squaw, saddled with a large brood, who had been pathetically deluded by a fast-talking "Negro" confidence man. This shift in her image reflects popular American ideas about Native women, in which the figure of the squaw was the inverse of the Indian princess. Squaws were degraded; they were described as undesirable, "overburdened" with Indian children, "fat, and unlike their Princess sisters, dark and possessed of cruder, more 'Indian' features."[47] Ironically, as criticism of her husband intensified, Laah Ceil's image suffered, but her claims to Indian identity were actually strengthened in the process.

Similar statements regarding the "Indian custom" of polygamy appeared in a variety of other papers as the news began to spread.[48] For example, carrying a reprint from New York papers, a Michigan publication reported that Tubbee claimed his first marriage was "consummated according to the laws of a savage people, to exist no longer than the parties should choose to have it, that the last marriage is according to the laws of civilization, and annuls the first."[49] This characterization of his first marriage as deficient and even uncivilized is particularly interesting since it disguises the Mormon sealing ceremony that united Okah Tubbee and Laah Ceil by cloaking it in Indian traits and customs rhetoric.

Area newspapers also tended to link the unfolding scandal to the recent case of alleged fugitive slave Daniel. When one Buffalo paper mentioned Tubbee's explanation that Choctaw custom permitted him take as many wives as he liked, the editor could not resist describing Tubbee as "a backwoods Daniel giving judgment to suit his own case," implying that in both circumstances a scheming person of color had tried to bend rules to his benefit.[50]

But why did Okah Tubbee take a second wife? Had he really met Marlett on a canal boat and charmed her in "a single hour"?[51] Had his first wife known about the nuptials? It is possible, of course, that Laah Ceil was completely unaware of this matrimonial drama. But given the Tubbees' earlier involvement in plural marriage, or some form of it, perhaps she had consented to or even arranged the nuptials. The Latter-day Saints Church would officially espouse plural marriage the following year, though some Mormons had been practicing it for nearly twenty years already. Perhaps the Tubbees had maintained an interest in the practice, anticipating its wider acceptance among their former religious community. In Cincinnati, the Tubbees had faced allegations of marital irregularity, accused of trying to "abolish marriage" among their followers, and they had been attacked for promoting unorthodox sexual sealing at Winter Quarters. It is thus possible that the Marlett affair was part of their ongoing marital idiosyncrasies, but Laah Ceil's perspective on the episode remains shrouded in mystery.

There was also a great deal of disagreement about the identity of Tubbee's new bride. She was unquestionably considered a white woman by press accounts, but descriptions of her character and background varied. By different accounts, she was a "deluded girl,"[52] "a lady of respectable connections,"[53] a "charming young white lady,"[54] and "particularly handsome."[55] Other characterizations insisted that, at age forty, she was certainly not young and that her appearance was decidedly ugly. In addition, she was apparently not in her right mind, having spent several years in the Utica insane asylum, to which she was committed for monomania regarding matrimony and from which, the papers claimed, she "evidently left too soon."[56]

Predictably, stories about the bigamy case were soon fused to stories about Tubbee's presumed race.[57] No paper evinced more disgust on both matters than the *Mississippi Free Trader* in Natchez. Under the heading "An Old Imposter," the story announced, "The Greatest Scoundrel now living *in human form in the United States is* Warner McCary, a negro born and raised in this city." The editors referred to the episode in Philadelphia when some southern men happened upon one of the Choctaw chief's performances, asserting, "Barnum exhibited the vagabond over the Eastern States as the son of an Indian Chief who was captured in this neighborhood and held to slavery for many years until he took flight." Like other southern accounts of "the Negro turned Indian," this one admitted his unmatched talent on the fife, but also referred to his involvement in barbering, though there's no evidence he ever worked in that trade. The Natchez paper then reprinted the now familiar account about the white woman who fell foolishly in love with the "Choctaw Chief (greasy negro)."[58]

The *Vicksburg Tri-Weekly Sentinel* was similarly harsh in its denunciation of both the imposture and the marriage. The editors described "Andrew Carey" as "a mulatto fifer" who had lived in Natchez for some time before departing for the North. The paper recounted a story from the spring of 1848 when a Mississippi man had bumped into Tubbee on the streets of Baltimore. According to his account, Tubbee informed him that he was successfully passing himself off as a Choctaw chief to "crowded houses" and then "implored us not to make an *expose*." The editors sneered at his gullible white bride and ridiculed the credulous northern press, remarking, "Wonder if she has dreamed yet that her Doctor Tibbee [*sic*]— the Choctaw chief is nothing but a mulatto barber of Natchez. He is nothing but an ignorant negro, and yet is reported to be a fine scholar in the northern papers, and speaks 24 different languages with ease."[59]

Despite the continuing critique of northern racial acuity and common sense by southern papers, the New York press quickly joined in the fray. One account from the *Buffalo Courier* stands out. The editor wrote with personal knowledge of and extraordinary contempt for the performer, claiming he could "speak feelingly of the events that have made [Tubbee's] life remarkable."

> The future historian of the nineteenth century will not fail to record, among the stirring events of 1851, and in the same chapter with the heroic deeds of the chivalrous Sutherland and the tribulations of "Daniel" and his hurried evasion to that soil, said to possess the quality of freeing from bondage any slave who sets foot upon it—will not fail, we say, to place alongside these events, in proper chronological order, the advent, nuptials, and exodu[s] of Okah Tubbee, the "big Ingin."[60]

Once again, Tubbee's "tribulations" were set alongside those of the alleged fugitive slave Daniel, whose apprehension had created such a stir in Buffalo, but in this case, the writer made explicit the racial resemblance of the two men.

The account also provided a detailed, if impressionistic, description of Tubbee's physical appearance:

> In person, Okah is short, and as his name denotes, tubby; his countenance is rather less Indian than African, being decidedly of a mulatto hue, and disagreeably pinguid, while the least experienced physiognomist would never pronounce his nose, aquiline: we should rather denominate that appendage an oleagenous [*sic*] bulb, than a nose, at all.[61]

The paper signaled the physical characteristics by which race was judged in the era, by both southerners *and* northerners, though they often arrived at different conclusions. The reference to the work of "physiognomists" reflects the rapid emergence of pseudoscientists who developed a new profession based on practices of racial classification, deemed all the more necessary in the context of imposture and fugitive suspicions. In hindsight, the editor suggested, it was easy to *see* that he was not an Indian.

The reactions of this editor (and others in western New York) were perhaps motivated in part by sympathy for Tubbee's first wife, who had very recently appeared on stage with her husband and young son. Because concurrent newspaper reports indicated that Laah Ceil was in Buffalo at the time of her husband's marriage to Sarah Marlett, it is possible that she had some supporters there. The *Courier* noted that the Indian musician's "matrimonial eccentricities" had been written about at length and that, among other things, his "constancy" was to be doubted since he was alleged to have several wives.[62] Despite his apparently disagreeable countenance, the "'big Ingin'" managed to woo one woman after another. The writer resignedly admitted, "Taken as a whole, the expression of his face was not such as to convey the idea of its belonging to a gay deceiver. We were not smitten with it, at all, though the result proves that we underestimated its powers of fascination." In much the same way that southern papers admitted Okah Tubbee's incomparable musical talents, while nevertheless dismissing his claims to Indian ancestry, the Buffalo paper offered a backhanded compliment to the gifted performer: "Okah 'did' us in the end, most satisfactorily, and we here publicly apologise to him for the uncomplimentary opinion we formed, of his suasive talent."[63]

Importantly, the emphasis on Tubbee's ethnic and marital impostures continued to deflect attention away from Laah Ceil's identity. Rather than becoming the subject of public scrutiny, she became a pathetic figure.

Although her relative status suffered as she was downgraded from a princess to a squaw, her claims to Indianness stood largely unexamined in the shadow of her husband's great humbug.

Given the high profile nature of Tubbee's various unveilings, it was perhaps predictable that he (or rather some interested patron or patroness) would attempt a public defense. Just one month after news of his Niagara Falls nuptials spread, the Syracuse *Daily Standard* addressed the various "statements, wide from the truth . . . concerning the character and nuptials of Okah Tubbee, head chief of the Choctaw nation." It is unclear who penned the response, but likely authors include Gardner, Marlett, or Laah Ceil. Okah Tubbee probably did not write it himself, since though the writer notes "he has few superiors in the world," as a linguist, "speaking fluently at least fifty dialects and several dead languages," he nevertheless could not "read a single word in any language." In order to address the "misapprehensions" and "false rumors," the account attempted to clarify the details of Tubbee's marriage to Marlett.[64]

The marriage was no accident or foolish mistake, the writer insisted. While traveling on the Erie Canal in western New York on a professional tour, Tubbee had seen a woman about whom he'd had a vision seven years before. When he played and sang for her, "his melody took hold of her heart" and the "marriage contract was perfected at once." Rather than emphasize the physical attractiveness of the pair, long since attacked in the papers, this story offered a different explanation for the sudden infatuation. "Since childhood," the writer explained, "Sarah Marlett has been an enthusiastic admirer of the Indian race. It had been the burden of her dreams by night, and her meditations by day. Even when a little girl, she longed to be stolen and carried off by the Indians."[65] In this fascinating description, Marlett's union with Okah Tubbee is explained not in terms of his attractiveness or even his impressive talents, but in terms of her desire for Indianness. Whether Marlett truly felt this way is hard to know, but the captivity fantasy seems intended, like the rest of the story, to reinforce Tubbee's identity claims. It explained her sudden and dramatic infatuation while brushing aside questions about his background. Because Marlett was obsessed with Indians, her marriage to Okah Tubbee must prove he was in fact an Indian. The story hinged in part on the proliferation and popularity of Indian captivity narratives in which white women were frequently the protagonists, making such tales even more popular among impressionable female readers. Despite the association of Okah Tubbee with savage Indian kidnappers, the *Daily Standard* emphasized that the Choctaw chief was a highly civilized, if not refined, Indian, who was at that very moment off on "a mission throughout the civilized world in behalf of his nation . . . [and that] Where he goes, his transcendant powers are acknowledged by all."[66] The story worked to defuse concerns about his "Negro" identity by depicting him as a legitimate object of white female desire—the civilized and heroic Indian man.[67]

In defense of his apparent infidelity and bigamy, Okah Tubbee also capitalized on popular beliefs about Indian marital practices. His assertion that taking multiple wives was an "Indian custom" appeared in a variety of papers as the news began to spread.[68] Vague references to Indian marriage traditions resonated with audiences accustomed to reading "Indian romances," attending lectures on "Indian manners and customs," and seeing performances of "Indian war and marriage dances."[69] In fact, it is possible, coming as it did on the heels of his exposure as a "negro barber," that Okah Tubbee (and perhaps Laah Ceil) devised the entire Sarah Marlett affair to affirm his Indianness by publicly performing a popular understanding of Indian masculinity and marriage practices.

While the Tubbees and their supporters apparently scrambled to spin the story to their benefit, accusations of bigamy gained steam. Although occasional accounts in the press suggested that Okah Tubbee was departing for a European tour, there is no evidence that such a plan was ever in motion.[70] Instead, he and Laah Ceil left for Canada, joining an exodus of fugitive slaves and free blacks who were fleeing the United States after the passage of the Fugitive Slave Act and recent high profile cases in Buffalo and Boston in which northern courts upheld the law.[71] Their departure took place against a backdrop of fear and intimidation, and the possible effect that this atmosphere had on the family should not be overlooked, particularly given the recent revelations about Okah Tubbee's past. Perhaps they also feared for their son, Mosholeh, and sought a new life across the border to prevent him from being endangered. In any case, it seems clear that their flight was also motivated by a desire to avoid further controversy stemming from the Marlett affair and to earn an income once more. By mid-September 1851, Tubbee was performing throughout the region known at the time as "Canada West" and known to us as Ontario.[72]

Although by this point, Okah Tubbee's secret past and his alleged bigamy with a lunatic white woman was well-known news from Vicksburg, Mississippi, to Bangor, Maine, he and Laah Ceil advertised performances to Toronto audiences apparently unaware of the couple's past. They were slated to appear at St. Lawrence Hall, a magnificent new 1,000-seat theatre, from January through March 1852. Although he was ill at the time, Okah Tubbee's first show was a rousing musical performance and he displayed his habit of "interspersing occasionally a witty remark . . . [and his] knack of pleasing his audience."[73] Within a month, Laah Ceil appeared on stage with him as she had so many times before. Three-year-old Mosholeh, however, was curiously absent.[74] Perhaps the Toronto audiences were exceptionally forgiving of the various accusations leveled at the Choctaw performer or perhaps the news of his misadventures still had not yet reached them.

By March, however, their stage shows ceased completely, and the Tubbees were solely dependent on their medical practice for income. It is unclear precisely why they retired from musical entertainments. Toronto was receptive to Native performers of various kinds: lecturers, musicians, and dancers frequently graced the city's stages. Indeed, the Tubbees may have found a fair bit of competition in the Indian business. One prominent figure who made frequent public appearances in the area was Maungwudaus, the Mississauga performer, often referred to as "the celebrated traveller."[75] Like George Copway and other professional Indians of the day, Maungwudaus was also a published author and had toured extensively in Europe and the United States, often in association with portrait artist George Catlin. Like Okah Tubbee, part of his appeal lay in his "stylized naïveté" and apparent natural talent; he called himself "The Self-Taught Indian of the Chippewa Nation."[76] In addition to these notable individuals, less famous Native troupes staged dances or gave concerts across western New York and into Ontario during the same era, suggesting that performances of Indianness still drew crowds in the region.[77]

The Tubbees took up residence in the building of a Toronto druggist named Swain and began to advertise that they could be "consulted on Chronic Diseases, and those of a private nature," and that the appropriate treatments would be prepared by Doctor Okah Tubbee himself.[78] They advised the public that the doctor had "recommendations from some of the most respectable citizens," and could provide "Genuine Indian Medicine!" for the afflicted. The notices further declared that they had determined to stay in Toronto for some time and could be found at 15 Victoria Street.[79]

Despite their apparent success in returning to Indian medicine, Sarah Marlett was not easy to shake. According to one western New York paper, she followed the Tubbees when they proceeded to Canada, where she became violent and threatened legal proceedings. Then, according to a description perhaps unknowingly suggestive of Mormon plural marriage, Marlett reportedly changed tacks and "besought Mrs. T. to allow her to at least share in the dark deceiver, offering to divide 'bed and board' with the lawful squaw," a proposition that was met with "prompt refusal."[80] Making good on her threat of a suit, Marlett then prevailed upon Canadian authorities to issue a warrant for Tubbee's arrest on the charge of bigamy. He was detained by Toronto police and the case, Regina v. Tubbee, came before the Ontario Court of Queen's Bench in August 1852.

Marlett appeared alongside the prosecutor, named Skelton, and provided testimony that she had consented to become Okah Tubbee's wife after hearing tales of his life and adventures. She became aware shortly after their nuptials at Niagara Falls that her new husband "had with him an Indian woman, by whom he had had a son; but she implicitly believed his statement, that this person was not his wife, but that in his capacity of chief, he might take any Indian woman he liked under his protection, as he called it." Tubbee had offered a similar defense when the story broke a year earlier, explaining that it was Indian custom to take as many women as one liked. Nevertheless, Marlett had decided to press the case against "her sable lord" on the advice of friends who insisted she defend her "offended virtue."[81]

Okah Tubbee appeared in court in his full Indian costume, sporting a broad mustache, large earrings, and several medals. On his head, he wore a tight-fitting beaded cap. At least one account explained that this head-covering was designed to hide his "woolly head" and remarked that the performer, who had been recently engaged in selling "quack medicines," was "nothing more nor less than a 'colored gentleman.'" Marlett took the stand and testified that she had lived as Tubbee's wife for nearly two months, during which time they traveled in western New York and were occasionally separated. At the end of that time, he left her at Cayuga and promised to rejoin her at Syracuse after a brief trip, but never returned.[82] Instead, he and Laah Ceil fled to Canada, stopping first in Lewiston, near the newly built suspension bridge spanning the Niagara River, and then proceeding to Toronto, where they had settled in early 1852.[83]

The case hinged on two elements: first, the prosecution had to provide sufficient evidence of bigamy; and second, if sufficient evidence existed, the court had to determine whether or not Tubbee could be extradited to stand trial for the charge in the United States, where the offence had allegedly occurred. Ultimately, the judge declared that bigamy could not be proved because the first marriage, although widely admitted, could not be shown to be a legal union. Neither could he proceed with extradition because even if bigamy had been proven, the offence was not covered under the Webster-Ashburton Treaty that governed the rendition of criminals across the U.S.-Canada border.[84] Tubbee was released from custody and resumed his medical practice in Toronto with Laah Ceil. Marlett presumably returned to the United States.

Although Okah Tubbee dodged extradition and imprisonment, by the time he was released from police custody in late August 1852, his fortunes in Toronto were on the decline. The bigamy case had been widely reported, and the revelations hurt his efforts to establish his trustworthiness as a physician.[85] The news even made it to Utah, where Willard Richards, Mormon apostle and church historian who had once examined the body of the man he referred to as "the nigger Indian," remarked in the *Deseret News*, "Okah Tubbee has been called in question by the Canadian courts, Toronto, for having added Sarah Marlett, to his broken ribs, while his old wife was living," referring to Tubbee's Adamic claims about a "missing rib." The brief story appeared amidst a growing national conversation about polygamy, initiated by the Utah Mormons' recent public declaration of plural marriage as official church doctrine.[86]

Perhaps to garner new business, later that fall, the Tubbees debuted a new advertisement for their medical practice in Toronto papers, touting the Indian doctor's "Scientific Principles" (a notable departure from the "Natural Principles" for which his music was known), but also his "Eclecticism."[87] The ad emphasized the variety of ailments the chief was known to have cured, including cancer, smallpox, cholera, and snake bites, drawing upon both the "simple, yet efficient medicines that the God of Nature has so abundantly supplied" and the maxim "'WASH and be Clean' . . . an ordinance laid down in THE Good Book."[88] While they were still operating out of the same building, the Tubbees had recently resumed their practice in rooms facing Yonge Street, having briefly consulted patients at their residence on the opposite side, facing Victoria Street.[89] (See Fig. 6.) But all was not well in the Indian medicine business.

In addition to lingering concerns about his apparent racial imposture and marital irregularities, the Tubbees' medical practice also began to suffer from both a general backlash against "quack" doctors and specific accusations of malpractice. Although Tubbee notably appeared in his full costume as the grand marshal for the 1852 Canadian National Exhibition, a splendid affair attracting nearly 30,000 people to Toronto, suggesting that he had managed to retain some respectability, he was simultaneously

FIGURE 6 The Tubbees' neighborhood in Toronto. Photographic view of the Toronto neighborhood where Okah Tubbee and Laah Ceil lived from 1852 until about 1856. The street along the left side is Victoria and the intersecting street is Adelaide. The Tubbees lived and worked at 15 Victoria Street. Booth & Son: north-east corner of Adelaide and Victoria Streets [1856 or 1857]. (Courtesy City of Toronto Archives)

busy deflecting criticism in the press.[90] While he continued to advertise his medical services in city papers, now claiming he was the head medicine man of the Choctaws and that his mother was Ojibwe, he could not ignore the charges against him.[91]

On the same day that the new ad appeared, the Tubbees also had the editor insert the following notice: "We have been requested to state that Matilda Thomson, of Agnes street, who died of consumption on Saturday last, the 20th ult., was not under the medical treatment of Dr. Okah Tubbee, although he had been solicited to attend, after some other medical gentlemen had given up hopes. The Chief stated that he could do nothing unless she was taken to his own dwelling and placed under the charge of Mrs. Tubbee. This was not complied with, and he only gave some medicines at the earnest request of her friends."[92] It is clear from this description of the medical business that Mrs. Tubbee was no mere assistant in treating patients. Indeed, Thomson's death is attributed to her unwillingness to submit to Laah Ceil's care, at which point Dr. Okah Tubbee simply supplied her some medicines, as he had done for patients from Missouri to Massachusetts. All along, Mrs. Tubbee had likely been playing a far more central role in administering medical advice and therapies than was apparent from the advertisements, drawing on a familiarity with both folk medicine and midwifery that was common among frontier women, as well as her particular interest in faith healing.[93] But her habit of boarding patients while they received care would soon bring further scrutiny.

In addition to the problem of malpractice accusations, the Tubbees faced expenses that had accrued from their legal troubles. For these reasons, and perhaps to offer a public defense against the many rumors circulating about them, they prepared another edition of the composite autobiography first published in 1848. *A Sketch of the Life of Okah Tubbee, (called) William Chubbee, Son of the Head Chief, Mosholeh Tubbee, of the Choctaw Nation of Indians, by Laah Ceil Manatoi Elaah Tubbee, His Wife*, was published in 1852 by Henry Stephens of Toronto and attributed to Laah Ceil's authorship. The new edition contained updated references to Tubbee's musical performances since 1848, including the insertion of testimonials from celebrities Anna Bishop and Nicholas-Charles Bochsa, a handbill from an 1851 performance in western New York, and most significantly, a new section explaining Okah Tubbee's education and talents in medicine.

The addition of material regarding Okah Tubbee's medical training under the tutelage of a white doctor, at whose office he learned "to read physiognomy," and testimonials from satisfied customers were designed to affirm his skills as a physician.[94] The following section of the autobiography reveals Tubbee's "calling" to heal, while explaining that although he studied under a conventional doctor, his lack of education effectively relegated him to the practice of Indian medicine:

> My heart longed to be of service . . . to one and all, I immediately
> determined to become a Physician, should an opportunity ever offer.
> At length I mentioned my wishes to my benefactor. He set before me
> the care and toil attendant on the profession, the envy and malice
> often returned where gratitude alone was due, and kindly hinted
> that I could not read, and consequently could not prepare for the
> task unless I could receive a liberal education. This served to dampen
> my newly created hopes, for I had already began to take pride in
> self-acquired abilities. At length he told me that the Indian Doctors
> were equally as successful as himself, that I could learn of them . . .

their manner of using roots and herbs, and probably benefit our race by the knowledge.[95]

The reference to "envy and malice" paid to physicians when "gratitude alone was due" suggests both the specific aspersions cast at Doctor Tubbee, but also the increasing backlash against so-called quack doctors, especially purveyors of Indian medicine.[96] They hoped the new edition of the autobiography would help protect them against such attacks.

In addition to including new background material designed to explain how a virtuosic flutist had also learned the physician's trade, the 1852 version included several testimonials from male and female patients in Missouri, Indiana, Massachusetts, New York, and Canada West, and a copy of licenses to practice medicine in Missouri, none of which made reference to Laah Ceil's apparently central role in their medical business. The Canadian testimonials included three from individuals living on Agnes Street, the same Toronto neighborhood in which unfortunate patient Matilda Thomson had died after refusing to board with the Tubbees during her treatment. Another Toronto endorsement referred to a gift of a "Silver Cup and Waiter," that an unidentified "Committee" had determined to give to the Indian Doctor in gratitude for having cured them of consumption and dyspepsia.[97]

Even with the new edition of the autobiography and its vigorous campaign on behalf of Okah Tubbee's medical credentials, as well as continuous advertising in city newspapers, problems continued. In August 1853, Okah Tubbee was arrested for assaulting a local man named G. L. Allen.[98] The details of the incident are obscure; it was apparently Tubbee's first offense in the city (though not his first arrest for assault—recall the brutal brick attack on a Natchez teen), and he was only required to pay a fine.[99] But the incident is suggestive of increasing disharmony in their lives. Perhaps as a result of this troubling episode and their need for more income, Okah Tubbee embarked on a "medical tour" during the winter of 1853. From Toronto, he traveled through other parts of Canada West, treating patients and interestingly, visiting First Nations settlements.

The following spring, a damning letter appeared in the Toronto *Globe* and shed light on the peripatetic Indian physician's activities during his tour. On April 10, 1854, a correspondent alerted the public to Tubbee's alleged misdeeds when he stopped in the southern Ontario town of Durham. Though locals later claimed they already suspected him of imposture, they nevertheless requested that Tubbee treat a local young man suffering a debilitating paralysis of the limbs. The patient's friends were induced to pay Tubbee ten dollars cash in advance for vital medicine that he then promised to have sent promptly from Hamilton or Guelph. Tubbee allegedly left with the money, stating that any advice he might offer on the case was "gratuitous," but he never delivered the medicine, a scheme reminiscent of the Waddell affair in Missouri. When the young man died, the townspeople of Durham swore that they would give Doctor Tubbee "a sound and wholesome thrashing."[100]

The letter carried weight. Not only was it believable, but it was written by Alexander B. McNab, a widely known local official in Grey County.[101] Two weeks later, Tubbee responded to his accusers. Ever eager to use his Indianness to explain and defend himself, he insisted that he had not merely been on a medical tour during the previous year. Instead, he claimed he had been solicited by the "Sugeen [Saugeen] and Chippawa [Ojibwe] Indians" to visit them at Colpoy's Bay and attend their council. During his journey to or from the Bruce Peninsula, he stopped at Durham, where, Tubbee claimed, McNab insisted on three separate occasions that he accept money to treat the ailing patient. Only under this extreme pressure did he accept the money, with the intent of forwarding it to Toronto or another locale for medicine. But he was unfortunately unable to attend to the matter because he became ill himself. After a convalescence of four weeks, Tubbee returned to his business in Toronto only to find that he was being accused of fraud. It is unclear from his rebuttal whether or not he ever sent the money as he claimed or made any further attempt to acquire the necessary medicine.[102]

Although it is difficult to believe Okah Tubbee's claims about the money and the missing medicine, he had indeed been invited to sojourn in Ojibwe villages at Saugeen and Colpoy's Bay. And according to the local Indian agent, he had also been denominated "Grand Council Chief" at Saugeen and among the Mohawks at Kahnawake. Although McNab had not mentioned it in his account of Tubbee's alleged misdeeds in Grey County, the doctor was also reported to have been traveling in the company of a white woman who, officials had been informed, was not his wife, though it is unclear if this was Laah Ceil absent her Indian garb or someone else. The local Indian agent worried that the itinerant physician was a bad influence on the First Nations people in the area, stating that "his object is to get all the money he can from them in one way and another and I am sorry to say that even the best informed among them is not proof against his wiles and pretensions." In addition to securing honorific titles among these groups, Tubbee was also selling them "charms" to protect them from cholera and other diseases that were at work in their communities. One wonders what combination of expert performance and intense desperation convinced the Native councils to endorse his claims and pay for his cures. In any case, evidence of his "cunning rapacity" among the Ojibwe settlements never made much impact in Toronto, where the death of an innocent white victim was more newsworthy than the follies of "foolish" Native people who might fall prey to his schemes.[103]

After his return to Toronto, Okah Tubbee resumed his residence on Victoria Street, and despite his recent illness, professional setbacks, and possible marital infidelity, he and Laah Ceil continued on as Indian doctors. According to the city tax assessment records for 1854, the Tubbees' personal property was worth about six pounds, not a large sum, by any means, but fair enough for people whose income had been so erratic.[104] The Indian medicine business was a lot like show business—appearance and reputation were everything. In such a profession, it was essential that they not let allegations of fraud go unchallenged, nor could they appear to take them too seriously, lest they give critics too much power and show themselves to be insecure. Even though they had already published a defense against the Durham accusations in local papers during April, the Tubbees decided to take the additional step of producing a handbill advertising their medical practice and offering a witty rejoinder to the allegations leveled at them. (See Fig. 7.)

Emboldened by his apparently successful visit to the Native councils at Colpoy's Bay and Saugeen, Okah Tubbee now referred to himself with the additional moniker "Council Chief Wah Bah Goosh, Head Council Chief. Caul Pois Bay Indians." The handbill was both advertisement and pointed defense, all delivered in lilting verse. It may have been composed by Laah Ceil, whose verse on long-distance love had graced the pages of the 1852 edition of the autobiography and whose own experiences of persecution may have partly inspired the barbed stanzas. And yet, some of the witticisms bear a striking resemblance to other examples of Okah Tubbee's distinctive sense of humor. In any case, its overall purpose, like that of the autobiography, was propagandistic. Shoring up Tubbee's claims to Indian ancestry was crucial and his essential Indianness was implied as the source of his medical knowledge. One verse proclaimed, "If you're sick I'll endeavor to cure you. / With the roots and the plants of the earth / 'Tis Dame Nature's own plan I assure you. / And to her we must all trace

FIGURE 7
Advertisement for the Tubbees' medical practice. Following public accusations of fraud, the Tubbees circulated this handbill, defending themselves and advertising "Cheap Medicine" from "Nature and God in the skies." Notice the use of both "Chief Okah Tubbee" and "Council Chief Wah Bah Goosh." Chief Okah Tubbee, No. 15 Victoria Street, Toronto, ca. 1856. (Courtesy Toronto Public Library)

our birth," suggesting not only a botanic approach to medicine that had broad appeal in the United States and Canada, but also subtly implying the equality of all humans as children of mother nature.

The verses also made reference to the recent McNab controversy, stating, "Of late I've been shamefully (M') *Nab'd* at / And cruelly held up to view / I'm now like a target to shoot at / Shoot on till your honors get through." When critics and false friends found their "poisonous arrows" spent, Tubbee invited all to visit him at Victoria Street: "You will find me quite snug in my clover, / *Friends or foes* I'll be happy to meet."[105] From his early efforts as a mimic, to his irreverent jokes before Mormon leaders, to his humorous stage asides on stage, Tubbee had learned the power of laughter to both endear audiences and deflect criticism.

Despite this notable effort to rescue Okah Tubbee's reputation and resuscitate their Indian medical business, no advertisements for the Tubbees' practice appeared in the Toronto newspapers during the remainder of 1854 and 1855. This may suggest that they were unable to pay for the ads, or it might indicate that they were sufficiently well-established and did not need to trouble with further advertising. Tax assessment data from 1855 imply that their fortunes had not changed materially. They still lived at No. 15 Victoria Street, and their personal property was valued at only one pound less than it had been in 1854. But problems persisted.

In August 1855, "Lucy Okah Tubbee" was arrested for keeping a "disorderly house," often a euphemism for operating a brothel.[106] In her defense, she argued that she was no madam, but a popular Indian physician and that a neighbor's complaint of people going in and out of her establishment at all hours was simply evidence of her successful business. She further explained that she often required patients to board with her during their treatments, perhaps unwittingly giving the appearance of multiple unrelated adults inhabiting the home on Victoria Street.[107] Arrests for keeping a disorderly house were relatively rare in Toronto during the 1850s ("drunk and disorderly" or just "drunk" were by far the most common offenses) and seem to have emerged from situations much like Laah Ceil's, in which a neighbor, or perhaps a competitor, reported the accused to authorities as a nuisance.[108]

The fact that no mention was made of her husband upon her arrest suggests that they were no longer living together. With his high profile, such an episode would surely have garnered the attention of the press. As interesting is the company she apparently kept. According to papers and crime reports, several other people were arrested at her home when

Mrs. Tubbee was taken into custody, including four "disorderly-looking females" and an Irish brawler named Bernard Kearney, who was wanted for a stabbing at a local tavern. There was no word of Okah Tubbee.[109]

By 1856, it seems clear that the Tubbees had split up. Near the start of the year, Chief "wah bah Goosh" appeared before a Masonic meeting in Boston in full Indian costume and addressed the congregation in English and German, suggesting that the performer formerly known as Okah Tubbee was using his new moniker and returned to his itinerant ways.[110] No mention was made of his wife.

Meanwhile, the Toronto city business directory for the year 1856 listed No. 15 Victoria Street as the residence of "Tubbee, Okah Leeheeil, Indian doctor," apparently a reference to Laah Ceil, now operating the medical practice on her own.[111] The former Mormon visionary and Indian performer, now using the aliases Lucy Okah Tubbee and Adelaide Okah Tubbee, seemed to be falling on hard times. In January 1856, she was arrested again, this time for "receiving stolen goods." She had been found in possession of black silk cloth pilfered from a local department store by a notorious gang of thieves that included the sister of Bernard Kearney, a black man known as Charles Shields, and an Irishman named Dillon who also used the alias "Shanghai." This motley group of criminals had first conspired to rob farmers in the countryside by stunning them with chloroform stolen from an apothecary shop, then later collaborated to break into clothing stores and plunder expensive fabrics.[112] The charges against Lucy/Adelaide Okah Tubbee appear to have been dropped, but her association with this gang suggests a hard fall. Again the papers were silent on her husband's whereabouts.

Later in the year, a series of notices inserted in a western New York newspaper during November 1856 indicate that the couple had ended their ten-year relationship. The ad stated, "I, WAH BAH GOOSH, notify all person or persons, or lending or trusting money or moneys, or harboring her in any shape whatever on my account, as I shall pay no debts of her contracting, by Saah Ciel Tubbee, by either of the said names." The following day, another notice indicated that the woman's name was "Sarah Tubbee," and this version ran for several more days.[113] While it is possible that these somewhat garbled announcements referred to Sarah Marlett, using some version of her husband's name (there is no evidence the marriage was annulled or otherwise rendered void), but it is likely that Wah Bah Goosh (aka Okah Tubbee) meant to distance himself from his former wife and partner, Laah Ceil. Although separated, by 1857, neither of them remained in Toronto.[114]

· · ·

I have found no record of Okah Tubbee (or Wah Bah Goosh) after late 1856. While he had some connection with First Nations groups in Ontario, it is difficult to imagine him settling among them, given the fact that local and provincial Indian Affairs officials vigorously opposed his effort to secure a grant of land from the tribes. Still, it is possible that he found a home amid the jumble of removed Indians and refugees, scattered in communities across Ontario. Or he could have settled among the thousands of free blacks and fugitive slaves who were busily establishing new towns and settlements along the U.S.-Canadian border, although his lifelong effort to distance himself from the stigma of African ancestry makes this unlikely as well. Maybe he headed west to seek his fortune and a new identity like so many other men of his day. Or maybe he died. It is perhaps fitting that the man born Warner McCary, a master of disguise who devised nearly a dozen aliases as he traveled the length of the continent, simply disappeared.

The woman born Lucy Stanton, however, is easier to track. By 1861, she was again working as a medicine woman or "Indian doctress," as she now preferred to be known, and operating a successful business in Buffalo, New York. Despite the hardships she'd endured, her Indianness remained intact, and she was once more making it pay.[115]

CHAPTER SIX

Practicing Indian Medicine

. . . .

Laah Ceil's Eventful Final Years

By the time Laah Ceil settled in Buffalo, New York, in 1861, the nation had already begun its bloody unraveling. The U.S. Civil War erupted quickly, but the issues that spawned it were not new. From the signing of the Constitution through the crises of Indian removal, the acquisition of massive western territories, and debates about slavery and emancipation, states' rights had been an important principle or a constant problem, depending on one's perspective, and had required a wide variety of "compromises" between slave and free states. Rapid national expansion brought these issues into further relief and highlighted sectional differences. When the Union-controlled Congress approved the Homestead Act and the Pacific Railroad Bill in 1862, it addressed both the promise and the problems of the West. Both pieces of legislation cut into the heart of American Indian lands in the interior of the continent, increasing the number of westward migrants, accelerating the destruction of buffalo herds, and hastening the effort to confine western Indians to reservations. By 1870, Laah Ceil would be among those migrants starting over in the West. But first, she made her way south from Toronto to Buffalo.

Situated at the western end of the Erie Canal, Buffalo was the terminus where travelers heading west left the canal for carriage, horse, boat, or rail. It was a commercial hub that helped power the industrial transformation of the West during the second half of the nineteenth century. During the war, the city's barons of industry made money hand over fist supplying the Union army and the unending tide of migrants, while the city's less fortunate sons were sent to fight in the South. The "Queen City of the Lakes," once known as a Seneca Indian settlement, jostled with sailors, peddlers, reformers, and seducers; some stayed, some passed through.

The canal district in particular catered to every need of the roiling masses with barrooms, barber shops, and brothels.[1]

The woman born Lucy Stanton settled in Buffalo under the name Madame Laahceil. Operating as an "Indian doctress," she occupied a large brick home near the Main and Hamburg canal, where she opened a medical business.[2] The facility employed a staff of servants and assistants who helped her attend to multiple patients who stayed in the home during their course of treatment. At least three people worked at the establishment full-time: a housekeeper named Bridget Kelly, a physician's assistant named Robert Harrod, and a "negro servant" named John Craig. Madame Laahceil also occasionally hired other temporary staff to help cook, clean, and do laundry. She provided a variety of medical services at her establishment, made regular trips to the druggist, prepared herbs and medicines, and instructed her employees how to provide for patients' needs. She had three, four, sometimes five patients staying with her—all women.[3] She was evidently successful and sufficiently well established that she had little reason to bother with advertisements.[4]

· · ·

Over the preceding fifteen years, Madame Laahceil had honed and refined her Native persona, adding and subtracting elements, often in response to the changing desires and expectations of those around her. She had accompanied husband Okah Tubbee on travels across the United States and into Canada, adjusting her role in each locale—wife of a Lamanite prophet, educated Indian advocating temperance reform, singer of Indian songs, Native missionary seeking contributions to help Christianize her people, partner in her husband's Indian medicine business. As their stage shows declined, the couple had increasingly come to rely on their medical practice for income. The Tubbees' life in Toronto had been filled with difficulties: harassment, arrest, and financial hardship. But perhaps more painful was her long separation from her children. Her daughters, Semira and Anne, had migrated to Utah in 1852 with their grandparents, and her eldest child Solon had apparently been living on his own since adolescence. When she returned to the United States from Canada at the beginning of the 1860s, Okah Tubbee was also gone— disappeared or dead. Curiously, their son Mosholeh was missing too. The young "brave" had previously appeared on stage with his parents but subsequent records say nothing of the boy. At the time Madame Laahceil,

Indian doctress, settled in Buffalo, Mosholeh would have been about eleven years old.

When she established herself in western New York then, Laahceil was alone. She could have easily dispensed with her Indian guise since she no longer needed to mask her relationship with a man of African descent or protect their child from scrutiny. Instead, she maintained her Indianness. Aside from whatever sense of personal fulfillment she may have gained from her Indian persona, she had learned in Toronto that the Indian doctoring business, however precarious, could provide her a way to earn a living. It allowed her to carve out a niche in a profession increasingly hostile to women practitioners and skeptical of those lacking credentials, ultimately permitting her to briefly attain a certain level of autonomy and financial success. And it provided an outlet for the practice of healing as an expression of Christian (if not Mormon) faithfulness.

In denominating herself an Indian doctress, Madame Laahceil was capitalizing on the ongoing popularity of all manner of "Indian" medicines, cures, and therapies across the United States and Canada. At the very same time that she was building her business in Buffalo, the popular Ojibwe entertainer Maungwudaus was embarking on his own highly successful medical tour through western New York. Broadsides advertising his services echoed the language found in the Tubbees' earlier advertisements: "Standing in Nature's vast laboratory, amid the ever changing scenery which the Great Spirit has created, I prepare the roots and herbs which render our mode of doctoring the sick a truly 'healing art.' My diploma is the knowledge and experience of my ancestors, handed down through a long line of 'Medicine Men.'" Likewise, a wide variety of Native and non-Native practitioners hawked their wares in newspaper pages, mail-order catalogs, and hotel lobbies, promising cures from the "laboratory of the Great Spirit."[5]

One reason Indian doctors, or "root and herb" practitioners, had met with steady success was because they offered an alternative to poorly trained and often incompetent licensed physicians.[6] The Thomsonian movement, whose motto was "every man his own physician," advocated the self-directed use of herbal remedies described in widely available home health manuals. Many patients believed that botanic medicines were a safer alternative to more invasive therapies and dubious treatments, such as bloodletting and calomel dosing. Samuel Thomson, the New Hampshire farmer who turned the "root-and-herb tradition into a full-blown medical sect," had been educated in these methods by a rural female herbalist. Thomsonianism, in turn, was extremely popular among antebellum women who sought to retain control of their bodies and their health and to avoid not only the prying eyes and hands of male doctors but also their frequently deadly medical treatments. The association between botanic medicines and esoteric indigenous knowledge was ubiquitous in the mid-nineteenth century, and both Native and non-Native practitioners capitalized on the popular image of Indians as skilled healers.[7]

Okah Tubbee's medical business, in which Laah Ceil had been his partner, if not his teacher, had relied on these same appeals. For instance, the many newspaper advertisements for their practice consistently emphasized the natural, herbal remedies that comprised their "Genuine Indian Medicine!"[8] Their poetic Toronto broadside had declared that "red men" offered superior remedies because they "trust to Nature and God in the skies."[9] But as was apparent during their time in Canada in the 1850s, the Tubbees' approach was more hands-on than the simple dispensing of medicine or advice. Although their advertisements had frequently referred to their practice as one of "Eclecticism," meaning that they relied primarily on botanic compounds often given in enormous doses, they may have also incorporated various other treatments, such as steam therapies and modifications to patients' "air, exercise, clothing, diet, and water."[10] That they frequently required patients to board with them during their treatment suggests that theirs was a varied practice.

Interestingly, Laah Ceil may have first learned about the benefits of botanic medicine and home remedies from both her female relatives and from Mormon faith healers years before. Doctor Willard Richards, a member of the Quorum of Twelve Apostles who had once examined Okah Tubbee's body in search of a lost rib, was trained as a Thomsonian practitioner, as were a number of other early Mormons.[11] They combined knowledge of herbal medicines with practices of healing through the laying on of hands.[12] Many such therapies are widely documented in Mormon diaries and letters and, at least during the antebellum period, were not limited to men only, but included the individual and community engagement of Mormon women. Joseph Smith's mother was recalled to have been a healer in Palmyra, New York, and the Mormon women in Kirtland were widely acknowledged to have engaged in ritual healing and folk cures. The formation of the Female Relief Society in Nauvoo inaugurated an expansion of women's participation in healing practices, and these roles continued prominently through the Winter Quarters years, when the Tubbees themselves had been simultaneously engaged in offering religious and medical services.[13]

Thus, when she resurfaced in Buffalo as an Indian doctress, "Mrs. Laahceil" was not so much reinventing herself as she was returning to her roots—both those she had shared with Okah Tubbee and those that long predated him. She could access power, influence, and status through healing, a vocation that had already been her primary means of income for nearly a decade. When she pronounced herself an "Indian doctress," however, she was also openly associating her business with a specific set of services that were increasingly criminalized in the United States.

In the nineteenth century, an "Indian doctress" was typically a fortune teller or a botanic physician (and sometimes both), but was also frequently understood to specialize in "cases of a delicate nature," or unwanted pregnancies.[14] Well before the 1860s, Indian doctors, female herbalists, and home health manuals had provided women in the United States and Canada with information on indigenous plant-based abortifacients, such as black cohosh or seneca root, as well as remedies for difficult childbirth, like blue cohosh.[15] Beyond the natural and native origins of these substances, Indian women were frequently linked with abortion in American ethnobotany and popular culture. The common nickname for black cohosh was "squawroot," and it was generally accepted that American Indian women openly practiced a variety of methods to prevent or terminate pregnancies. Among non-Native American women, the popularity of botanic means of abortion stemmed in part from women's desire to avoid dangerous instrumental operations that were more often performed by male practitioners who were increasingly taking the place of midwives, particularly in the urban Northeast.[16] Patients praised indigenous plant-based treatments for their effectiveness, while reformers denigrated them as evidence of Native women's moral inferiority.[17] Within this context, Indian doctresses came to occupy a relatively specialized and often lucrative but frequently controversial niche.[18]

Although abortion (and contraception) had long been practiced among women in the United States, the mid-nineteenth century was an era of increasing regulations regarding women's reproduction. In most states, terminating a pregnancy was not illegal if it took place prior to "quickening," the first movement of the fetus. But starting in the 1840s, states including New York were pressured by moral crusaders and professional guilds to begin enacting harsher and more restrictive abortion laws.[19]

Antiabortion campaigns swept through the Northeast in the 1850s and had a twofold purpose: to reduce women's reproductive control (and thereby limit their sexual freedom) and to restrict women and other "irregular" practitioners from the medical profession.[20] Madame Laahceil's position as an Indian doctress thus made her especially vulnerable to new laws and social reforms, not only because she was delivering alternative medicine but also because her success threatened her professional male competitors and because her contemporaries associated abortion with illicit sex.

It was only a matter of time before Madame Laahceil's medical practice in Buffalo raised concerns. In February 1861, she was arrested on suspicion of manslaughter in the death of one of her patients. Harriet Wagner, a free black woman whose husband had run off to California, had allegedly appealed to Madame Laahceil for an abortion and then died from complications. Although it is not clear from the reports whether the operation involved instrumental or merely botanic means, a postmortem examination confirmed that an abortion had been attempted and that it ultimately led to the patient's death. When Wagner's eighteen-year-old daughter was interrogated, she claimed that "Madame Laacheil Manitou Elah" had been the physician. The charges were ultimately dropped, but not before the local press could inform readers that the alleged abortionist was the former wife of "a 'Big Injum [sic] chief,' who will be recollected, by many of our citizens, as having given a musical entertainment, some dozen or more years ago, at Concert Hall, under the name of Oakee Tubbee."[21]

Interestingly, the paper asserted that both Okah Tubbee and his former wife were "impostors, as he, so far from being a red son of the forest, was a full-blooded black man; and she, instead of the 'doctress' for which she has been hailing, is one who has been engaged in a line of practice forbidden by the law," meaning, of course, abortion. It seems possible from Laah Ceil's arrests in Toronto that she was probably already catering to women seeking such services, even though she did not use the appellation "Indian doctress" at that time. But while this newspaper referenced the now-familiar narrative of her husband's racial masquerade, her Indian identity remained unquestioned and uninspected. Instead, her crime was in posing as a legitimate physician.[22] In fact, while an editorial in the *Buffalo Medical and Surgical Journal and Reporter* made specific mention of Madame Laahceil's case, calling for better regulation of death certificates to prevent cover-ups, as well as a broad rejection of quacks and impostors who prey on the "stupid and uninformed," it contained no suggestion that she was not an Indian.[23]

If Madame Laahceil was concerned about her business or reputation following the Wagner inquiry, however, she did not let on. Once cleared of criminal charges, she expanded her practice and drew in new clients. When she was arrested again in the summer of 1862, she hardly needed an introduction to western New Yorkers, and many newspapers referred to her as simply "the notorious Indian doctress." There was considerable demand for her services, and her relative success makes it clear that fears of malpractice did not dissuade patients from seeking her out. Many of the women who came to her probably did so in part to avoid the embarrassment of consulting male practitioners on any ailment. But those seeking treatment for unwanted pregnancies may have predominated. On finding information about abortion and contraception, one essayist wryly observed, "Notwithstanding the pretended squeamishness of the American people on this subject, no class of books finds a readier sale, or is more eagerly sought after in private."[24] No doubt some of Madame Laahceil's patients came to her hoping to find someone with knowledge of methods and means for ending (and possibly preventing) pregnancy. But she also advised patients on a variety of other conditions and illnesses. Although the information surrounding her second New York arrest suggests that she was exclusively an "abortionist," the sensationalism of the case overshadows what was likely a more varied and often mundane medical business.

The *Buffalo Courier* was the first to report on "A Human Slaughter House" discovered on the corner of Washington and Carroll streets, across from the prominent Bonney House hotel. On Thursday, June 5, 1862, police learned that a hearse had suspiciously parked in front of the Indian doctress's residence. After the cart bore a body away, officers contacted the coroner, who in turn opened an investigation. The deceased was Naomi Hamilton, a married twenty-nine-year-old mother of three from the town of Alabama, New York. Her husband was away fighting for the Union army, and she was brought to the Indian doctress by an older Michigan man purporting to be her uncle, but "undoubtedly her paramour."[25] Convinced after the coroner's inquest that something was amiss, police returned to the home of Madame "Laahceil Manitou Elaah, generally known as Mrs. Laacheil" with a search warrant. Inside, they discovered two desperately ill young women, one of whom, Mary Louisa Byer, would die within the day. Initially, both Byer and Hamilton were determined to have died from complications arising from abortion, allegedly performed by the Indian doctress.

The police investigation into this scandal was breathlessly recounted in Buffalo newspapers, and the accounts emphasized the scale of Madame Laahceil's business ("a human slaughterhouse of the hugest proportions").[26] Indeed, the papers noted that during the few days police occupied her dwelling, "no less than twenty women, married and single, had appeared at the door and inquired for Madame Laahceil."[27] Clearly, neither attacks from professional medical men, a history of malpractice suits, nor accusations of manslaughter in 1861 had done much to stem the tide of clients who sought the services of the Indian doctress. On the contrary, Madame Laahceil was doing quite well for herself. Her relative success as a female physician in a city suddenly overrun with male doctors and the various guilds that represented their interests may help explain the scrutiny she faced. The movement to professionalize American medicine in this era boiled down to competition, a truth of which Madame Laahceil was all too aware.[28]

Starting in the 1850s, Indian doctors and other "irregular" practitioners were increasingly denounced by emergent professional organizations such as the American Medical Association (founded in 1847), but the fervor of their campaigns indicates how popular such alternative physicians and treatments were.[29] One writer declared in the *Boston Medical and Surgical Journal*, "So wide, varied and extensive is the range of quackery, that in considering its follies and impositions, one hardly knows where to begin or where to end." But the "various nostrum venders" were undeterred, finding eager customers despite the accusations leveled at them by reformers.[30] With Thomsonian self-help books, patented devices, and mail-order medicines, as well as traditional networks of midwifery and community support, women had preserved some control over their reproductive health through mid-century, particularly where licensed doctors were scarce. By increasingly criminalizing methods of reproductive control, such as abortion and contraception, states like New York began to shift the balance of power over women's bodies away from women themselves. And Buffalo was a key site in this search for "social purity" that motivated crusades led by "energetic, driven men," who, along with their various professional organizations and enthusiastic supporters, "assumed the role of custodians of the public good."[31] The presumed and often real connection between sex out of wedlock (whether consensual or coerced) and abortion amplified the concerns of the reform-minded and added fuel to their moralizing fire.

As professional physicians tried to differentiate themselves from "ir-regular" and amateur doctors in the 1850s and following decades, they denigrated "doctresses" alongside Indian herbalists, homeopathic thera-pists, and patent medicine hucksters. But doctresses—whether Indian or not—were not merely seen as medical impostors; they were regarded as "transgressive women" who operated outside the bounds of both professional standards and gender norms.[32] The persecution of Madame Restell, the nation's most notorious abortionist, whose wildly successful Fifth Avenue business had launched satellite offices in Philadelphia and Boston, is prob-ably the best-known of the nineteenth-century antiabortion crusades. Although Restell, a midwife from England, did not proclaim indigenous ancestry or knowledge, her successes were nevertheless depicted by oppo-nents as a sign of moral decrepitude, seduction, and vice. Some other female physicians even referred to Restell and her ilk as engaged in the "'gross perversion and destruction' of womanhood."[33]

Although antiabortionists targeted both male and female practition-ers, their campaigns were explicitly "antifeminist" because they proscribed narrower roles and choices for women, partly in reaction to industrializa-tion and urbanization that increasingly pulled women into workplaces and the cities.[34] Of course, this was not the first time that Laahceil had found herself at the margins of acceptable women's behavior.

When charged with manslaughter in the case of Mary Byer and Naomi Hamilton, Madame Laahceil could thus hardly have expected an impar-tial verdict. Just a few years before, another Indian doctress had been charged with murder following a botched abortion in a similarly high-profile episode. In both situations, papers drew clear connections between abortion, seduction, and the battle for control of women's bodies. Laah Ceil's case was particularly remarkable for the detail and relish with which the public "feast[ed] upon the loathsome details," but both stories were made even more sensational by the professed race of the doctresses.[35] Both women were depicted as dusky, unwomanly villainesses who viciously deprived other women of their lives through the most invasive and pene-trating means, as if they were themselves the seducers.

From the beginning, new revelations about the Indian "abortoreum" in their midst sent Buffalonians into hysterics. In addition to Naomi Ham-ilton, whose hearse had first attracted attention to Madame Laahceil's house, and Mary Byer, who died shortly after police entered the premises, twenty-year-old Jenny Johnson had also been discovered convalescing with the Indian doctress. When she was found at Madame Laahceil's house, she was described as "skeletonic," but she had apparently not received an abortion. She had worked as a cook in a Buffalo saloon and like Hamilton, she was from out of town. Local papers said very little on her condition, however.[36]

By contrast, the tragic story of twenty-three-year-old Mary Byer occupied considerable space in the columns of local newspapers, perhaps because she was the most "respectably connected" of the women discovered at Madame Laahceil's house. Byer, like Hamilton, was identified as a victim of "the seducer's art."[37] She had lived most of her life in the city and was the sister of a prominent tugboat captain. She boarded with a respectable family and was known as an industrious dressmaker. Byer was conveyed to the Indian doctress by William Barr, in whose middle-class household her sister boarded and who had reportedly taken an unusual interest in young Mary recently.[38]

As Byer's case suggests, Laahceil's business probably touched the households of the city's elite far more than they wanted to admit. Wives, daughters, cooks, and servants were among the women who turned up seeking the help of the Indian doctress, sometimes escorted there in secret by wayward sons or philandering patriarchs of the state's leading families. Indeed, the clients of such "abortionists" were typically white, married, Protestant, middle- or upper-class women.[39] Thus, while criticism of both women doctors and Indian medicine converged in the case of Madame Laahceil, the investigation also threatened to expose the open secret of illicit sex and the unwanted pregnancies it produced. One newspaper predicted that details revealed in the unfolding inquiry would shake the "dry bones . . . in various circles in this city."[40] Another paper surmised, "Startling disclosures are expected to grow out of this arrest which may involve those holding respectable positions in society."[41]

It is hard to overstate the sensational quality of the reports that spread word of the unfolding scandal. Such cases, like the notorious murder mystery surrounding New York prostitute Helen Jewett, fed the reading public's appetite for stories of sex and death.[42] The discovery of a "slaughter house" run by an "Indian wretch" pretending to be a doctor, whose dangerous and illicit operations help to hide the sexual misdeeds of the city's denizens, provided nearly unlimited fuel for both yellow journalists and officious reformers. In addition to proposing a more rigorous check on death certificates, the papers variously blamed the coroner, the police chief, the patients, and the seducers, all while lamenting the sad moral state of a society in which a vile murderess could convince desperate young women to put their lives in her hands.[43]

Like other popular tales of imposture that captivated readers, the public was titillated by stories that exposed poseurs of one sort or another. Audiences mitigated their anxieties about identity and imposture by producing and reproducing narratives of revealing, unmasking, or exposing pretenders. The more integrated the impostor was within the community, the more eagerly the story was consumed. So the papers printed not only the outlines of the investigation, indictment, and trial, but also aired Madame Laahceil's dirty laundry—literally. Among other revelations, several papers included salacious details about the profusion of bloody linens and undergarments "scattered promiscuously," linking the alleged filth of the house with both its "brutal transactions" and the suggestion of illicit sex.[44]

The "vile den" was described in vivid detail, painted as a bordello of blood, where a fiendish "she devil" preyed upon vulnerable young women.[45] In addition to describing the various apartments in which her patients boarded, all of which were deemed insalubrious for one reason or another, one paper's reporter recounted his observations when he accompanied the police into Madame Laahceil's chambers:

> On the first floor, entering from Washington street, was the office
> and bed-room of the doctress herself. The office, which comprised
> the entire front apartment, was occupied by a table, chairs, stand
> and cases, all littered, piled and filled with every variety of Indian
> medicines—barks, roots, herbs and decoctions—and with instruments
> of a trade so enormously wicked that we scarcely care to name it.
> Books, papers, letters, &c., all filled with fearful evidence, were
> scattered on the table, and in the back room were found, besides
> a further lot of medicines and instruments, trunks, boxes, &c.,
> containing either papers, little clothes, trinkets, and even portraits—
> to redeem which, what would their original owners not give in
> promises and gold? The couch of Madame, upon which her susian
> form had rested through the night, stood "not half made up" in the
> furthest corner, and a stand was near laden with bottles and cups,
> full of many colored fluids.[46]

The presence of "Indian medicines," as well as medical books and instruments, confirms that Madame Laahceil was engaged in a variety of therapies and operations and was probably performing instrumental abortions, as well as providing herbal or chemical abortifacients. The writer's description of "papers, little clothes, trinkets, and even portraits" implied that she robbed her pitiful patients of their cherished belongings, but it is impossible to know whether such was the case. Perhaps instead these were the cherished possessions of the Madame herself, accumulated over years of travel with and without her family.

This same account also provided a description of Madame Laahceil's appearance, saying that she was in her late forties, with dark, but graying, hair and "a very dark expressive eye." The reporter guessed that she weighed about 200 pounds and appeared to be of foreign extraction, though he noted that she claimed to be an American Indian.[47] Other papers simply stated that she "pretends to be an Indian doctress," more suspicious of her professional abilities than her ethnicity.[48] These stories come closer than any before to scrutinizing Madame Laahceil's claims to Indianness. But in each case, the authenticity of her Native persona was subordinated to the villainy of her occupation. Although Laahceil still asserted her Indian identity, in the eyes of observers, it may have been the least important thing about her.

A decline in the importance and cachet of Laahceil's Indianness was partly the result of a broader shift in representations of Native people within American popular culture. Whereas she had once been able to convince discriminating audiences that she was a delightful Mohawk princess, if anything, she was now regarded as Indian squaw—fat, venal, ignorant—an image that had first been sketched during the bigamy case a decade before.[49] During her youth, Indian impersonation had been important in the expression of her religious beliefs; in her young adulthood, Native-themed performances still inspired the sympathy and excited the imagination of theatregoers. But by the end of the 1850s, much of the value of professional Indianness had depreciated. Performances by Native people still continued, to be sure, and American writers still returned to the well of Indian themes in their literary expressions, but broadly speaking, the capacious Indianness of earlier decades had diminished.

The narrowing of the Indian aura was attributable in large part to the consequences of continued national expansion. At the close of the Mexican War, the United States annexed vast territories filled with thousands of Native and mixed-ancestry people. An ascendant racial Anglo-Saxonism held that these people would pollute the nation, so it was only right that they be exterminated or confined. Lingering faith in the possibility of improving and uplifting Native peoples and the vague sentimentalism of the removal era gave way to ethnic cleansing in places like California and Texas. Whereas Indianness once provided a woman like Laahceil some measure of social mobility, by the start of the Civil War, the new order hinged on racial purity. The turn away from interest in Indian welfare and well-being is evident in the legislation passed by northern representatives after their southern peers departed the Congress, particularly the massive railroad subsidies that were a "dagger in the heartlands" of Indian country. The first groups victimized in the new push for the West were those like the Delawares who had already been removed more times than most could remember.[50] Being an Indian might continue to be profitable in some professions—as it still was in some ways for Madame Laahceil—but whatever emancipatory potential it had once offered was largely eroded by the time she found herself facing policemen at her front door in Buffalo in 1862.

Five people were arrested in the June raid on the Indian doctress's house: servants John Craig and Bridget Kelly, assistant Robert Harrod, suspected seducer William Barr, and Madame Laahceil herself.[51] Craig and Kelly were questioned and then released when it was determined that they were "not seriously identified with the criminal workings of the institution," being primarily involved in handling meals, laundry, and general maintenance.[52] Madame Laahceil's assistant, Robert Harrod, had been found crouching behind a shed door during the police raid. Suspected of intimate involvement in the treatment of patients, he was arrested. Although Harrod was initially implicated as an accomplice in the deaths of Mary Byer and Naomi Hamilton, at least one witness later testified that he never actually treated the women, but instead labeled medicines at Madame Laahceil's instruction and sometimes served food to patients.[53] He apparently feared the worst, however. While police were gathering more evidence, Harrod managed to escape custody and flee the city.[54]

After first having been suspected as an accessory for his role in delivering Mary Byer to the "abortoreum," William Barr was released on bond until trial. Barr claimed that he was not Byer's seducer, but merely a family friend because her sister boarded with the Barr family. His relative position within the community may explain his acquittal. He worked for the Central R. R. Company, overseeing the cattle yards and stock trains, and appears to have been generally respected. Byer's sister testified that Barr had been intimate with Mary Byer, although she had tried to repel his advances. Mary herself had confirmed these suspicions in her deathbed conversation with the chief of police, telling him that Barr had brought her to Madame Laahceil, but that she did not think he was a bad man. For his part, Barr implicated himself in a desperate last-minute attempt to visit Mary Byer before her death. When confronted by police and prevented from entering the room, he told the chief, "Some of these days I will tell you all about this." Barr's brother testified that William was not the father of the child, but that Mary Byer had merely come to him seeking help when she discovered her pregnancy. Barr said he had tried to prevent her from going to Madame Laahceil's, but had visited her there out of concern when he failed to change her mind. Perhaps reflecting his "respectable connections," Barr was ultimately acquitted, to the great relief of his friends in the city.[55]

The Indian doctress, however, was confined to the Erie County jail immediately upon her arrest on June 5, and she remained there through her trial in October.[56] Initially, she was accused of killing both Mary Byer and Naomi Hamilton. A man named Aaron Burnett was also charged in Hamilton's death when it was discovered that he had brought her to Madame Laahceil's and was the "uncle" mentioned in earlier testimony. The papers reported that he was a loquacious fellow of about sixty years old, married, with grown children, and according to one account, betrayed "no embarrassment whatever" for his crimes.[57] But ultimately, the charges in the case of Ms. Hamilton were dropped, whereas the Byer case continued.

Upon her arrest, Madame Laahceil was initially described as "sullen" and "uncommunicative," but once sequestered in the jailhouse, she began to open up. She admitted that she had been married to Okah Tubbee, but said she did not know his whereabouts and supposed he might have gone to England, a reference to his chimerical 1851 scheme of touring Britain with agent Frank Gardner. She indicated that her parents were still living, as was her son, who she said was probably fighting in "the rebel army," an apparent reference to her twenty-eight-year-old son, Solon. He was living in Memphis and working as a newspaper man at the time, though whether she had direct communication with him remains unclear.[58] She apparently made no mention of her two daughters, Ann (age 26) and Semira (24), or her youngest child, Mosholeh (13).

Despite her generally downcast demeanor, she displayed a certain indignation at her arrest, as she had during the Harriet Wagner episode a year earlier, and declared that she was "the victim of jealousy on the part of the medical faculty, who were desirous of driving her from the city." She and her husband had experienced such scrutiny many times before, and she was at least partially right that her apparent success in the business had brought the unwanted attention.[59] Indeed, in the years just before and after her trial, arrests for abortion in Buffalo were exceedingly rare, implying that competition rather than morality was at the heart of her persecution.[60]

On October 8, 1862, Madame Laahceil was found guilty of manslaughter in the second degree in the death of Mary Byer. It took the jury mere minutes to reach a verdict; the judge sentenced her to seven years' hard labor at the New York state women's prison, to begin immediately. But Laah Ceil was determined to have her say first. She responded to her sentence with a poem, apparently addressed to her victim.

> O, must I to that prison go?
> Is there no hope for me below?
> How can I meet this foul disgrace
> For taking you into my place?
>
> Is there no justice in our laws?
> Have I no right within my cause?
> One single moment ere I go,
> I still will hope from courts.
>
> I did not harm you, lady fair,
> So much as was one single hair.
> My sentence, I'll receive it meek,
> A prisoner hath leave to speak.
>
> But if they tear me from my knee,
> And this free spirit sorely tried,
> To the courts of Heaven I must appeal,
> Where Justice can be found, I feel.
>
> Before His face, by night and day,
> In silence I will work and pray.
> His Son my counsellor shall be,
> And there the witnesses set me free.
>
> Oh Mary, Mary, did you know
> The trials we must undergo,
> Were you in Heaven among the blest,
> I think your spirit could not rest.

I succored those in time of need,
Your every want I strove thee,
May you be blest in Eternity,
I feel your spirit pities me.

Full nineteen weeks in sorrow sore,
Foul slanders, prison, all I bore,
Trusting in God I shan't be,
Where Judge and Jury set on.

They found me guilty of sin
Which you well know
Did not begin within my house;
Within my house, or by my hand,
Or yet by her who accused stand.[61]

Although observers described Madame Laahceil as uncaring, if not malicious, toward her patients, the verses suggest that she pitied Mary Byer
and even mourned her. Her unwavering faith and her sense of herself as a
respectable and caring healer are also apparent. But the often tender poem
is also indignant. She rightly pointed out that she was not the author of
the sins that led Mary to her demise, but merely the scapegoat. While she
had languished in the Erie County jail for nineteen weeks, alleged seducer
William Barr walked free on bond and was later acquitted. Meanwhile,
the newspapers heaped scorn on the Indian doctress with slanderous and
sensational allegations that she made Lucretia Borgia look like "an angel
of mercy" and that her business was surely "one of the most cursed human
slaughter-houses ever known to any community."[62]

Using the name Celeste La Salle, the former Madame Laahceil was
committed to the female prison at Sing Sing where she would remain for
the next seven years. Very few detailed records exist to document her
years as an inmate. But prison regulations made attendance at chapel
compulsory, so she may have found solace in worship, though the singing
during services was reportedly very bad. Like other convicts, she worked
to produce goods for use in the prison and for sale on the outside. While
incarcerated men worked in the manufacture of iron castings, files, augurs,
shoes, carpets, and horse blankets, the women made clothing for convicts
and for private contractors.[63] "Celeste" may have sought a pardon or re-
prieve from the governor's office (the records for this period have been

lost), but if she did, they were not granted because she apparently served her full sentence. Upon her release in 1869, she joined thousands of other migrants and headed for the West, possibly traveling on the newly completed transcontinental rail line.

She arrived in Utah in August and was reunited with her parents, Daniel and Clarinda, and her daughter Semira, now grown and with a family of her own. She settled down in Springville with her daughter, son-in-law, and their seven children.

The next few years must have been bittersweet. Just as she had done in Winter Quarters, Laah Ceil, once known as an accomplished Delaware/Mohawk princess and a wretched Indian doctress, shed her Indian persona and resumed life as Lucy Stanton. Despite her persecution in New York, she once more worked as a midwife, though whether she provided abortions is unclear. The following year her daughter Ann and her son Solon both turned up in Springville, and the family was reunited for the first time since 1850. Still, there was no sign of Mosholeh and no mention made of her former husband, Okah Tubbee. Within the space of two years, whatever relief she may have felt in her family's reunification was shattered as Ann, Solon, and her father, Daniel Stanton, all died in rapid succession.[64]

In March 1873, Lucy moved out of her daughter's house and married Heman Bassett, the brother of her first husband Oliver.[65] Heman had been among the followers of "Black Pete" in Kirtland, demonstrating his faith by behaving "like a baboon" and telling others he had received a revelation from an angel, before being excommunicated. In addition to having once been in-laws, Lucy and Heman shared the memory of youthful exuberance and spiritual excesses in Ohio. Perhaps they also shared a sense of estrangement from the church. Both of them had also endured a history of voluntary and involuntary separation from their families. In fact, when Heman Bassett married his erstwhile sister-in-law Lucy Stanton, he still had a wife and children in California.[66]

Interestingly, Lucy Stanton Bassett's time in Springville likely brought her back into contact with some of her former followers. For instance, by the early 1870s, Sisson Chase, whose wife had driven him to muteness with her description of the Lamanite prophet's sexual sealing ceremony, was an elder in the Springville ward.[67] Did her Mormon neighbors remember her? Did they blame her for their troubles? Surely some of them had read news of Okah Tubbee's escapades following the Winter Quarters episode, or seen notice of the Marlett affair when it traveled west in 1852.[68] Lucy's marriage to Heman Bassett might also have raised eyebrows. But her daughter Semira's status in the town of Springville probably helped to shield her from scrutiny. Semira Bassett Wood had been among the earliest Mormon settlers in the area and was married to Lyman S. Wood who was a prosperous businessman and later mayor of Springville.[69] Perhaps unknowingly following in her mother's theatrical footsteps, Semira was also well known for promoting dramatic and musical entertainments in the fledgling town situated just south of Provo.[70]

By 1876, Lucy Stanton Bassett was once more a woman alone among the Mormons. Heman died while on a transcontinental trip to Philadelphia, and she did not remarry. Perhaps seeking the support of her community, she was rebaptized and reconfirmed as a member of the Latter-day Saints Church, and her reentry into the fold was complete.[71] But she was not well. She suffered from intermittent paralysis that may have been related to diabetes and finally died after a long bout with the ailment in 1878.[72] Her daughter, Semira, wrote a sentimental verse on the occasion of her mother's death, a poem very much like those her mother had penned at various moments of trial and tragedy.[73] Lucy Celesta Stanton Bassett, aka Laah Ceil Manatoi Elaah Tubbee, aka Madame Laahceil, is buried in the city cemetery in Springville, Utah, next to her three oldest children. (See Fig. 8.)

Among the others who paid their respects at Bassett's funeral was her adopted grandson Frank Wood, a Paiute Indian. Ostensibly to rescue him, Semira's husband Lyman Wood had purchased the boy from a group of Utes during a Lamanite mission and brought him home. The Mormons, expelled from the East in part because of their attitudes toward both Indians and slavery, had entered a region where an entrenched indigenous slave trade baffled the popular cultural American association of Indians with freedom. Although the Emancipation Proclamation had freed enslaved people of African ancestry, in the Mountain West, Paiutes and other Great Basin Native peoples were still caught in a web of bondage and kinship, infinitely complicated by the pressure that Mormon migrants exerted on their lands and resources. For their part, some Utah Mormons like the Wood family believed that purchasing Paiute children was a path to salvation—for the unfortunate youths and for themselves. Separated from their people, many of these indigenous children were never fully accepted into or accepting of their new homes.[74] Standing at Lucy's grave

FIGURE 8 Grave of Lucy Stanton Bassett. Laah Ceil again became Lucy Stanton Bassett when she joined her Mormon family in Utah and married Heman Bassett in 1873. When she died in 1878, she was buried in the Springville city cemetery. She lies beside her three eldest children, Ann, Semira, and Solon in the shadow of the Wasatch Mountains. (Photograph by the author, 2012)

in the looming shadow of the Wasatch Mountains, Frank Wood was nearly the same age as her mysteriously absent son Mosholeh would have been. One wonders what he knew about his grandmother's life as an infamous Indian doctress, her years as stage performer, or her tumultuous marriage to a man who had also spent his youth in bondage among people who were family in name alone.

Epilogue

· · · · · · · · · · · · · · ·

Maybe entertainment is the story of survival.
—Thomas King, *The Truth about Stories*

In the years after Laah Ceil's death, the meanings of Indianness in American popular culture continued to shift. Nevertheless, the idea of the Indian remained central to a wide variety of discourses about identity. Indians and non-Indians alike participated in the definition of Indianness. The 1880s were the high water years of Buffalo Bill's Wild West, a raucous but predictable spectacle that relied for its authenticity on the nightly participation of indigenous Americans, including Sitting Bull, as well as gunslingers like Annie Oakley and genuine Indian fighters such as Bill Cody himself. The late nineteenth century was also a time in which American Indians in the United States were being aggressively confined to frequently barren reservations, their treaty rights eroded and their lands carved up into allotments preyed upon by land speculators. Along the way, measures such as blood quantum and physical phenotype became the basis for authenticity and formal enrollment in a tribe, as bureaucrats used supposedly "scientific" markers of race and racial inferiority to further dismantle tribal sovereignty. As in the removal era half a century earlier, representations of Indianness proliferated while Indian people were perceived to be vanishing.[1]

The last quarter of the century also witnessed the increasingly brutal treatment of African Americans. Reconstruction-era reforms helped spark a widespread, violent backlash against people of African descent, ultimately codified in Jim Crow laws. Interracial relationships were a particular target for the vitriol of white supremacists who wanted to protect the "purity" of their race at all costs; the race science that had grown in importance during the antebellum period matured after Reconstruction into full-blown eugenics. The dangers of "race mixing" led more than a few people to try to disguise their ancestry to escape the stigma of blackness.

Yet some communities were able to creatively express the complexity of their genealogy, both real and symbolic, as a means of resisting the laws and policies that sought to categorize and dehumanize them. In the late 1880s in New Orleans, for example, when African-descended and mixed-heritage people were subjected to brutal discrimination and even denied the right to participate in Mardi Gras parades, they created their own carnival, costuming themselves in the imagined attire of indigenous forbearers. Their subsequent performances signaled their connection to Native southerners like the Choctaws and Chitimachas while harnessing the symbolic and liberating power of stereotypical Indian play. They riffed on the indigenous cultural influences that permeate the food, music, and language of the South, while reflecting the influence of contemporary Native performers such as those appearing in Buffalo Bill's Wild West shows. In so doing, the Mardi Gras Indians devised an alternative mode of civic participation, social power, and cultural redemption, even as their performances relied on narrow visions of Indianness that arguably contributed to misperceptions of Native people.

For their part, indigenous people across the continent also devised creative ways to profit from America's fascination with Indians in an era of extraordinary poverty and despair for most tribal nations. Whether traveling with wildly popular medicine shows, appearing at world's fairs, or publishing popular autobiographies, American Indians represented themselves both within and against the narrow typology that claimed to define them.[2] Native men and women used what leverage they could find to affect federal and local policies on behalf of their people—still very much alive.[3] Some, like Ely Parker, the first Native American head of the federal Commission on Indian Affairs, did so within the halls of government power. Others mirrored the professional Indians of the antebellum era and made painful compromises like shedding one's business suit for buckskin and leggings if it would bring attention to the cause. For instance, when the newly formed Society of American Indians held its first conference in 1911, the organizers arranged an "Indian concert" for spectators and even shipped in "blankets and feathers," which they knew would "add to the attractiveness" of their cause. And it worked: the concert drew fifteen hundred people and raised seven hundred dollars.[4]

• • •

If we are to understand representations of American Indians, we must acknowledge that they are often not about Native people at all; they more frequently reflect the dominant ideologies within American society. That said, under this wide umbrella, it is important to examine variations and continuities in how Americans other than empowered white men—slaves, free blacks, women, and Mormons, for example—thought about Indians. These ideas were and are influential, not because they are accurate or sensitive portrayals of diverse indigenous peoples, but because Native people have frequently had to define themselves within or against such perceptions.

The incredible story of the two individuals in this book lays bare a complex of popular nineteenth-century beliefs about American Indians. Details, events, and episodes in the lives of the man born Warner McCary and the woman born Lucile Stanton illustrate how diverse audiences across North America understood "Indianness" during the middle of the century, an era during which the United States dispossessed Native people east of the Mississippi River of nearly all of their lands, and the role that race, gender, faith, music, and medicine played in these myriad understandings. At times, I have suggested how Okah Tubbee and Laah Ceil themselves might have thought about Indians and Indianness, and both the origin and the import of those ideas. And I have argued that while they sometimes escaped or exceeded the limits imposed upon them by constrictive ideologies of race and gender operating within the United States and Canada, they also contributed to a system of Indian representation and stereotypes that was (and is) detrimental, if not deadly, for American Indian societies.

What is most important about Okah Tubbee and Laah Ceil's "Indianness" is how and why they constructed and performed alternative personas that allowed them to transcend their proscribed identities, while capitalizing (sometimes literally) on popular cultural beliefs about what it meant to be an Indian. This strategy was not without its complications. Like the Mardi Gras Indians of later years, the Tubbees' actions may have subverted some discourses of race and gender, but they emphatically endorsed others. Their representation of themselves *as Indians* relied on popular cultural tropes and antebellum stereotypes that offered a narrow, inaccurate, and homogenized image *of Indians* and inherently limited the subversive potential of their actions. As one scholar puts it, "images in negotiation with power are often ambiguous, complicated, and implicated in the crimes they seek to address."[5] And yet, by confronting their lived experiences in all their messy complexity, many of those "crimes" are laid bare.

The legacies of white supremacy and settler colonialism in North America that enabled—even encouraged—Warner McCary and Lucy Stanton to become professional Indians continued after their deaths and remain relevant in our own time. The realities of mixed ancestry continue to vex bureaucratic efforts to categorize people on the basis of biological race (like the federal census), even as questions of indigenous sovereignty are being answered today with continued reliance on blood quantum and disenrollment. Despite a flourishing of scholarship on black-Indian relationships throughout the western hemisphere over the past decade, local tensions and considerable blind spots persist. Tribes disfranchise the descendants of their former slaves, while descendants of other enslaved people participate in the appropriation of tribal cultures.

And it is only natural that race would remain a central concern for the most successful homegrown religion of the United States: Mormonism. When the ban on men of African descent in the priesthood was finally lifted by revelation in 1978, the influence of both "secular and sacred variables" was undeniable. Although there was increasing pressure within the United States to rescind the prohibition in the context of domestic civil rights, the issue came fully to light in the context of colonialism. LDS mission work in South America, particularly Brazil, was hampered by the problem of the priesthood ban because the vast majority of church members in the region had some African ancestry.[6] Many of these people were probably also kin to the indigenous peoples of the western hemisphere. And, as we've seen, the history of the ban on blacks in the LDS priesthood was partly shaped by Mormon attitudes toward Native peoples. Then as now, the intertwined legacies of slavery and colonialism reverberate through social relations in the western hemisphere.

• • •

Despite the potentially wide-ranging significance of the issues raised in this book, what little was previously known about the figures at its center has tended to focus on three largely isolated concerns. One common assertion about Okah Tubbee is that he was a fugitive slave who used claims to Indian ancestry to escape bondage.[7] But, it was not until *after* his manumission that he began to perform as an Indian. Nevertheless, this widely reproduced misinterpretation sheds light on the association of Indianness with "freedom" that is pervasive in American culture, as well as its insidious obverse, the association of African-descended Americans with slavery.

Another common assumption about the pair was that while Okah Tubbee's indigeneity was doubtful, Laah Ceil was the Indian she claimed to be. Many works describe Laah Ceil Manatoi Elaah Tubbee as Delaware and Mohawk, as she consistently asserted, or sometimes Mahican or Stockbridge. Despite the absence of corroborating evidence for such claims, some scholars have crafted elaborate arguments based on presumptions about Laah Ceil's Indian ancestry.[8] Her ability to pass as Indian in even very recent literature suggests the ways in which "white Indians" are more readily accepted than "black Indians," even among modern scholars.

A third mode of thinking about the pair centers on the role of McCary's "misbehavior" at Winter Quarters and its relationship to the Mormon priesthood ban, but often without adequate consideration of ideas about Indians or the key role of McCary's white wife. And most people outside Mormon history have labored in complete ignorance of this parallel line of inquiry.[9] These discrepancies reveal blind spots in Mormon history, but also the continued marginalization of Mormon stories within broader U.S. history.

With this book, I have tried to unite frequently isolated topics (slavery, Mormonism, popular culture, and medicine, among others) and demonstrate that representations of American Indians were critical to each. In addition to underscoring the centrality of ideas about Indians to American culture writ large, I also want to suggest two other conclusions. The first is the paradox in antebellum thinking about identity—that it was both fluid and fixed—and the way that Indianness functioned within the contradiction. The second is the fallacy of considering American cultural history within silos that parse intersecting aspects of identity (such as race, gender, and religion) and consider them separately instead of approaching them as interdependent parts of complex lived experiences.

That I had labored so long on this project before becoming aware of its connections to Mormon history and that so many scholars knew either William McCary and Lucy Stanton or Okah Tubbee and Laah Ceil but not both suggests to me that our frameworks of inquiry are still too often isolated from one another. My hope is that this work can help illuminate where connections exist and what we have to gain by occasionally visiting others' fields.[10]

Many mysteries in the fascinating lives of Okah Tubbee and Laah Ceil still remain unexplained, but one thing is certain: Indianness mattered. But it mattered (and still matters) to different people in different, overlapping, and sometimes contradictory ways, depending on the contexts in which it is expressed and received. Far from being a distraction from "real" challenges facing Native peoples in the past and present, understanding how ideas of Indianness emerge and operate is a crucial step toward dislodging the often dangerous misperceptions that flow from them.

Notes

ABBREVIATIONS

ACPC   Adams County Probate Cases, MDAH
CHL   Latter-day Saints Church History Library, Salt Lake City, Utah
CTA   City of Toronto Archives, Toronto, Ontario
LTPSC   L. Tom Perry Special Collections, Brigham Young University Library, Provo, Utah
MDAH   Mississippi Department of Archives and History, Jackson, Miss.
MSA   Missouri State Archives, Jefferson City, Mo.
NARA   National Archives and Records Administration, Washington, D.C.
OIA   Office of Indian Affairs, NARA
WRP   Willard Richards Papers, 1821–54, CHL
RG10   Record Group 10, Central Toronto Superintendency, Correspondence, 1845–79, Library and Archives Canada, Library and Archives Canada, Ottawa, Ontario
RG75   Record Group 75, Records of the Bureau of Indian Affairs, Letters Received by the Office of Indian Affairs, 1824–51, NARA

PROLOGUE

1. Regina v. Tubbee, 1 P.R. 98, Westlaw Canada, http://canada.westlaw.com. Accounts of their nuptials and the ensuing controversy appeared in numerous papers, including but not limited to the *Buffalo Commercial Advertiser*, Aug. 18, 26, Sept. 1, 1851; *Brooklyn Daily Eagle*, Aug. 30, 1851; *Cleveland Herald*, Sept. 1, 1851; *Hartford Daily Courant*, Sept. 3, 1851; *Barre Gazette*, Sept. 5, 1851; *Adams Sentinel*, Sept. 8, 1851; *Milwaukee Daily Sentinel and Gazette*, Sept. 8, 1851; *The Sun*, Sept. 8, 1851; *Covington Journal*, Sept. 13, 1851; *Vermont Patriot & State Gazette*, Sept. 18, 1851; *Democratic Expounder*, Sept. 19, 1851.

2. Many newspapers carried news of Tubbee's background, including but not limited to the *Louisville Courier*, June 28, 1851; *Daily Picayune*, July 8, 1851; *Adams Sentinel*, July 14, 1851; *Bangor Daily Whig & Courier*, July 19, 1851; *Mississippi Free Trader*, Sept. 13, Dec. 10, 1851; *Cleveland Herald*, Sept. 17, 1851; *Vicksburg*

Tri-Weekly Sentinel, Sept. 18, 1851; *Independent American*, Oct. 3, 1851; *Farmer's Monthly Visitor* 12:1, Jan. 1852; *New York Times*, Aug. 24, 1852; *Newport Daily News*, Aug. 26, 1852; *Daily Missouri Republican*, Aug. 28, 1852; *Detroit Daily Free Press*, Aug. 30, 1852.

3. Two such figures were murdered New York prostitute Helen Jewett and self-proclaimed prophet Matthias, examined in Cohen, *Murder of Helen Jewett*, and Johnson and Wilentz, *Kingdom of Matthias*, respectively.

4. James McCary, Will, 1813, box 27, microfilm roll 5646, Estate of James Mc-Cary, Adams County Probate Cases (hereafter ACPC), Mississippi Department of Archives and History (hereafter MDAH).

5. Staker, *'Hearken, O Ye People,'* 81–82. On Mormon relations with Indians, see Farmer, *On Zion's Mount;* Reeve, *Making Space on the Western Frontier*; Duffy, "Use of 'Lamanite' in Official LDS Discourse."

6. There were especially compelling reasons to conceal their intermittent involvement in plural marriage. On non-Mormon reactions to polygamy, see Gordon, *Mormon Question*.

7. For McCary and Stanton's varied influences, see Mielke and Bellin in their edited collection *Native Acts*. In the introduction, Mielke explains that they "adopt the term *Native acts* (rather than *Indian play*) as shorthand for American Indian participation and agency in a tradition of Indian performance . . . a critical intervention in the scholarship treating the performance of Indianness because [it] restore[s] Indian peoples to the intercultural matrix from which such performances arose." Mielke, introduction to *Native Acts*, 10.

8. Halttunen, *Confidence Men and Painted Women*, xv. Related works include Streeby, *American Sensations*; Mihm, *A Nation of Counterfeiters*.

9. See, e.g., Watson, *Liberty and Power*; Sellers, *Market Revolution*; Perry, *Boats against the Current*.

10. Elliott, "Telling the Difference."

11. Lott, *Love and Theft*; Green, "Tribe Called Wannabee."

12. Though we might debate whether Okah Tubbee was considered a freak by antebellum standards, his appearance among Barnum's other displays of human deformity and animal curiosity is striking. And, as Reiss has asserted, "Freak shows, perhaps more than any other popular antebellum practice, helped disseminate the lessons of racial solidarity because they acted as a hinge between scientific inquiries into racial essence and the popular desire for images of white domination. Exhibits typically highlighted the physical anomaly, grotesque features, extreme disability, or exotic racial and cultural difference of the displayed human object, and often more than one such quality at a time." Reiss, "P. T. Barnum," 85–86.

13. Horsman, *Race and Manifest Destiny*, 139–57. On manifestations of scientific racism in American literature, see for example, Putzi, *Identifying Marks*. On the role of scientific racism in American empire abroad, see Jacobson, *Barbarian Virtues*.

14. Horsman, *Race and Manifest Destiny*, 149–56.

15. On transatlantic Native travelers, see Weaver, *Red Atlantic*; Thrush, *Indigenous London*.

16. Artists F. O. Lewis, Karl Bodmer, Charles Bird King, and George Catlin, among others, contributed to the burgeoning industry of Indian portraiture. See Berkhofer, *White Man's Indian*; Truettner, *Painting Indians*; Pearce, *Savagism and Civilization*.

17. Moody, *America Takes the Stage*, 79.

18. On Jones, Copway, and Maungwudaus, see D. Smith, *Mississauga Portraits*.

19. I treat identity as essentially, but not exclusively, performative. For an insightful application of performative theories of identity in relation to racial categorization, see Rottenberg, "Passing: Race, Identification, and Desire." On gender as performative, see Butler, *Gender Trouble*. On "performance" as a "medium of cultural definition and transmission," see Roach, "Slave Spectacles and Tragic Octoroons."

20. Green asserts that playing Indian is "one of the oldest and most pervasive forms of American cultural expression." Green, "Tribe Called Wannabe," 30. Other important work on the phenomenon includes Deloria, *Playing Indian*; Huhndorf, *Going Native*; Trachtenberg, *Shades of Hiawatha*; Bird, *Dressing in Feathers*.

21. There are a few exceptions to the aforementioned lack of emphasis on people of color playing Indian, the most notable of which is L. Browder, *Slippery Characters*.

22. Berlin, *Slaves without Masters*, 161. One of the most fascinating cases of double-passing, in which an enslaved woman passed as both male and white, is that of Ellen Craft, *Running a Thousand Miles for Freedom*.

23. *Cincinnati Commercial*, Oct. 27, 1846.

24. *Daily National Intelligencer*, Nov. 23, 25, 1847.

25. The text went through three editions: Rev. L. L. Allen, *A Thrilling Sketch of the Life of the Distinguished Chief Okah Tubbee Alias, Wm. Chubbee, Son of the Head Chief, Mosholeh Tubbee, of the Choctaw Nation of Indians* (New York, 1848); Laah Ceil Manatoi Elaah Tubbee, *A Sketch of the Life of Okah Tubbee: Alias, William Chubbee, Son of the Head Chief, Mosholeh Tubbee, of the Choctaw Nation of Indians* (Springfield, Mass., 1848); Laah Ceil Manatoi Elaah Tubbee, *A Sketch of the Life of Okah Tubbee . . .* (Toronto, 1852). For a composite version, see Littlefield, *Life of Okah Tubbee*. Littlefield was the first modern scholar to seriously research Okah Tubbee and Laah Ceil, compiling the autobiography's three editions and providing in-depth annotations.

26. Schlicher, "Terre Haute in 1850," 259.

27. *Buffalo Commercial Advertiser*, Aug. 9, 1851. Tubbee was also acknowledged as a possessor of musical "genius" in other accounts: *Weekly Reveille*, Oct. 27, 1845; *Daily Picayune*, July 8, 1851.

28. Deloria, *Playing Indian*, 74–76. See also Granqvist, *Imitation as Resistance*; McCloskey, "Campaign of Periodicals"; Shank, "Theatre for the Majority."

29. I address the discrepancies in scholarly treatments of Laah Ceil in the epilogue.

CHAPTER ONE

1. Schulz, *Travels on an Inland Voyage*, 2:132–33, 135; Carson, *Searching for the Bright Path*, 74.

2. Martha Jane Brazy notes that in 1810, the population was 1,684, and ten years later, it had increased to only 2,184. The surrounding Natchez district, however, saw its population quadruple. Schulz may have based his estimate on the wider district. Brazy, *American Planter*, 8.

3. Hodgson, *Letters from North America*, 1:208–10.

4. Brazy, *American Planter*, 6.

5. McCary appears in the 1810 Adams County tax list. *Mississippi, Compiled Census and Census Substitutes Index, 1805–1890*, http://www.ancestry.com.

6. James, *Antebellum Natchez*, 44; Brazy, *American Planter*, 7–8.

7. For evidence of Indian sailors on the Mississippi and Ohio Rivers, see Asbury, *Reminiscences of Quincy, Illinois*, 7; Quick and Quick, *Mississippi Steamboatin'*, 14–15.

8. Schulz, *Travels on an Inland Voyage*, 2:138; Janson, *Stranger in America*, 438–39.

9. Hodgson, *Letters from North America*, 1:168.

10. Schulz, *Travels on an Inland Voyage*, 2:139. The Natchez Trace was established as a federal roadway following the Treaty of Fort Adams (1801), between the Choctaws and the United States. It involved cessions of land for the road, as well as providing agreements for the ownership and operation of ferries and other establishments. Hudson, *Creek Paths and Federal Roads*, 62.

11. Schulz, *Travels on an Inland Voyage*, 2:144–45. Warner McCary might have seen some of these ancient Indian mounds firsthand when accompanying one of his employers into the backcountry, or perhaps at the plantation of Walter G. Irvine, executor of the McCary estate, whose property included a notable earthwork. According to the Report of the Committee on Plantations of the Agricultural, Horticultural and Botanical Society of Jefferson College, "Mr. Irvine's plantation lies about twelve miles North East of Natchez, near the village of Selser-town, and embraces the large and ancient Indian Mound near that place so famous for its gigantic dimensions," possibly a reference to Emerald Mound. *Western Farmer and Gardener*, 2:187.

12. Grafton, "Natchez," 2.

13. In the borderlands of the lower Mississippi valley, we find what Evan Haefli describes as a place "where autonomous peoples of different cultures are bound together by a greater multi-imperial context." Haefli, "Note on the Use of North American Borderlands," 1224.

14. On Choctaw stories and their animating power for both people and lands, see Howe, "Ohoyo Chishba Osh." On early Choctaw history and especially the importance of travel and journey worlds, see Galloway, *Choctaw Genesis, 1500–1700*.

15. Chateaubriand's work was composed, along with another called "René," as half of his Romantic masterpiece, *The Natchez*, but published separately. It describes the ill-fated love affair between Chactas, a Natchez man, and Atala, a French-Indian Christianized woman. *The Natchez* was eventually published in its entirety in 1826 and is considered to be an influential depiction of the figure of the "noble savage." In Simms's story, "Oakatibbee; or, the Choctaw Sampson," the narrator describes a conversation between himself and a planter (Col. Harris), as they stand watching

laborers pick cotton. Some of those working in the field or bringing their baskets to be weighed are Choctaws, and the two white men discuss the so-called Indian character at length. They muse about whether a young Indian boy could be taken from his tribe and raised among a different people and whether he would come to know of his true birth or pass unknowingly into the other culture. Simms, "Oakatibbee; or, the Choctaw Sampson." Carson uses this story as the framing device for his book on pre-removal Choctaw history and notes that it is ostensibly based on Simms's actual experiences in the area. Carson, *Searching for the Bright Path*, 1–2.

16. Carson, "Greenwood LeFlore," 222–23. Carson calls this intermixture foundational to understanding *creolité*, a concept that has been used in very limited ways within North American scholarship to signal "mixed race" peoples, but theorized more broadly within Caribbean studies as a complex of identity practices in which Natives and newcomers interweave their cultures. I have stopped short of labeling Tubbee a Creole in the same sense that Carson uses it to analyze Choctaw leader Greenwood LeFlore, but the concept usefully illuminates the ways that people become enmeshed in the cultures of others, whether or not their biological origins are "mixed."

17. James McCary, Will, 1813, Estate of James McCary, ACPC.

18. Berlin, *Slaves without Masters*, 150.

19. Allen, *Thrilling Sketch*, 15. Littlefield makes this powerful assertion: "There is no reason to doubt that at a young age the boy began to question his identity. A mind as clever as Okah Tubbee's would quickly have perceived the distinction society made between him and his mother and siblings. . . . Such a mind . . . might easily have concluded that something was amiss, that the arrangement was inherently unfair." Littlefield, *Life of Okah Tubbee*, x. Wilma King makes a similar argument in *Stolen Childhood*, 124.

20. Allen, *Thrilling Sketch*, 9.

21. Carson, *Searching for the Bright Path*, 70–74; Carson, "Native Americans, the Market Revolution, and Culture Change," 188–89.

22. Also contained in this section of Okah Tubbee's autobiography is a sketch of "the present condition of the Choctaw Indians, written in 1846, by a highly respected and devoted Missionary, and teacher at Fort Coffee Academy, Iowa Territory [*sic*], Rev. W. G. Montgomery." Allen, *Thrilling Sketch*, 12–15.

23. Ibid., 12, 15, 33. "Comfortable fictions" is a term used by Vine Deloria Jr. in "Comfortable Fictions and the Struggle for Turf."

24. As Littlefield observes, "Though there may be some question about who Okah Tubbee was, it is less difficult to say who he was not." Littlefield, *Life of Okah Tubbee*, xi–xii.

25. Krauthamer, *Black Slaves, Indian Masters*, 28–29.

26. Carson, *Searching for the Bright Path*, 74, 80; Lincecum, *Pushmataha*, 26, 28.

27. On African-Indian interactions in the context of slavery in the early South, in addition to Carson and Krauthamer, see Usner, *Indians, Settlers, and Slaves in a Frontier Exchange Economy*; Miles, *Ties that Bind*; Gallay, *The Indian Slave Trade*; Snyder, *Slavery in Indian Country*.

28. Allen, *Thrilling Sketch*, 22.

29. Brooks, *American Lazarus*, 87–114; Byars-Nichols, *Black-Indian in American Literature*, 9–10, 16–34; VanDerBeets, *Held Captive by Indians*, 177–78.

30. Another parallel case was that of Elizabeth Taylor Greenfield, who lived as a slave in Natchez, but later was known as "The Black Swan" when she became a minor celebrity singing sensation in 1851. She frequently claimed that one or both of her parents were of Indian, specifically Seminole, ancestry. LaBrew, *The Black Swan*.

31. James McCary, Will.

32. See, e.g., *Village Doctor*, 6; Cobbett, *Thirteen Sermons*, 172–84; Bowers, *The Politics of Motherhood*, 95.

33. On the representation of enslaved mothers as deficient, negligent, or unnatural, see Schwartz, *Birthing a Slave*. These depictions existed uneasily alongside the widespread use of enslaved wet nurses and midwives in the South. See also Schwartz, *Born in Bondage*.

34. Allen, *Thrilling Sketch*, 31. This woman, Sally Kelly, may or may not have been the same Sally manumitted with Franky, Bob, and Kitty in James McCary's will. James McCary, Will.

35. Allen, *Thrilling Sketch*, 18–19. Interestingly, such moments of childhood realization, particularly of one's own enslaved status, were practically axiomatic in slave narratives. For a sample, see the excerpts in chapter 6 of Mintz, *African American Voices*.

36. Tubbee, *Sketch of the Life* (1848), 20.

37. Allen, *Thrilling Sketch*, 16.

38. McCary's paternity is explicitly acknowledged in two separate documents: an 1817 deed of sale for a several lots of land in which Bob is referred to as "Robert McCarey son of the late James McCarey deceased" and a receipt for medical services provided to "McCary's Son Bob" by Dr. Samuel Gustine. William Barland's Execr. to Robert McCarey, Deed, 1817, Deed Book K, 146, MDAH; Receipt, Estate of Jas. McCary to Saml. Gustine, April 7, 1821, Estate of James McCary, ACPC. As Littlefield has noted, "The sexual chasm between white and black in Natchez was not nearly so wide as the social chasm." Littlefield, *Life of Okah Tubbee*, x.

39. Littlefield, *Life of Okah Tubbee*, xi.

40. A brief but useful discussion of *partus sequitur ventrem*, the legal principle dictating that the child of an enslaved mother follows the mother's condition, can be found in Kennedy, *Born Southern*, 164–66.

41. Allen, *Thrilling Sketch*, 21.

42. In addition, if Warner McCary had been born to a Choctaw mother, he would have had a clan identity and a network of maternal relatives to care for him, even if a father (of whatever background) had forsaken him. The decision to emphasize his paternal rather than maternal ancestry seems to signal a fundamental misunderstanding of southeastern Indian kinship and lineage patterns, though admittedly, by 1810, these were changing under pressure from settler colonial apparatuses like the civilization plan. On Choctaw gender relations and their impact on diplomacy, see Galloway, "'The Chief Who Is Your Father'"; on Choctaw gender and culture change more broadly, see Carson, *Searching for the Bright Path*.

43. Allen, *Thrilling Sketch*, 10.

44. Ibid., 16.

45. Berlin, *Slaves without Masters*, 197–98. Berlin further observes, "While whites allowed these free Negroes to prosper, those who stood outside these relations with whites were viewed with intense hostility" (215). This caste system was also evident in Charleston, where the free black community likewise used social institutions like marriage and education, along with their ties to powerful whites, to maintain their precarious status. Marshall, "'They Will Endeavor to Pass for Free,'" 164–66.

46. Littlefield, *Life of Okah Tubbee*, ix–x; Berlin, *Slaves without Masters*, 179–80, 197–98, 215.

47. Berlin, *Slaves without Masters*, 222; Thomas, *From Tennessee Slave to St. Louis Entrepreneur*, 113–15.

48. Even ties of family and prosperity could not protect against the rigid racial codes of the later Jim Crow era. A female descendant of Robert McCary's (Clara McCary Dwyer) was involved in a 1919 legal case in Nebraska in which she was accused by her new husband of concealing her "Negro ancestry" and passing as a white woman. Gatewood, "The Perils of Passing."

49. See receipts and accounting lists, 1813–27, Estate of James McCary, ACPC.

50. Receipt for tuition, Oct. 1823, Estate of James McCary, ACPC. Other receipts indicate that Bob and Kitty also received instruction (from various tutors and for varying lengths of time) in 1816, 1817, 1818, 1821, 1824, and 1825.

51. List of accounts payable, Sept. 1818, Estate of James McCary, ACPC.

52. Ibid. See also List of accounts payable, 1825–27, Estate of James McCary, ACPC.

53. Receipt for payment of damages to [Zucofes?] from Walter Irvine, 1826, Estate of James McCary, ACPC. The receipt indicates that [Zucofes?] received the sum of "sixty dollars in full satisfaction for a violent assault commited upon Lucian Adam[s] by Warner a yellow boy slave belonging to said Estate the injury done, three teeth lost or broken out." Although there's no mention of McCary being treated for similar injuries in his youth, his difficulties included occasional illnesses, such as when he was treated by local physician Dr. Samuel Gustine in 1825, along with Bob and Kitty, for ailments that may have related to yellow fever outbreaks in the area. See Receipt for medical services of Samuel Gustine, Mar. 13, 1826, Estate of James McCary, ACPC.

54. Allen, *Thrilling Sketch*, 20.

55. Hogan and Davis, introduction to *William Johnson's Natchez*, 12; Brazy, *American Planter*, 13-14.

56. Hogan and Davis, introduction, 11.

57. Ibid.; Schweninger, "Prosperous Blacks in the South," 36–37.

58. Berlin, *Slaves without Masters*, 197–98. In this crucial passage, Berlin asserts, "The greater the distinction whites were able to make between slaves and free Negroes, the greater their willingness to accept Negro freemen as a distinct part of the social order. . . . The close connections with whites, light skin, urban residence, comparatively high occupational status, and the very name 'free people of color'

distinguished Lower South free Negroes from the overwhelmingly black, rural slaves and raised the free Negro's standing in Southern society."

59. During this particular journey, Warner McCary narrowly escaped being attacked by bears in an episode that bears a striking resemblance to a popular story told about Choctaw headman, Pushmataha. Lincecum, *Pushmataha*, 43.

60. Allen, *Thrilling Sketch*, 16–17.

61. Brazy, *American Planter*, 25. Camp and Krauthamer have both shown how such physical mobility and freedom to travel was largely denied African-descended women slaves. Camp, *Closer to Freedom*; Krauthamer, *Black Slaves, Indian Masters*.

62. Allen, *Thrilling Sketch*, 17.

63. James, *Antebellum Natchez*, 242–51. In addition to the Methodist establishments, the predominant denominations were Baptist and Episcopal, but James concludes, based on numerous sources, that Schulz had the gist of it right and most Natchezians seemed indifferent to religion.

64. Littlefield, *Life of Okah Tubbee*, xvii. See Alford, *Prince among Slaves*. As both authors note, the story of the long-lost African prince was widely covered in Natchez and across the nation.

65. Nearly thirty years later, a Natchez newspaper reporting on the debut of "Black Swan" songstress Elizabeth Greenfield in the North, placed her alongside Ibrahima and Okah Tubbee, observing, "Adams County has been somewhat remarkable as the residence of noted colored individuals." *Mississippi Free Trader*, Dec. 10, 1851.

66. Indeed, the system of slavery itself often meant that "slaves did not equate the idea of family with a particular form of household composition," and when enslaved parents tried to hold their families together, according to their own concepts of familial relations, their efforts were derailed by the involvement of owners. Schwartz, *Born in Bondage*, 53, 74. Reflecting on Okah Tubbee's autobiography and its depiction of the slave family, Murray observes, "One of the most distinctive features of this particular account is the way that the basic family relationships are so confused and threatening. Rather than, for instance, the black mother being a positive, and the absent white father being the enigma, the black woman here represents the brutality of slavery itself." Murray, "Racial Identity and Self-invention," 87–88.

67. Camp notes that truants were far more common than runaways and argues that their short trips to nonauthorized locations created a "rival geography" that upset their owners' attempts to constrict their mobility and provided slaves with time and space for "independent activity" as well. Camp, *Closer to Freedom*, 36.

68. Allen, *Thrilling Sketch*, 18.

69. Usner, *Indian Work*, 46.

70. Ibid., 48–57; Libby, *Slavery and Frontier Mississippi*, 93; Carson, *Searching for the Bright Path*, 73.

71. Allen, *Thrilling Sketch*, 25.

72. Ibid., 26.

73. Schulz, *Travels on an Inland Voyage*, 2:140–41.

74. Rousey, "Aliens in the WASP Nest."

75. Former Nashville slave and later entrepreneur James Thomas put it this way: "The old time barber shop was the best of all places to learn the ways and peculiarities of the old time gentlmen," which included how they ran their households, with whom they did business, what political affairs concerned them, and what advice they had. Thomas, *From Tennessee Slave to St. Louis Entrepreneur*, 73. See also Hogan and Davis, introduction.

76. Alford, *Prince among Slaves*, 66.

77. On the Creek War, see among others, Waselkov, *Conquering Spirit*; Braund, *Tohopeka*.

78. The literature on Indian removal is considerable. For a glimpse of the southern debates, see Green, *Politics of Indian Removal;* Garrison, *Legal Ideology of Removal*.

79. Wimsatt, introduction to *Tales of the South*, 1–2, 8; Carson, *Searching for the Bright Path*, 1–2. See also O'Brien, "Writing with a Forked Pen."

80. Free notes that the first permanent theater, on Main Street, was built on the site of an abandoned graveyard, and Smith confirms the grisly setting, remarking, "The dressing-rooms for the gentlemen were under the stage, the earth having been excavated to make room for them. Human bones were strewn about in every direction. The first night, the lamplighter being a little 'pushed' for time to get all ready, seized upon a skull, and, sticking two tallow candles in the eye-sockets, I found my dressing-room thus lighted." Free, "Ante-bellum Theatre," 19, 21–22; Smith, *Theatrical Management*, 52.

81. Free, "Ante-bellum Theatre," 19, 22.

82. Quick and Quick, *Mississippi Steamboatin'*, 172. According to a retrospective engineer's report, the number of steamboats on the Mississippi River grew from 231 in 1834 to approximately 1,000 by 1849.

83. The Erie Canal was opened in 1825 and contributed mightily to what George Rogers Taylor called, in his classic work, the "transportation revolution." Taylor, *Transportation Revolution, 1815-1860*. See also Sheriff, *The Artificial River*.

84. S. Smith, *Theatrical Journey-Work*, 26–28.

85. Ibid.; James, *Antebellum Natchez*, 229. In 1833, Caldwell sold his interest in the Natchez theater to Richard Russell, who would later become the manager of the Tremont Temple in Boston, where, some fifteen years later, Okah Tubbee and his wife, Laah Ceil, would make their debut as "temperance activists" speaking on behalf of "their red brethren." See chapter 4.

86. Free, "Ante-bellum Theatre," 21.

87. James, *Antebellum Natchez*, 137.

88. Ibid., 168, 175, 178; Hogan and Davis, introduction, 12–13; Berlin, *Slaves without Masters*, 189–90.

89. Board of Police Minutes, 1832, 12, 19, Adams County Records, MDAH.

90. William Johnson noted that Ann Perkins of Natchez successfully fought a bid to revoke her "free negro license" by proving her Indian ancestry. Johnson, *William Johnson's Natchez*, 342. James Thomas likewise noted that "early in the forties the people were earnestly enforcing the contravention act prohibiting free Negroes from

coming in the state," and he asserted that some proved themselves by "Christining [*sic*] papers," and others "proved themselves Indians." Thomas, *From Tennessee Slave to St. Louis Entrepreneur*, 113–14.

91. James, *Antebellum Natchez*, 179; Buchanan, *Black Life on the Mississippi*, 24. The urban South's elite whites, more secure in their own social standing, tended to be those who provided testimony of the good character of free blacks, perhaps owing to frequent ties of kinship.

92. Allen, *Thrilling Sketch*, 25.

93. See Buchanan, *Black Life on the Mississippi*.

94. Allen, *Thrilling Sketch*, 29, 37.

95. Ibid., 35.

96. Adams, "Autobiography of William Adams," 4, L. Tom Perry Special Collections (hereafter LTPSC). Mormons migrated via steamer from Liverpool to New Orleans before proceeding upriver. These migrations began in the late 1830s and continued well into the late nineteenth century. For another Mormon journey on the Mississippi River roughly contemporaneous with McCary's early travels, see C. Smith, "Journal, 1843," 14, Charles Smith Papers, 1840–1905, LTPSC.

97. Allen, *Thrilling Sketch*, 34–35.

98. Littlefield notes that a wave of reform targeting slave conspiracies and "immoral" activities like gambling swept Natchez during the mid-1830s. Littlefield, *Life of Okah Tubbee*, xv.

99. Music was so important that it was given its own section in militia handbooks. See, e.g., Cooper, *Concise System of Instructions and Regulations*.

100. Allen, *Thrilling Sketch*, 39.

101. On the social function of militias in this era, see Laver, "Rethinking the Social Role." Among other roles, Laver asserts, "The militia's public appearances reinforced the social hierarchies of race, class, and gender, while maintaining the cross-class hegemony of white males," 780. Prominent Masons in Natchez included John A. Quitman, who also participated widely in militia activities. James, *Antebellum Natchez*, 117.

102. Tubbee, *Sketch of the Life* (1848), 84.

103. Treaty with Choctaw, 1830, in Kappler, *Indian Affairs*.

104. Walker, "Public Dinner Given in Honor of the Chickasaw and Choctaw Treaties."

105. Ibid.

106. Satz, "The Mississippi Choctaw," 7.

107. Power, *Impressions of America*, 2:113.

108. Wells, introduction to *After Removal*, vii.

109. Satz points out that "state courts offered the Indians a vehicle for seeking redress, but the legal process was costly, time consuming, and often incomprehensible," especially for those Choctaws who did not speak English. Satz, "Mississippi Choctaw," 8–9. The definitive account of removal era fraud and speculation in the Southeast remains M. E. Young, *Redskins, Ruffleshirts, and Rednecks*.

110. See, e.g., *New-York Morning Herald*, July 3, 1830. The story was also carried in *Raleigh Register and North Carolina Gazette*, July 5, 1830; *Providence Patriot*,

Columbian Phenix, July 7, 1830; *Boston Courier*, July 8, 1830; *Carolina Observer*, July 15, 1830; *Daily National Journal*, July 17, 1830; *Dover Gazette & Strafford Advertiser*, July 20, 1830; *Maryland Gazette*, July 29, 1830.

111. Bellin offers an innovative read of Catlin's works, with an emphasis on an antebellum "struggle for the meaning, control, and use of Indian sacred performance." Bellin, *Medicine Bundle*, 21–77.

112. Thomas, *From Tennessee Slave to St. Louis Entrepreneur*, 112–13.

113. *Daily Picayune*, July 23, 1839.

114. Robert McCary P. Atty. Almon Baldwin, 1839, Deed Book BB, 228–29, MDAH. Although Warner is referred to in the document as "James Warner," a subsequent appearance before the police court in 1843 confirms his identity. It refers to "Warner McCarey alias James Warner, a free man of Color of mulatto complexion, aged about 29 years." Board of Police Minutes, 1843, 374, MDAH.

115. Hogan and Davis, *William Johnson's Natchez*, 146. McCary claimed in the autobiography that he worked at Leed's Foundry, which specialized in accoutrements of sugar production. Allen, *Thrilling Sketch*, 34, 40-43; "Leed's Foundry," [broadside], Merchants of New Orleans Print Collection, 1840s–50s, Box 1, Folder 12, Tulane University, Louisiana Research Collections.

116. Hogan and Davis, *William Johnson's Natchez*, 186.

117. Littlefield, *Life of Okah Tubbee*, viii.

118. Either McCary lied about his age or the court reporter made a guess. He was either thirty-three or thirty-four at the time.

119. *Cincinnati Commercial*, Oct. 27, 1846.

120. In the autobiography, he claims to have witnessed the 1840 tornado that destroyed Natchez before returning to New Orleans for a stay of three or four years. Tubbee, *Sketch of the Life* (1852), 44.

121. *Daily Picayune*, Oct. 21, 1843.

122. Tubbee, *Sketch of the Life* (1848), 45; Minute Book, Louisiana Volunteers, Apr. 22, 1843–Nov. 29, 1845, James H. Dakin Papers, 1816–1973, box 1, folder 22, Tulane University, Louisiana Research Collections. Dakin was a well-known architect in both New Orleans and the northern states. Scully, *James Dakin, Architect*.

123. *Daily Picayune*, July 9, 1844. The *Picayune* was quoting from the *Concordia Intelligencer*.

124. *Weekly Reveille*, Oct. 27, 1845.

125. S. Smith, *Theatrical Journey-Work*, 27–28.

CHAPTER TWO

1. Staker, *'Hearken, O Ye People,'* 49–52.

2. Westbrook, *Mormonism*, 93.

3. Fluhman, *'Peculiar People,'* 28.

4. Johnson and Wilentz, *Kingdom of Matthias*, 6.

5. Fluhman notes that Mormonism was "not merely another in a long line of democratizing religious movements, but also a feature of a society newly acclimating to the very idea of diversity." Fluhman, *'Peculiar People,'* 17.

6. See, e.g., Snow, *Personal Writings of Eliza Roxcy Snow*, 8–10.

7. Bushman, *Joseph Smith*, 64, 82–83, 93.

8. Gutjahr, *Book of Mormon*, 5.

9. The Book of Mormon is a living document of religious faith. The original passage was "white and delightsome," appeared sometimes as "light and delightsome," and now reads "pure and delightsome." Both the logic of the original wording and the subsequent changes are a matter of considerable debate. For a comprehensive discussion of the phrase over many editions, see Campbell, "'White' or 'Pure': Five Vignettes."

10. *History of the Church*, 1:118, quoted in Staker, *'Hearken, O Ye People,'* 49.

11. Smith, *Personal Writings of Joseph Smith*, 273. See also Duffy, "Use of 'Lamanite,'" 124. Duffy further suggests that linking American Indians to the Lost Tribes of Israel was a way of defending the truth of the Bible against skeptics who used the existence of this formerly unknown people to cast doubt on the veracity of the Bible's account of creation.

12. Walker, "Seeking the 'Remnant,'" 3.

13. Farmer, *On Zion's Mount*, 16. Joy Porter echoes these characterizations, asserting that Indians, as well as Freemasons, held a special place in Smith's "spiritual imagination" and referencing the widespread antebellum discussions about Indian origins (in relationship to the biblical account of Genesis) as an important influence on him. Porter, *Native American Freemasonry*, 96–97. See also C. C. Smith, "Playing Lamanite."

14. Walker, "Seeking the 'Remnant,'" 6.

15. Gutjahr, *Book of Mormon*, 115.

16. Johnson and Wilentz, *Kingdom of Matthias*, 64–67. The authors further note that shortly after this ceremony, a procession of steamboats sailed from Grand Island (where the cornerstone of Noah's planned asylum, Ararat, had been laid) to New York harbor in celebration of the opening of the Erie Canal. "Not to be outdone, the Messiah of the Jews outfitted a steamboat—dubbed, naturally, Noah's Ark—and filled it, one newspaper reported, 'with all manner of animals and creepy things.' But the Ark never made it, as planned to Manhattan, and Ararat attracted increasing public criticism and ridicule."

17. On this point, I am especially indebted to Joy Porter's clear articulation of what is at stake in the Lost Tribes thesis. Porter, *Native American Freemasonry*, 99–101.

18. Johnson and Wilentz, *Kingdom of Matthias*, 6.

19. Ibid., 11.

20. Kennedy, *Early Days of Mormonism*, 3.

21. Quinn, *Mormon Hierarchy*, 9–10, 12; Johnson and Wilentz, *Kingdom of Matthias*, 7.

22. The 1830 census of Kirtland, Geauga County, Ohio, shows Daniel Stanton living among several other families on the land of Isaac Morley. Stanton's household included five daughters and his wife, Clarinda. U.S. Bureau of the Census, *Fifth Census of the United States, 1830*, http://www.ancestry.com; Staker, *'Hearken, O Ye People,'* 45, 56; G. A. Smith, "Historical Discourse," 3.

23. The principle of common ownership was most popularly represented in the reform movement of Robert Owen, a Scottish entrepreneur who came to the United

States promoting social reform and assistance for the poor. Owen's followers became known as "Owenites" and advocated a communal economic system. Staker, '*Hearken, O Ye People,*' 37–41, 46.

24. Cook, *Revelations of the Prophet Joseph Smith,* 156. For other references to Daniel Stanton's participation in the early church, see Cannon and Cook, *Far West Record.*

25. Clarinda Stanton's baptism is confirmed in her obituary. *Deseret News,* Feb. 22, 1882. I am grateful to Connell O'Donovan for alerting me to this source.

26. Late nineteenth-century writer J. H. Kennedy elaborated, "Those remarkable nervous manifestations . . . were yet other evidences of the mood in which certain of the more emotional sections of America were preparing to receive whatever of truth, or alleged truth, might be spoken unto them. Very many of the religious meetings of the day were attended by these remarkable physical and mental phenomena that were looked upon by the ignorant mass as the moving of a divine power upon the bodies and minds of men." Kennedy, *Early Days of Mormonism,* 3.

27. Taves notes that in addition to the Methodists, the Separate Baptists helped to develop the "shout tradition" in American styles of worship. Taves, *Fits, Traces, and Visions,* 50, 76–117.

28. Johnson and Wilentz, *Kingdom of Matthias,* 9; Quinn, *Mormon Hierarchy,* 7–15; and generally Staker, '*Hearken, O Ye People.*'

29. Staker, '*Hearken, O Ye People,*' 5–92. See also G. A. Smith, "Historical Discourse," 3–4; Bringhurst, "The 'Descendants of Ham' in Zion," 301–2.

30. Harmon, "[Statement of] Reuben P. Harmon," 1.

31. Miller, "Joel Miller's Statement," 2; Harmon, "[Statement of] Reuben P. Harmon," 1.

32. The Shakers provide the closest analogue. Erik Seeman argues that Shaker women used Indian spirit narratives (recorded as messages from dead Indians) to express "nuanced views about the legacy of colonialism and white male violence." Seeman, "Native Spirits, Shaker Visions."

33. Staker, '*Hearken, O Ye People,*' 81–82.

34. Walker, "Seeking the 'Remnant,'" 7.

35. Duffy, "Use of 'Lamanite,'" 126.

36. On the centrality of women in these practices, see Newell and Avery, "Sweet Counsel and Seas of Tribulation," 151–62.

37. Jesse Moss, 1938, quoted in Staker, '*Hearken, O Ye People,*' 83.

38. Vogel and Dunn, "'Tongue of Angels,'" 4.

39. The first quote is from John Whitmer, and the second quote is from Josiah Jones, both in Staker, '*Hearken, O Ye People,*' 85.

40. U.S. Bureau of the Census, *Fourth Census of the United States, 1820,* http://www.ancestry.com. For additional genealogical information respecting the Stantons, I am deeply indebted to Connell O'Donovan. O'Donovan, personal email communication to the author, May 12, 2012. O'Donovan suggests that Clarinda was pregnant with Lucy at the time of her marriage to Daniel Stanton. There does not appear to be any evidence to support Laah Ceil's claim that her mother was Delaware and her father Mohawk.

41. See Larson, *Internal Improvement.*

42. Staker, *'Hearken, O Ye People,'* 82.

43. See Bowes, *Pioneers and Exiles*; Buss, *Winning the West with Words*; Hurt, *The Ohio Frontier*; Miller, *Forced Removal of American Indians from the Northeast.*

44. According to the Utah Cemetery Inventory, which is based on contemporary death notices, "Lucy C. Bassett" was born on Dec. 28, 1816. *Utah Cemetery Inventory*, http://www.ancestry.com. Altering her place of birth from Manlius to an unnamed locale in western New York did not necessarily lend credence to her claim that her father was a Mohawk chief. The eponymous Mohawk valley and other portions of the traditional homelands of the Iroquois people known as the "Keepers of the Eastern Door" are situated across the central, northern, and northeastern portions of present-day New York. On Iroquois history in New York, see Hauptman, *Conspiracy of Interests.*

45. Tubbee, *Sketch of the Life* (1852), 77.

46. Ibid., 15.

47. Walker asserts out that while Smith "reigned in the unregulated Kirtland charisma that focused on the Indian," the "hope of Indian destiny and Zion remained unabated in the Mormon mind." Walker, "Seeking the 'Remnant,'" 9.

48. Tubbee, *Sketch of the Life* (1848), 77.

49. Walker, "Seeking the 'Remnant,'" 8, 10.

50. In her autobiographical account, she says she was baptized before she was ten years old, which, if true, suggests she was baptized into something other than the Mormon Church, since the missionaries first brought the new religion into Ohio only in 1830, when she was fourteen. She does not indicate when she was first baptized into the Mormon Church. Tubbee, *Sketch of the Life* (1848), 78.

51. Ibid.

52. Walker, "Seeking the 'Remnant,'" 11. Stanton's patriarchal blessing does not appear in the only compendium of such blessings from the Kirtland era, but the collection is not comprehensive. See Marquardt, *Early Patriarchal Blessings.*

53. Harmon, "[Statement of] Reuben P. Harmon," 1.

54. Stapley and Wright, "Female Ritual Healing in Mormonism."

55. Newell and Avery, "Sweet Counsel and Seas of Tribulation," 158.

56. Harmon, "[Statement of] Reuben P. Harmon," 1. Pete's last name is uncertain. He was owned by the Kerr family for a time, but it is unclear if he ever used that surname. He is almost universally referred to by the moniker "Black Pete." A few scholars have connected him to other people of color in early Mormonism, including Okah Tubbee. In addition to Staker, see, e.g., Bringhurst, "'Descendants of Ham' in Zion" and *Saints, Slaves, and Blacks.*

57. Staker's interpretation of Pete's influence is that "by drawing on the slave shout experience, Black Pete played a significant but heretofore unrecognized role, directing worship during Mormonism's earliest weeks of worship in Ohio in a direction previously unknown to the Disciples of Christ and the community at large." Staker, *'Hearken, O Ye People,'* 29, 77–78.

58. G. A. Smith, "Historical Discourse," 4.

59. Staker, 'Hearken, O Ye People,' 105.

60. Hill, Rooker, and Wimmer, *Kirtland Economy Revisited*, 1–15; Larson, *Internal Improvement*, 71–147.

61. Snow, *Personal Writings of Eliza Roxcy Snow*, 10.

62. Tubbee, *Sketch of the Life* (1848), 80.

63. Cannon and Cook, *Far West Record*, 6–7; Cook, *Revelations of the Prophet*, 156–57; Walker, "Seeking the 'Remnant,'" 9.

64. Walker, "Seeking the 'Remnant,'" 12–13.

65. Staker underscores the point that few Ohio Mormons had much contact with living Native peoples in the period prior to their exodus to Missouri. 'Hearken, O Ye People,' 82.

66. Walker, "Seeking the 'Remnant,'" 9–10, 13–14.

67. Staker, 'Hearken, O Ye People,' 95.

68. On accusations of interfering with slaves, see Fluhman, 'Peculiar People,' 53; on "Indian tampering," see Walker, "Seeking the 'Remnant,'" 15. In 1840, Parley P. Pratt offered a point-by-point refutation of the charges against the Mormons. Pratt, *History of the Late Persecution*, 6–7.

69. Fluhman, 'Peculiar People,' 56–57.

70. Winn, "Missouri Context of Antebellum Mormonism," 23; Bushman and Bushman, *Building the Kingdom*, 26; Walker, "Seeking the 'Remnant,'" 15–16.

71. In 1870, Solon Bassett, then living in Springville, Utah, was listed as age 36, placing his birth sometime in 1834. U.S. Bureau of the Census, *Ninth Census of the United States, 1870,* http://www.ancestry.com.

72. Curtis, *1836 Clay County, Missouri State Tax List*, 8–9, 40. This record indicates that both Oliver Bassett and Daniel Stanton paid their poll taxes, as did Heman Bassett, Oliver's brother, who also had one cow valued at $10.

73. Cannon and Cook, *Far West Record*, 88–90.

74. Vogel and Dunn, "'Tongue of Angels,'" 5–6. Smith continued to refine his thinking on the matter over the succeeding decade.

75. Quinn, *Mormon Hierarchy*, 7. In his chapter "The Evolution of Authority," Quinn asserts that "the official account of Mormon origins obscures . . . the egalitarian nature of the church before 1835," by retroactively naturalizing, editing, and revising early inconsistencies to produce a more seamless account of the church's development.

76. Cannon and Cook, *Far West Record*, 89.

77. Miller, "Joel Miller's Statement," 2.

78. Daniel Stanton was among those Crandall claimed to perceive in this way. He testified at the August church conference that she had told him, "she saw his heart and saw two books in it, and that there was a Nephite standing behind him to push him into his duty." Cannon and Cook, *Far West Record*, 79–93.

79. Cannon and Cook, *Far West Record*, 63n2.

80. Launius and Hallwas, introduction to *Kingdom on the Mississippi Revisited*, 3–4.

81. Staker, 'Hearken, O Ye People,' 111–14.

82. Launius and Hallwas, introduction, 4.

83. The reasons for the fall of Kirtland are detailed in voluminous literature and largely revolve around the failures of Smith's ambitious economic programs, including Mormon banking and currency schemes, in the context of the Panic of 1837, as well as rumors of polygamy, and personal animosities. See Hill, Rooker, and Wimmer, *Kirtland Economy Revisited*; Fluhman, *'Peculiar People'*; and Quinn, *Mormon Hierarchy*.

84. Wood, "Abridged Sketch of the Life of Semira L. Wood," in Mitchell, "Biographies, 1935," LTPSC, 1.

85. *Far West*, Aug. 11, 1836, 1:27; Bushman and Bushman, *Building the Kingdom*, 22, 26.

86. The causes and circumstances of the conflict have been detailed, analyzed, and debated at great length by historians. For a start, see LeSueur, *1838 Mormon War in Missouri* and Spencer, *Missouri Mormon Experience*. Among the more intriguing analyses is that of Walker because he argues that local fears about a Mormon-Indian combination were at the root of the Missourians' attacks on the Saints. Walker, "Seeking the 'Remnant,'" 20.

87. Walker, "Seeking the 'Remnant,'" 18–19.

88. Bushman and Bushman, *Building the Kingdom*, 26.

89. One narrative by Elias Hutchings describes the Mormon expulsion: "Trule the seens to those who witnessed what my eyes have beheld was heart rending how we left this state being forced amediately away and not all having teams at their comand and the few teams that was with us was very busy carrying families perhaps one days journey then unloaded on the ground to do the best they could the teams then returning for others. Thus were the saints exposed to the cold rain, and the inclemency of the weather." Hutchings, "Autobiography, ca. 1842," 30, LTPSC.

90. Stephen Aron draws a similar comparison in *American Confluence*, 237.

91. In addition to Hutchings, see, e.g., Pratt, *History of the Late Persecution*, 22–23; U.S. Congress, House, "'Latter-day Saints', alias Mormons," 2–4. The footprints were mentioned, e.g., in Mulholland, *Address to Americans*, 3–4, and are ubiquitous in American Indian oral histories of removal.

92. Tubbee, *Sketch of the Life* (1848), 80.

93. Kettley, Garr, and Manscill, *Mormon Thoroughfare*, 95.

94. Asbury, *Reminiscences of Quincy, Illinois*, 76.

95. Black and Bennett, *City of Refuge*; Hallwas and Launius, *Cultures in Conflict*; Woods, "Two Sides of a River."

96. Wood, "Abridged Sketch," 1.

97. U.S. Bureau of the Census, *Sixth Census of the United States, 1840*. http://www.ancestry.com. The census does not list Oliver Bassett's occupation but confirms that he and Lucy were living in Quincy with their children Solon (age 6), Ann (4), and Semira (2).

98. Hutchings, "Autobiography, ca. 1842," LTPSC.

99. Cannon and Cook, *Far West Record*, 290; Cook, *Revelations of the Prophet Joseph Smith*, 157. A "stake" is a group of LDS congregations in a particular area, not unlike a diocese within the Catholic Church. Today, stake presidents oversee their

congregations, including meetings, ordinances, conferences, and the fiscal matters of the stake, though these responsibilities have changed somewhat over time. They are not paid for their service. Kettley, Garr, and Manscill note that the Quincy stake was short-lived, since many Mormons left to follow Smith to Commerce, where he established Nauvoo. Within one year, the stake had been reduced to an "ordinary branch" numbering only seventy members. *Mormon Thoroughfare*, 108.

100. Stapley and Wright, "Female Ritual Healing," 4–6.

101. Wood, "Abridged Sketch," 1.

102. Stapley and Wright, "Female Ritual Healing," 6–7.

103. In addition to Sally Crandall, the witnesses subpoenaed were Carter Graham, Mr. Whitney "the carpenter," and Warren Cook, in whose own divorce case Oliver H. Bassett had been a witness earlier the same year. Cook had initiated his divorce on the grounds that his wife was adulterous and did not perform appropriate household and wifely duties. The divorce immediately preceding the Bassetts' case was initiated on the grounds of bigamy. No reason was given in the case of the Bassetts' divorce. Divorce, Bassett, Harmon (C) [and] Bassett, Lucy Ann (D), Sept. 6, 1843, case 294, box C9, Adams County, Ill., Clerk of the Circuit Court, Chancery case files, 1827–54, Family History Library, Salt Lake City, Utah.

104. Wood, "Abridged Sketch," 1.

105. Daniel and Clarinda Stanton took the girls, Ann and Semira, to Lima, Iowa Territory, where Daniel had been appointed a seat on the high council in 1843. In the second 1848 edition of the autobiography, Laah Ceil states that she met William McCary in Iowa, where her father "made a visit" with his family. But is unclear if she was living with them there or was just visiting and returned to Quincy. Semira's later recollection suggests that the girls went to Iowa without their mother and perhaps without their brother, Solon. Ibid.; Tubbee, *Sketch of the Life* (1848), 78, 80.

106. Tubbee, *Sketch of the Life* (1852), 73.

107. Tubbee, *Sketch of the Life* (1848), 79.

108. Kimball, "Captivity Narrative on Mormon Trails," 82. Kimball asserts that Louis Dana and Shawnee convert Joseph Herring were ordained in 1845. Walker suggests that Dana was the unnamed Oneida man ordained in 1840. Walker, "Seeking the 'Remnant,'" 22–24. On Dana, see also Palmer, "Did Joseph Smith Commit Treason," 52–58; Allen, "One Man's Nauvoo," 46. According to Ronald K. Esplin, Smith's call for Dana to unite and missionize the western Indians was confidential and would not have been known to most within the church. Esplin, "'A Place Prepared,'" 98.

109. Walker, "Seeking the 'Remnant,'" 25–29.

110. Ibid., 91.

111. *Voree Herald*, Oct. 1846, 1:10. Hyde's role in marrying the couple is also referenced in the *True Latter Day Saints' Herald*, Mar. 1861, 2:1, 5. It should be noted, however, that both of these publications were critical of Hyde and may have overstated his role in bringing McCary into the church.

112. Tubbee, *Sketch of the Life* (1848), 80.

113. *The True Latter Day Saints' Herald*, Mar. 1861, 2:1, 5. By this time, there were about 15,000–17,000 people living in Nauvoo, and Brigham Young was launching a

plan to lead them to the Rocky Mountains. Bennett, "Lamanism, Lymanism, and Cornfields," 46.

114. Reeve makes a similar observation in *Religion of a Different Color,* chapter 5.

115. Tubbee, *Sketch of the Life* (1852), 75.

116. Wood, "Abridged Sketch," 1.

117. Tubbee, *Sketch of the Life* (1852), 92.

CHAPTER THREE

1. According to historian Ruth M. Alexander, "Washingtonianism marked the first time that American women of relatively low rank joined and played a prominent role in reform. The thousands of women who established Martha Washington societies in the 1840s throughout the Northeast and Midwest were . . . primarily from the homes of laborers, artisans, shopkeepers, and clerks . . . [and while] women of higher standing and privilege were not absent from the movement . . . the leadership of most female Washingtonian societies was probably in the hands of women of humble background and social standing." Alexander, "'We Are Engaged as a Band of Sisters,'" 764.

2. *Weekly Reveille,* May 4, 1846. Interestingly, the autobiography also makes oblique reference to the Martha Washington societies. Allen, *Thrilling Sketch,* 12–14.

3. Conyers, *Brief History,* 3–4.

4. Ibid., 31.

5. Robert McCary P. Atty. Almon Baldwin, 1839, Deed Book BB, 228–29, MDAH.

6. Pusey, *Builders of the Kingdom,* 51–56; Samuel Whitney Richards, Diaries, 1:4–15, LTPSC. See also Speek, *"God Has Made Us a Kingdom."* Quinn points out that the ascendancy of the Quorum was not immediate or absolute but a matter of considerable negotiation and adjustment over many years. Quinn, *Mormon Hierarchy,* 61.

7. Thomas and Sarah Colborn, Iowa, to Daniel Bowen, Lansingville, Post Office, Tompkins County, New York, June 2, 1846, Thomas Colborn Letters, LTPSC.

8. *Voree Herald,* Oct. 1846, 1:10. This publication was critical of Hyde and thus may have overstated his role in bringing McCary into the church.

9. *Gospel Herald,* Oct. 5, 1848; *True Latter Day Saints' Herald,* Mar. 1861, 2:1–6. Thompson would later become an adherent of Nachash theology that sought to justify the subservience of blacks and likened them to orangutans. See Davis, "Negro a Beast."

10. *Cincinnati Commercial,* Oct. 27, 1846.

11. *Gospel Herald,* Oct. 5, 1848.

12. *Cincinnati Commercial,* Oct. 27, 1846.

13. *The Weekly Reveille,* Mar. 30, 1846.

14. Fluhman, *'A Peculiar People,'* 97–98; Bushman, *Joseph Smith,* 530–31.

15. *Gospel Herald,* Oct. 5, 1848.

16. *Cincinnati Commercial,* Oct. 27, 1846.

17. Louisville was also a locus for Indian sympathetic societies. The Board of Indian Missions published a weekly paper there, announcing such events as the "annual meeting of the American Indian Mission Association" where "the friends of the Indian race, from all quarters of the land, are most earnestly entreated to meet with and aid this society in prosecuting its noble cause." *Indian Advocate*, Sept. 1847. This particular paper emphasized "causes" among the Choctaws and Creeks.

18. *Cincinnati Commercial*, Nov. 17, 1846. A similar account was carried in *Nauvoo New Citizen*, Dec. 23, 1846. A compendium of patriarchal blessings from this era is available in Marquardt, *Early Patriarchal Blessings*.

19. *Cincinnati Commercial*, Nov. 17, 1846.

20. The Walum Olum or "Red Record," is recognized by neither modern Delaware people nor anthropologists as a genuine record of Lenape history. It was first discovered, translated, and publicized in 1836 by Constantine Samuel Rafinesque, a scientist and doctor who worked to convince contemporaries that it was an ancient text of Delaware origin. Rafinesque, *American Nations*; Brinton, *The Lenâpé and their Legends*; Oestreicher, "Anatomy of the Walam Olum."

21. Jennings, "First Mormon Mission to the Indians," 294–96. See also Pratt, *Autobiography of Parley Parker Pratt*.

22. Deloria, *Playing Indian*, 76–85, 90–91.

23. Among others, see Berkhofer, *White Man's Indian*; Bank, "Staging the 'Native'"; Bellin and Mielke, *Native Acts*; Sayre, *Indian Chief as Tragic Hero*.

24. *Semi-Weekly Eagle [Weekly Eagle]*, Mar. 1, 1849.

25. Michael Oberg uses "professional Indian" to describe contemporary figure Eleazer Williams (Kahnawake Mohawk) who was "a descendant of an unredeemed Puritan captive carried away to the Catholic Mohawk town of Kahnawake early in the eighteenth century, a Mohawk missionary to the Oneida Indians in central New York and Wisconsin, and an active supporter of the effort beginning early in the nineteenth century to 'remove' eastern Indians to new homes in the American West." Oberg, *Professional Indian*, ix.

26. Bank, "Staging the 'Native,'" 461–86; *Democratic Telegraph and Texas Register*, Apr. 5, 1849. The Houston paper was reprinting news of one of Copway's lectures in New York.

27. A useful study of this phenomenon in New England is Jean M. O'Brien, *Firsting and Lasting*.

28. Deloria, *Playing Indian*, 78.

29. Renato Rosaldo describes "imperialist nostalgia" as a paradox: "In any of its versions, imperialist nostalgia uses a pose of 'innocent yearning' both to capture people's imagination and to conceal its complicity with often brutal domination." Rosaldo, "Imperialist Nostalgia," 108. Gordon Sayre argues, conversely, that "analyzing the resistance of Native Americans to colonization as a tragedy and its leaders as tragic heroes yields a better explanation . . . than do the concepts of the vanishing Indian or of imperialist nostalgia." Sayre, *Indian Chief as Tragic Hero*, 5. Benjamin F. Reiss has described a similar nostalgia expressed in the popularity of P. T. Barnum's exhibition of Joice Heth, reputedly George Washington's formerly enslaved

nursemaid, which he asserts, "expressed a conservative longing for a place and time in which blacks were perfectly in their place." Reiss, "P. T. Barnum," 88.

30. Tubbee, *Sketch of the Life* (1852), 4.

31. This phrase appeared as the title of an article in the *Nauvoo New Citizen,* Dec. 23, 1846. The article was basically a reprint of the *Cincinnati Commercial* piece from Nov. 17.

32. *Zion's Reveille,* Feb. 25, 1847.

33. There were nearly 90 settlements in the area known as Winter Quarters, in addition to the central church headquarters, near present-day Florence. Contemporaneous accounts sometimes use "Winter Quarters" to describe one or more of these other encampments. For accounts of the Winter Quarters experience, see The Winter Quarters Project, Brigham Young University, http://winterquarters .byu.edu.

34. Bennett, "Lamanism, Lymanism, and Cornfields," 47.

35. H. H. Cole, Letter, Franklin Township, Lee County, Iowa, to James Winans, Milton, Trumbull County, Ohio, Nov. 26, 1846, LTPSC; Bennett, "Lamanism, Lymanism, and Cornfields," 47; Wood, "An Abridged Sketch," 1.

36. Wood, "An Abridged Sketch," 1–2.

37. Stout, *On the Mormon Frontier,* 244; Willard Richards, Journal, 1847, n.p., Willard Richards Papers, 1821–54, Latter-day Saints Church History Library (hereafter CHL); Lee, *Journals of John D. Lee,* 100–103; Campbell, *Robert Lang Campbell Journal,* 56, LTPSC, http://lib.byu.edu/collections.

38. Cazier, "A copy of the Sketch of the Life," 3, LTPSC; Kimball, *Heber C. Kimball,* 145; see also Bennett, "Lamanism, Lymanism, and Cornfields" and *Mormons at the Missouri.*

39. Purdy, "They Marched Their Way West," 20–23.

40. Lee, *Journals of John D. Lee,* 100–103.

41. Newell and Avery suggested that sending a husband on a mission was a source of pride and status for Mormon women. How much more so to have a prophet for a husband? Newell and Avery, "Sweet Counsel and Seas of Tribulation," 154.

42. Campbell, *Robert Campbell Journal,* 56, LTPSC, http://lib.byu.edu/collections.

43. Ibid., 58.

44. Bathsheba B. Smith (1846) and Mary Ellen Kimball (1847), both quoted in Kimball, "Captivity Narrative on Mormon Trails," 82.

45. It is unclear from the context of the entry whether or not Richards meant to indicate that McCary and his wife came into the meeting with a stranger or that McCary, accompanied by his wife, *was* a stranger. Both interpretations could be sustained. Church Historian's Office, General Church Minutes, 26 Mar. 1847–6 Apr. 1847, CHL. It is possible, though not probable, that the stranger was L. L. Allen, the Methodist preacher who would help pen the first edition of the autobiography in 1848 and may have been acting as their manager as early as 1847.

46. Ibid.

47. Campbell, *Robert Campbell Journal,* 56, LTPSC, http://lib.byu.edu/collections.

48. Stout, *On the Mormon Frontier,* 243–44.

49. Lee, *Journals of John D. Lee,* 162n41. Bennett estimates the total number of followers as two hundred for Wight/Miller and two hundred for Cutler. Bennett, "Lamanism, Lymanism, and Cornfields," 49–55.

50. Willard Richards, Journal, 1847, n.p., CHL.

51. Bennett, "Lamanism, Lymanism, and Cornfields," 54.

52. Campbell, *Robert Campbell Journal,* 56, LTPSC, http://lib.byu.edu /collections.

53. Gross, *What Blood Won't Tell,* 30. On the frequency of and reaction to interracial unions from the colonial period through the mid-nineteenth century, see, e.g., Brown, *Good Wives, Nasty Wenches, and Anxious Patriarchs;* Fowler, *Northern Attitudes Towards Interracial Marriage;* Hodes, *White Women, Black Men;* Robinson, *Dangerous Liaisons.*

54. Pascoe, *What Comes Naturally,* 22–27. The 1845 Illinois law is cited on 329n44.

55. Whipple, *"Autobiography and Journal of Nelson W. Whipple,"* 31, CHL.

56. Church Historian's Office, General Church Minutes, Mar. 26, 1847–Apr. 6, 1847, CHL. On the curse of Ham and the emergence of a scriptural rationale for slavery and white supremacy, see Haynes, *Noah's Curse.*

57. Young, *Journal of Brigham,* 213.

58. Church Historian's Office, General Church Minutes, Mar. 26, 1847–Apr. 6, 1847, CHL.

59. Allen, *Thrilling Sketch,* 20.

60. Church Historian's Office, General Church Minutes, Mar. 26, 1847–Apr. 6, 1847, CHL.

61. Ibid.

62. Hosea Stout, head of the Winter Quarters police, regarded the Omahas as idle thieves. Stout, *On the Mormon Frontier,* 244; Kimball, "Captivity Narrative on Mormon Trails," 84–85.

63. Deloria, *Playing Indian,* 90.

64. *True Latter Day Saints' Herald,* Mar. 1861, 2:1.

65. Bringhurst, *Saints, Slaves, and Blacks,* 84–85.

66. Church Historian's Office, General Church Minutes, Mar. 26, 1847–Apr. 6, 1847, CHL.

67. Ibid.

68. *True Latter Day Saints' Herald,* Mar., 1861, 2:1.This is a retrospective account of the events, couched within a scathing condemnation of church leader Orson Hyde, who was accused of marrying McCary "to a white sister, and [telling] him to go forth among the Gentiles to deceive them."

69. Church Historian's Office, General Church Minutes, Mar. 26, 1847–Apr. 6, 1847, CHL.

70. On the rise of scientific racism and its association with both American Indians and physical examination, see Horsman, *Race and Manifest Destiny.*

71. Church Historian's Office, General Church Minutes, Mar. 26, 1847–Apr. 6, 1847, CHL.

72. Ibid.; Bringhurst, *Saints, Slaves, and Blacks*, 90–91, 98; O'Donovan, "Mormon Priesthood Ban," 82–90. Reeve provides a more elaborate explanation of the scriptural origins of Young's statements in *Religion of a Different Color*, chapter 5.

73. Berlin, *Slaves without Masters*, 236.

74. Church Historian's Office, General Church Minutes, Mar. 26, 1847–Apr. 6, 1847, CHL.

75. When Young and other church leaders confronted an analogous situation involving interracial marriage—the case of the union of "African" Elder Lewis's son, Enoch, with a white woman in 1846—Young asserted that it was against both law and nature for their seed to be amalgamated. O'Donovan, "Mormon Priesthood Ban."

76. Church Historian's Office, General Church Minutes, Mar. 26, 1847–Apr. 6, 1847, CHL.

77. Ibid.

78. Young, *Journal of Brigham*, 213.

79. Stout, *On the Mormon Frontier*, 244.

80. Bennett, "Lamanism, Lymanism, and Cornfields," 48, 57n10. Bennett refers to these crises as "doctrinal brushfires" compared to the larger problem of defection from the church.

81. Brown, *Journal of Lorenzo Brown, 1823–1900*, 1:31–32; Campbell, Robert Campbell Journal, 56, LTPSC, http://lib.byu.edu/collections.

82. Whipple, "History of Nelson Wheeler Whipple," 30, 37, Nelson Wheeler Whipple Diaries, 1863–87, LTPSC. Whipple was first counselor to Springville branch president Samuel Williams, who was apparently incapacitated by illness to such a degree that Whipple was the de facto branch president.

83. Bushman and Bushman, *Building the Kingdom*, 30.

84. Jackson, *Adventures and Experience of Joseph H. Jackson*, 14.

85. Fluhman, *'A Peculiar People,'* 97–98.

86. Bennett, "Lamanism, Lymanism, and Cornfields," 48.

87. Fluhman aptly summarizes, "Mormonism functioned like a screen upon which Americans could project their crises." Fluhman, *'A Peculiar People,'* 104.

88. Ibid., 98.

89. Jackson, *Adventures and Experience of Joseph H. Jackson*, 14–15.

90. Bushman, *Joseph Smith*, 440–41.

91. Whipple, "History of Nelson Wheeler Whipple," 37.

92. Ibid.

93. Ibid.

94. Ibid., 38. The one member who Whipple could not account for was Sylvanus Calkins. According to another witness, Calkins's wife left him because he was a follower of the "Negro prophet" and married another man the following year. Stout, *On the Mormon Frontier*, 307.

95. Bringhurst, *Saints, Slaves, and Blacks*, 90–91; O'Donovan, "Mormon Priesthood Ban." As evidence of the taint of black blood, he later referred specifically to William McCary, calling him "the negro prophet" and averring that he was cast out by the Potawatomis because of his "negro blood." Minutes of the Quorum of the Twelve, Dec. 3, 1847, 6–7, CHL, cited in O'Donovan, "'I Would Confine Them to

Their Own Species.'" See also Turner, *Brigham Young*, 221–23; Reeve, *Religion of a Different Color,* chapter 5.

96. A List of Licenses, From Grand Jury, Nov. Term 1848, Lafayette County Records, Individual Licenses Granted, 1843–50, Missouri State Archives (hereafter MSA).

97. William W. Waddell v. William McChubby, Lafayette County Records, Circuit Court, May Term 1848, MSA.

98. McCary didn't submit a plea in his defense until the summer of 1849, and when he did so, he signed only with a mark, suggesting that he remained illiterate as he claimed in the autobiography. William McChouby v. Talmon Tripp, Lafayette County Records, Circuit Court, 1849–51, MSA.

99. Whipple, "History of Nelson Wheeler Whipple," 38.

CHAPTER FOUR

1. Tubbee, *Sketch of the Life* (1852), 79; Konkle, *Writing Indian Nations,* 163–64.
2. *Daily National Intelligencer,* Nov. 23, 1847.
3. Young, *Journal of Brigham Young,* 213.
4. *Baltimore Clipper,* Nov. 24, 1847.
5. As one scholar put it, "Slaveholders in Maryland considered free blacks a standing incitement to servile disorder and placed elimination of them on the order of the day from the post-Revolutionary period right up to the eve of emancipation." Fields, *Slavery and Freedom,* 2–4.
6. *Daily National Intelligencer,* Nov. 23, 25, 1847.
7. On Williams, see Oberg, *Professional Indian.* Littlefield also notes the similarity of Tubbee's claim to those of other Lost Dauphin poseurs and the story of Ibrahima. Littlefield, *Life of Okah Tubbee,* xvii.
8. *Baltimore Clipper,* Nov. 24, 1847.
9. Ibid.
10. *Baltimore Clipper,* Dec. 21, 1847.
11. *New York Herald,* Mar. 9, 1848.
12. Konkle, *Writing Indian Nations,* 165; Round, *Removable Type,* 160–61.
13. Moody, *America Takes the Stage,* 79.
14. See O'Brien, *Firsting and Lasting.*
15. Moody, *America Takes the Stage,* 86–89, 104.
16. See, e.g., a notice about a new hotel to be erected along the Indian border in Wisconsin, where "Indian dances" could be easily seen: "The Niagara of the Far West," *New-Bedford Mercury,* Sept. 29, 1837. A Pawnee Indian dance in Washington, D.C., was advertised in "From the New-York Statesman, from One of the Editors, Washington, Jan. 2, 1823," *Norwich Courier,* Jan. 22, 1823.
17. Deloria, *Playing Indian,* 73.
18. "Grand Exhibition," [1842]. Another specific reference to "Indian warriors and squaws" appears in an 1841 Boston notice; see Clapp, *Record of the Boston Stage,* 470. Maungwudaus's advertisement appeared in *Buffalo Commercial Advertiser,* Mar. 11, 1851.

19. Rourke, *American Humor*, 104, quoted in Jones, *Native Americans as Shown on the Stage*, 89.

20. *Weekly Reveille,* Apr. 6, 1846. One traveling act that made a big splash in the Ohio River city that fall and may have acted as a foil against which Warner and Lucy determined to define their own emergent stage show was the Christy's minstrels. *Cincinnati Commercial*, Nov. 5, 1846. While it is unclear whether Mormons living in and passing through Cincinnati went to the minstrel shows, at least one account confessed that while on a mission trip, they attended the theater to see some shows for the middling sorts. Richards, "Diaries, 1846–76," typescript, 1:68, LTPSC.

21. Moody notes that "many factors contributed to the deterioration of the Indian drama in the forties and fifties. The age of 'critical realism' was opening up, and audiences were no longer willing to accept the trite and overworked themes that had been popular for so many years. . . . As with the monotonous pattern of the minstrel show, the sameness of the plot in the Indian dramas and the strains on verisimilitude became intolerable." Moody, *America Takes the Stage*, 109.

22. *Baltimore Clipper*, Dec. 20, 1847.

23. Allen, *Thrilling Sketch*, 43.

24. *Brooklyn Daily Eagle*, Mar. 27, 1851.

25. Green, "Pocahontas Perplex," 703–4. In 1844, there had even appeared an autobiographical account of a man claiming to be the descendant of Pocahontas on the one side and an African king on the other. Archer, *Compendium of Slavery*. I am grateful to Arika Easley-Houser for bringing this source to my attention.

26. Murray, "Racial Identity and Self-invention in North America," 96.

27. Naylor, *African Cherokees in Indian Territory*, 218.

28. Deloria, *Playing Indian*; Green, "Tribe Called Wannabe."

29. Green, "Tribe Called Wannabe," 36–37.

30. Deloria, *Playing Indian,* 65–66.

31. *Baltimore Clipper*, Dec. 20, 1847. The "science" music anecdote was carried in the *Semi-Weekly Eagle*, Mar. 12, 1849. On his renown as a virtuoso or prodigy, see May, "May's Dramatic Encyclopedia of Baltimore, 1750–1912," 23; *New Hampshire Patriot and State Gazette*, Dec. 7, 14, 1848.

32. Beckert, "Bourgeois Institution Builders," 107.

33. May, "May's Dramatic Encyclopedia of Baltimore, 1750–1912," 13–14; *Baltimore Clipper*, Dec. 24, 1847.

34. *Baltimore Clipper*, Dec. 28, 1847.

35. Ibid., Dec. 31, 1847.

36. One scholar sums up the custom, saying, "Only the great favorites . . . ever profited by their benefits." Grisvard, "Final Years," 128. Barnum was apparently opposed to such benefits for his employees.

37. Allen was from St. Louis and had been the chaplain for the Louisiana Volunteers, the same militia group for which Tubbee claimed he had been appointed fife major, during the Mexican War. Whether they met in New Orleans, Missouri, or the eastern states is unclear. In addition to publishing the Tubbees' autobiography, in 1848, Allen also wrote and published an account of his Mexican war expe-

rience, titled *Pencillings of Scenes upon the Rio Grande*. Littlefield, *Life of Okah Tubbee*, xxiv.

38. Allen, *Thrilling Sketch*, 5.

39. Green, "Tribe Called Wannabe," 36. See also Scheckel, *Insistence of the Indian*.

40. Browder asserts, "Both the reader and the writer of an ethnic autobiography understand the implied contract: the memoirist is not telling his or her own story as much as the story of a people. In order to be heard, the ethnic autobiography must often conform to his or her audience's stereotypes about that ethnicity. . . . Ethnic autobiographies, called upon to be representatives, to be the voice of their people, have sometimes even borrowed memories." L. Browder, *Slippery Characters*, 5.

41. Deloria identifies James Fenimore Cooper's *The Redskins: Indians and Injins* (1846) as exemplary of this turn from an emphasis on Indian savagery to a "friendlier, more nostalgic image." Deloria, *Playing Indian*, 63.

42. Allen, *Thrilling Sketch*, 3.

43. Ibid., 3, 5.

44. Ibid., 5.

45. L. Browder, *Slippery Characters*, 8–9.

46. Allen, *Thrilling Sketch*, 29.

47. Ibid., 12–13.

48. L. Browder, *Slippery Characters*, 5. "Imagined community" is a term used by Benedict Anderson to explain how nationalism works. He argues that national belonging is rooted in the belief that individuals, often separated by space and circumstances, are simultaneous members of a fictive community, articulated and reinforced through forms of mass communication, most notably, newspapers. See Anderson, *Imagined Communities*.

49. D. Smith, *Mississauga Portraits*, 185–88. See Copway, *Life, Letters, and Speeches*. Toward the end of his life, Copway too became an "Indian doctor."

50. Allen, *Thrilling Sketch*, 15.

51. *The Sun*, Jan. 22, Feb. 1, 1848.

52. Tubbee, *Sketch of the Life* (1848), 81.

53. "The Chinese collection," [broadside].

54. *Daily Picayune*, July 8, 1851.

55. *Mississippi Free Trader and Natchez Gazette*, Mar. 11, 1848.

56. *New York Herald*, Mar. 9, 1848; Mason, *Performing America*, 48.

57. Thomas, *From Tennessee Slave to St. Louis Entrepreneur*, 130.

58. Castle Garden was situated on the former West Battery, once a War of 1812 fort, accessible from Manhattan Island via drawbridge. Landfill later fused the island to the tip of Manhattan. After its years as a theater and amusement park, in 1855 Castle Garden became a U.S. immigration depot. It loomed so large in the oral history of late nineteenth- and early twentieth-century European immigrants that the word "kesselgarden" in Yiddish came to mean a place where a confusing babel of languages is spoken. Castle Clinton National Monument, http://www.nps.gov/cacl.

59. *New York Herald*, July 10, 1848.

60. Ibid., July 12, 1848.

61. Green, "Tribe Called Wannabe," 31.

62. *New York Herald*, July 16, 1848. This account and the one that precedes it on July 15 suggest an air of desperation at Castle Garden, whose promoters lamented that "we are often surprised to find the attendance at this invigorating, healthy location so limited."

63. Lott, *Love and Theft*, 76.

64. *New York Herald*, July 16–21, 29, 1848.

65. Ibid., July 29, 1848.

66. Cook, *Arts of Deception*; Reiss, *Showman and the Slave*.

67. Indeed, in the subsequent edition of the autobiography, they obscured the circumstances of their sojourn in New York entirely. Tubbee, *Sketch of the Life* (1852), 79.

68. Fretz, "P. T. Barnum's Theatrical Selfhood," 98.

69. Guest Register, Tontine Hotel, Aug. 28, 1848, New Haven Hotels Collection, 1847–1973, New Haven Museum.

70. Jones, quoted in Konkle, *Writing Indian Nations*, 188. See generally D. Smith, *Sacred Feathers*.

71. Tubbee, *Sketch of the Life* (1852), 80.

72. See O'Brien, *Firsting and Lasting*.

73. Deloria, *Playing Indian*, 72–73.

74. *Boston Daily Atlas*, Nov. 8, 18, 1848.

75. *Farmer's Cabinet*, Nov. 16, 1848.

76. *Ibid*.

77. Tubbee, *Sketch of the Life* (1848), 74–77.

78. "Masonic Chit Chat," *Freemason's Monthly Magazine* 8, no. 1 (Nov. 1, 1848): 384; vol. 9 (1850): 64. Also referred to in Pratt, *Historical Sketch of Early Masonry in Michigan*, 14; *Proceedings of the Grand Lodge of the Most Ancient and Honorable Fraternity*, 363; *Transactions of the Grand Lodge of Ancient York Masons*; 15; *Masonic Signet and Literary Mirror* 3 (1850): 119–20.

79. Clarke, *Manchester, A Brief Record of its Past*, 215; *Proceedings of the Grand Lodge of Freemasons of New Hampshire*, 194, 224.

80. Porter, *Native American Freemasonry*, 94–96. Porter disputes Clyde R. Forsberg's contention that the Book of Mormon is "a well-crafted defense of Christian Masonry." Another useful critique of Forsberg is Duffy, "Clyde Forsberg's *Equal Rites*."

81. According to Oliver H. Olney, Emma Smith, Joseph Smith's first wife, organized a women's temperance society in Nauvoo in 1842 with "degrees" that mirrored the structure of Masonic orders. Oliver H. Olney, "Journal," April 6–12, 1842, Oliver H. Olney Papers, 1842–43, Yale Collection of Western Americana, Beinecke Rare Book and Manuscript Library.

82. Porter, *Native American Freemasonry*, 119.

83. The relationship between Tubbee's Masonic connections and his subsequent downfall are addressed in Chapter 5. See, e.g., *Masonic Signet and Literary Mirror* 3 (1850): 119–20.

84. Bringhurst describes Lewis's role in the church, as well as McCary's but does not posit contact between them. Bringhurst, *Saints, Slaves, and Blacks*, 90–91.

85. *Proceedings of the One Hundredth Anniversary of the Granting of Warrant 459 to African Lodge*, 19; Hinks, *To Awaken My Afflicted Brethren*, 70.

86. Tubbee, *Sketch of the Life* (1852), 92–93. They also purported to treat several Native people in New Bedford. Robbins provided a testimonial included in the 1852 edition of the autobiography. In addition to his participation in Christian temperance activities in New Bedford, Robbins was a local constable. Crapo, *New Bedford Directory*, 14, 35.

87. The earliest testimonials are from March 1849 in New Bedford and appear in Tubbee, *Sketch of the Life* (1852), 92–93.

88. *Daily Journal and Courier*, Dec. 4, 1848, Jan. 22, 1849.

89. *Semi-Weekly Eagle*, Mar. 12, 1849; see also *Boston Courier*, Feb. 8, 1849; *Saturday Evening Post*, Feb. 10, 1849; *Massachusetts Ploughman and New England Journal of Agriculture*, Feb. 10, 1849; *Maine Farmer*, Feb. 15, 1849; *Boston Investigator*, Feb. 21, 1849.

90. Tubbee, *Sketch of the Life* (1852), 80.

91. Ibid., 80–81.

92. Ibid. Littlefield points out that the fire was so extensive that it spread from city buildings to ships in the Missouri River. Such destruction would have further hampered the Tubbees' efforts to continue their travels via steamboat. Littlefield, *Life of Okah Tubbee*, 145n105.

93. *Sanitary Survey of St. Louis*, 41–42.

94. Woods, "Between the Borders," 157. Woods notes that the Mormons in St. Louis were hit hard by the cholera epidemic. When Laah Ceil mentions in the autobiography that death visited the "next room to mine," one wonders if she was referring to lodgings in the Mound House Hotel, where local Mormon migration agent Nathaniel H. Felt had found temporary housing for emigrating Saints.

95. Laah Ceil says they left St. Louis around the first of July. Tubbee, *Sketch of the Life* (1852), 80–81.

96. Ibid., 76.

97. William W. Waddell v. William McChubby, Lafayette County Records, Circuit Court, May Term 1848, MSA. Littlefield states that "McChubby" had purchased the farm from Hosea and Mary Ashcraft in August 1847 for $240 and that he hired the lawyers Wood, Sharp, and Ridgley to countersue. Littlefield, *Life of Okah Tubbee*, 145–46, 146n106.

98. Tubbee, *Sketch of the Life* (1852), 81.

99. Ibid.

100. Wood, "Abridged Sketch," 2.

101. D. D. Mitchell, St. Louis, to William Medill, Commissioner of Indian Affairs, Washington, D.C., Apr. 25, 1849, enclosing a petition of the Munsee Chiefs to the President of the United States, March 1849. Letters Received by the Office of Indian Affairs, 1824–51, Record Group 75 (hereafter RG75), National Archives and Records Administration (hereafter NARA).

102. Silverman, *Red Brethren*, 16, 207.

103. Woods, "Between the Borders," 156–59.

104. Tubbee, *Sketch of the Life* (1852), 82. Ceil implies in the autobiography that their possessions were burned, but it is clear from letters to the Indian commissioner that their belongings had instead been stolen.

105. Luke Lea, Fort Leavenworth Agency, to D. D. Mitchell, Commissioner of Indian Affairs, Washington, D.C., Jan. 26, 1850, Office of Indian Affairs (hereafter OIA), NARA.

106. Ibid. They also claimed that they had paid some expenses for Fanny Beach, daughter of Parish LeClair, but when they requested payment of the note, Beach instead demanded $100 from them, asserting that they owed her father money instead of the other way round.

107. Tubbee, *Sketch of the Life* (1852), 82–83, 87, 89–90. A transcription of his licenses to practice medicine in Missouri appears in the 1852 edition of the autobiography, one from Platte County in 1849 and another from Jackson County in 1850. These licenses were not indications of training or education but merely business or merchant licenses for which applicants had simply to pay a fee or tax in order to certify their practice. As Littlefield also notes, while Laah Ceil's eldest child Solon was with the family during early 1850, because the autobiography claims he accompanied Okah Tubbee to St. Louis in an attempt to seek redress for their losses from the Indian agent there, by the time the census taker arrived in September 1850, he was apparently no longer living with them. Littlefield, *Life of Okah Tubbee*, 146–47, 147n110; Bureau of the Census, Seventh Census, 1850, http://www.ancestry.com.

108. "Masonic Chit Chat," *Freemason's Monthly Magazine* 9 (1850): 64.

109. For example, when McCary (Tubbee) appeared before the Natchez police board in 1843 to give evidence of his good standing, John A. Quitman was among the Natchez notables who gave testimony on his behalf. Quitman, a Whig politician, was a well-known Mason in the city and also participated in the local militia. Tubbee, *Sketch of the Life* (1852), 41; Clayton, *Antebellum Natchez*, 119.

110. Tubbee, *Sketch of the Life* (1852), 83–84.

111. *Masonic Signet and Literary Mirror* 3 (1850): 119–20.

112. Ibid.

CHAPTER FIVE

1. Johnson, *William Johnson's Natchez*, 2:727n13.

2. "Masonic Chit Chat," *Freemason's Monthly Magazine* 9 (1850): 64.

3. U.S. Bureau of the Census, *Seventh Census*, 1850, http://www.ancestry.com.

4. Tubbee, *Sketch of the Life* (1852), 83; Schlicher, "Terre Haute in 1850," 259–60.

5. *Daily Ohio Statesman*, June 10, 1851. For early published versions of the "oak tub" story, *Independent American*, Oct. 3, 1851; *Cleveland Herald*, Sept. 17, 1851; *Spirit of the Times*, Sept. 30, 1851, June 26, 1852. Sol Smith's first published mention of the "oak tub" story was in the 1854 edition of his memoir. S. Smith, *Theatrical Journey-Work*, 26–28.

6. I have seen only one other reference to Tubbee as a guitar player: *Daily Standard*, Sept. 30, 1851.

7. *Daily Ohio Statesman*, June 10, 1851.

8. Schlicher, "Terre Haute in 1850," 260.

9. *Daily Picayune*, July 8, 1851.

10. *Louisville Courier*, June 28, 1851.

11. Ibid., *Daily Picayune*, July 8, 1851. The Franklin *Examiner* story was carried in both these newspapers.

12. Tubbee, *Sketch of the Life* (1848), 26.

13. See, e.g., *Maine Farmer*, Aug. 26, 1847. The same Montague ad ran in this paper repeatedly during 1847–48.

14. A wide variety of advertising cards for Indian medicines can be found at Patent Medicine Labels and Advertisements, Library of Congress, http://www.loc.gov /pictures/item/2002696083.

15. Fryer Jr., *Indian Guide to Health*; *Indian Doctor's Family Physician*; *House-Keeper's Guide, and Indian Doctor*; Greene, *Dr. R. Greene's Indianopathy*.

16. See, e.g., Skinner, "Domestic Medicines"; "Medical Profession," *North American*, July 23, 1852; *New York Ledger*, Jan. 29, 1859.

17. *Louisville Courier*, June 28, 1851. This piece is the first time a paper cast any doubt on Laah Ceil's stage persona, but it is unclear whether the editor doubted her Indianness or her royalty.

18. *Daily Picayune*, July 8, 1851.

19. Ibid., July 23, 1839.

20. Ibid., July 8, 1851. An identical story was carried again on July 9, 1851.

21. Ibid. The incident apparently occurred in Philadelphia during 1848.

22. After describing his costume, the men concluded that he "looked Choctaw, all over," but they were still able to recognize him.

23. *Masonic Signet and Literary Mirror* 3 (1850): 120.

24. Horsman, *Race and Manifest Destiny*, 151–57.

25. Clayton, *Vindication of the Recent and Prevailing Policy*, 18. O'Brien points out that the prominence of New England voices in the opposition to Indian removal prompted their southern and western counterparts to ask, "'What happened to *your* Indians?'" O'Brien, *Firsting and Lasting*, xviii.

26. *Louisville Weekly Democrat*, Sept. 10, 1851. This piece was also carried in the *Covington Journal*, 1851. Gross observes that racial "experts" sometimes had their opinions overturned by juries who arrived at different determinations on the basis of "common sense" and how "these supposedly solid ways of knowing race were surprisingly indeterminate and unreliable, particularly within a society where race was such a crucial aspect of identity." Gross, *What Blood Won't Tell*, 38, 46.

27. *Choctaw Intelligencer*, Oct. 15, 1851.

28. See, e.g., *Adams Sentinel*, July 14, 1851; *Bangor Daily Whig & Courier*, July 19, 1851.

29. The ad stated that Gardner was "introducing" Tubbee to "his audience." *Buffalo Daily Courier*, Aug. 4–5, 1851. Bishop and Bochsa's tawdry Victorian romance was said to be the basis of George De Maurier's 1894 novel *Trilby*. Bochsa was also rumored to be a forger and a bigamist. Pick, *Svengali's Web*, 98.

30. *Buffalo Commercial Advertiser*, Aug. 9, 1851.

31. The playbill is printed on unnumbered pages preceding the text itself. Tubbee, *Sketch of the Life* (1852). The account referred to the toddler as the Tubbees' "YOUNG BRUCE," an allusion to Robert the Bruce, Scottish independence hero. "Bruce's Address to his Army" was one of Tubbee's original flute arrangements on the program that night. The phrase "young Bruce" was thus not meant to indicate Mosholeh's nickname, but a way of introducing their little "brave," while also riffing on the Scottish flavor of the evening's entertainments. In addition to this piece, Tubbee also performed "Bonnie Woods and Braes," a popular bagpipe tune, and Robert Burns's popular "Auld Lang Syne" and "Killey Cranky," a Scottish anthem alluding to a battle during the Jacobite uprising. Bantock, *Sixty Patriotic Songs of All Nations*, 14–15.

32. *Buffalo Commercial Advertiser*, Aug. 16, 18, 1851.

33. Landon, "Negro Migration," 22–36. Among many other cities and locales that experienced an exodus of free blacks in 1851, Landon notes, "Out of one Baptist church in Buffalo more than 130 members fled across the border, a similar migration taking place among the Negro Methodists of the same city though they were more disposed to make a stand." Apparently, there were concerns in Buffalo that blacks from Canada were actively inciting discontent within the city. The *Buffalo Commercial Advertiser* reported that "It is understood that quite a number of negroes have come over from Canada for the avowed purpose of assisting in creating a disturbance, and to obstruct the execution of our laws. Of course, if it is true, and any manifestations are made, they will be made to know that they are in a land of 'law and order.'" *Buffalo Commercial Advertiser*, Aug. 19, 1851.

34. Thomas, *From Tennessee Slave to St. Louis Entrepreneur*, 5–6.

35. *Buffalo Commercial Advertiser*, Aug. 18, 1851. An update on the case of Daniel also appears in this issue.

36. Ibid., Aug. 26, 1851.

37. *Spirit of the Times*, Aug. 26, 1851.

38. *Daily Standard*, Aug. 26, 1851. Interestingly, the writer observed that a "smart negro barber" would be preferable to a "gross, uneducated Indian," but granted that if Sarah Marlett was satisfied with her choice, "no one else ought to complain."

39. Taves, "Sex, Race, Gender, and Religion," 40–41. See also Gaul, *To Marry an Indian*.

40. *Brooklyn Daily Eagle*, Aug. 30, 1851. The actual language from the account reads, "The case narrated below, is somewhat similar, save that the matrimonial attack was more sudden and violent, and seized both parties like a raging epidemic, and run its course in a few days." Tubbee would cross paths with Jones a year later when he performed for a group of First Nations people in Ontario.

41. Ibid.

42. Ibid.

43. The Medina story was reproduced in the following papers: *Buffalo Daily Courier*, Aug. 25, 1851; *Evening Journal*, Aug. 27, 1851; *Syracuse Standard*, Aug. 27, 1851; *Oneida Chief*, Sept. 4, 1851; *Barre Gazette*, Sept. 5, 1851; *The Sheboygan Mercury*, Sept. 6, 1851; *Adams Sentinel*, Sept. 8, 1851; *The Globe*, Sept. 9, 1851; *Daily Morning News*, Sept. 9, 1851; *Mohawk Courier*, Sept. 11, 1851; *Covington Journal*,

Sept. 13, 1851; *Mississippi Free Trader,* Sept. 13, 1851; *Schenectady Cabinet,* Sept. 16, 1851; *Manchester Guardian,* Sept. 17, 1851; *Vermont Patriot & State Gazette,* Sept. 18, 1851; *Democratic Expounder,* Sept. 19, 1851; *German Reformed Messenger,* Oct. 1, 1851.

44. *Daily Gazette,* Aug. 30, 1851. This story was apparently reprinted from the Rochester, N.Y., *Advertiser.*

45. Because Laah Ceil had three children from her first marriage to Oliver Harmon Bassett and one child with Okah Tubbee, it is unclear which three children are referred to in these accounts.

46. *Buffalo Commercial Advertiser,* Sept. 1, 1851.

47. Green, "Pocahontas Perplex," 711.

48. See *Hartford Daily Courant,* Sept. 3, 1851; *The Sun,* Sept. 8, 1851; *Cleveland Herald,* Sept. 17, 1851; *Spectator,* Sept. 11, 1851; *Cattaraugus Republican,* Sept. 17, 1851; *Mississippi Free Trader,* Sept. 24, 1851.

49. *Democratic Expounder,* Sept. 19, 1851.

50. Ibid., *Hartford Daily Courant,* Sept. 3, 1851. Both these papers reprinted a story originally carried in the *Buffalo Republic.*

51. *Brooklyn Daily Eagle,* Aug. 30, 1851.

52. *Daily Gazette,* Aug. 30, 1851.

53. This description came from the first report in the Medina paper and was reproduced in the sources cited in note 43.

54. *Adams Sentinel,* Sept. 8, 1851.

55. *Mississippi Free Trader,* Sept. 24, 1851.

56. *Buffalo Commercial Advertiser,* Sept. 1, 1851; *Hartford Daily Courant,* Sept. 3, 1851; *Weekly Wisconsin,* Sept. 10, 1851; *Democratic Expounder,* Sept. 19, 1851.

57. An example appears in the *Independent American,* Oct. 3, 1851.

58. *Mississippi Free Trader,* Sept. 13, 1851.

59. *Vicksburg Tri-Weekly Sentinel,* Sept. 18, 1851.

60. *Buffalo Courier,* Sept. 4, 1851.

61. Ibid.

62. *True Latter Day Saints' Herald,* Mar. 1861, 5.

63. *Buffalo Courier,* Sept. 4, 1851. Perhaps the account was even penned by Laah Ceil herself.

64. *Daily Standard,* Sept. 30, 1851.

65. Ibid.

66. Ibid.

67. In his analysis of the marriage of Ely Parker (Seneca) to white woman Minnie Sackett, Genetin-Pilawa argues that Indian men could represent embodiments of "primitive masculinity," that were nevertheless understood as "non-threatening object[s] of public fascination for a sentimentalized, feminized, middle-class audience." Genetin-Pilawa, "'All Intent on Seeing the White Woman Married to the Red Man,'" 57–58.

68. See *Hartford Daily Courant,* Sept. 3, 1851; *The Sun,* Sept. 8, 1851; *Cleveland Herald,* Sept. 1, 17, 1851; *The Spectator,* Sept. 11, 1851; *Cattaraugus Republican,* Sept. 17, 1851; *Mississippi Free Trader,* Sept. 24, 1851.

69. See, e.g., advertisements and stories in these disparate papers: *Daily Ohio Statesman,* June 10, 1851; *Hartford Daily Courant,* May 27, 1850; *Democratic Telegraph and Texas Register,* Apr. 5, 1849.

70. *Brooklyn Daily Eagle,* Aug. 30, 1851; *Covington Journal,* Sept. 13, 1851; *Vicksburg Tri-Weekly Sentinel,* Sept. 18, 1851.

71. On the Boston case, see Barker, *Imperfect Revolution.*

72. Tubbee, *Sketch of the Life* (1852), 88–89.

73. *North American,* Jan. 30, 1852. See also *The Globe,* Jan. 29, 1852.

74. *North American,* Feb. 3, 6, 10, 13, 17, 20, 24, Mar. 2, 5, 1852. Their son's disappearance from the stage does not necessarily indicate a decline in the popularity of child performers in Toronto. For example, a Grand River Mohawk family appeared at the Royal Lyceum and included two costumed child "prodigies" who performed "a variety of little tricks." *The Globe,* Feb. 14, 1852. Maungwudaus also appeared on stage with his children "much to the amusement of the audience." *The Globe,* Apr. 22, 1852.

75. *Buffalo Commercial Advertiser,* Mar. 11–13, 15, 1851; *The Globe,* Apr. 19, 22, 1851.

76. Konkle, *Writing Indian Nations,* 209–10.

77. Other advertisements for Indian shows during 1851–52 can be seen in the *New York Daily Times,* Jan. 31, 1852; *The Globe,* Feb. 14, 1852; *New-York Daily Tribune,* Jan. 19, 1852.

78. *North American,* Apr. 16, 20, 1852. The business that hosted the Tubbees was known as Swain & Co.'s, and the proprietor of the building was James Howard. City of Toronto, Assessment Roll for St. Patrick's Ward, 1852, 12, City of Toronto Archives (hereafter CTA).

79. *North American,* Apr. 23, 27, 30, May 5, 7, 11, 14, 21, 25, 28, June 1, 4, 8, 11, 15, 18, 22, 25, 29, July 2, 6, 9, 13, 16, 27, 30, Aug. 3, 6, 10, 13, 17, 20, 24, 31, Sept. 7, 10, 14, 17, 21, 24, 28, Oct. 8, 12, 15, 19, 22, 26, Nov. 12, 16, 19, 23, 26, 30, Dec. 17, 21, 1852, Jan. 7, 13, 1853.

80. *Onondaga Gazette,* Nov. 20, 1851.

81. *New York Herald,* Aug. 20, 1852.

82. Ibid. A version of this specific story also appeared in the *Daily Standard,* Aug. 18, 1852; *New-York Daily Tribune,* Aug. 21, 1852; *Daily Missouri Republican,* Aug. 28, 1852.

83. *Onondaga Gazette,* Nov. 20, 1851.

84. Regina v. Tubbee, 1 P.R. 98, 1851, Westlaw Canada, http://canada.westlaw .com. I am grateful to Daniel Johnson for his assistance in locating this docket. The case is also discussed in Clarke, *Treatise upon the Law of Extradition,* 81.

85. News of the case appeared in the *Daily Standard,* Aug. 18, 1852; *New-York Daily Tribune,* Aug. 21, 1852; *New York Times,* Aug. 24, 1852; *Newport Daily News,* Aug. 26, 1852; *Schenectady Cabinet,* Aug. 30–31, 1852; *Detroit Daily Free Press,* Aug. 30, 1852; *Maine Farmer,* Sept. 9, 1852; *Daily Missouri Republican,* Aug. 28, 1852; *Hartford Daily Courant,* Aug. 27, 1852; *Detroit Daily Free Press,* Aug. 30, 1852; *Deseret News,* Dec. 11, 1852; *Fredonia Censor,* Aug. 28, 1852; *Onondaga*

Gazette, Aug. 19, 1852; *United Empire*, Aug. 19, 1852; *Farmer's Monthly Visitor* (Jan. 1852): 347.

86. *Deseret News*, Dec. 11, 1852. I am grateful to Connell O'Donovan alerting me to this source.

87. The "eclectic" system was one of several forms of medical practice in Toronto at this time. Other "systems" included allopathic, homeopathic, hydropathic, botanic, and Thomsonian therapies. "An Act for the Better Organization of the Medical Profession in Upper Canada, and for the Protection of the Public against Quackery," published in the *North American*, July 23, 1852. See also discussion of "eclecticism" in Chapter 6.

88. *North American*, Nov. 5, 1852.

89. City of Toronto, Assessment Roll for St. Patrick's Ward, 1852, 12, CTA; *North American*, Apr. 23, 27, 30, May 5, 7, 11, 14, 21, 25, 28, June 1, 4, 8, 11, 15, 18, 22, 25, 29, July 2, 6, 9, 13, 16, 27, 30, Aug. 3, 6, 10, 13, 17, 20, 24, 1852. From April 23 until May 14, the ads directed patients to the Yonge and Adelaide office. From May 15 until August 24, the ad indicated Yonge and Adelaide as the location of the Tubbees' office, but also mentioned their residence around the corner on Victoria. From August 12 until August 28, the ads in *The Globe* mentioned only the Yonge and Adelaide office address. *The Globe*, Aug. 12, 14, 17, 19, 24, 26, 28, 1852. From August 31 until October 8, the ads in the *North American* only referred clients to the Tubbees' residence on Victoria Street.

90. *New York Times*, Oct. 2, 1852. The *Times* referred to Tubbee as the "pseudo Indian chief."

91. A simple ad appeared in the *North American*, Aug. 26, 31, Sept. 7, 10, 14, 17, 21, 24, 28, Oct. 8, 12, 15, 19, 22, 26, 1852, with a more elaborate one appearing in the same publication for the rest of the year. Littlefield, *Life of Okah Tubbee*, xxxiii.

92. *North American*, Nov. 5, 1852.

93. Faragher, *Sugar Creek*, 91–93.

94. Littlefield, *Life of Okah Tubbee*, xxxiii–xxxiv.

95. Tubbee, *Sketch of the Life* (1852), 21–22.

96. One newspaper notice that appeared during his imprisonment for bigamy referred to him specifically as "an Indian quack doctor." *United Empire*, Aug. 19, 1852.

97. Tubbee, *Sketch of the Life* (1852), 87–96.

98. Advertisements for "Doctor Okah Tubbee" appeared in the *Toronto Patriot*, Jan. 10–Aug. 22, 1853.

99. City of Toronto, Register of Criminals, 1853–57, 36, CTA.

100. *The Globe*, April 10, 1854.

101. Littlefield, *Life of Okah Tubbee*, xxxiv–xxxv.

102. *The Globe*, Apr. 24, 1854.

103. Richard Carney, Addenda, [1853?], Central Toronto Superintendency, Correspondence, 1845–79, Record Group 10, Library and Archives Canada (hereafter RG10), vol. 411, 697; Mr. Harrison's report and account for expenses in examining a mill site near Colpoys Bay, RG10, vol. 411, 694–702; [Council meeting with Supt. of Indian Affairs and Colpoy's Bay Indians, Ontario, Aug. 17 1853], RG10, vol. 205,

121234–121236; T. G. Anderson, [Report on Doctor Okah Tubbee, Anderson to Bruce, Dec. 9, 1853], RG10, vol. 207, 122530–122532; Robert Bruce, [Replies to report on Okah Tubbee, Dec. 26–27, 1853], RG10, vol. 516, 145; [Reply to report on Okah Tubbee, Dec. 27, 1853], RG10, vol. 411, 230–31.

104. City of Toronto, Assessment Rolls, Ward of St. James, 1854, CTA.

105. "Chief Okah Tubbee, No. 15, Victoria Street, Toronto," [1854], Toronto Public Library.

106. City of Toronto, Register of Criminals, 1853–57, 129, CTA. News of the arrest was carried in *Toronto Patriot*, Aug. 24, 1855. Interestingly, the person who lodged the complaint against Mrs. Tubbee was William McGann, who, according to the 1856 Toronto city directory, was the proprietor of a boarding house adjacent to the Tubbees' residence. *Brown's Toronto General Directory*, 84.

107. *Toronto Patriot*, Aug. 23, 1855.

108. Toronto Jail Registers, 1852–64, Archives of Ontario.

109. *Toronto Patriot*, Aug. 23, 1855. A follow-up story on Kearney's case appears in the same paper on August 24.

110. Lenning, *Allgemeines Handbuch der Freimaurerei*, 31–32. I am grateful to Adam Seipp for help in translating this source. Another compendium claimed the Masonic meeting in question had actually been held in the fall of 1855. *Proceedings of the Grand Lodge of New Hampshire*, 2:530.

111. *Brown's Toronto General Directory*, 84. A similar entry in the alphabetical index to the directory is equally confusing: "Tubbe, Okah Leeheeit, indian doctor. 15 Victoria-street, w.s.," 234.

112. She was arrested on January 31, 1856. Toronto Jail Registers, 1852–64, Archives of Ontario. As with the arrest for keeping a disorderly house, the absence of a follow-up in the local papers suggests that either the charges were dropped or that she simply paid a fine to discharge them. *Daily Leader*, Jan. 30–31, 1856; *The Globe*, Jan. 28, 30–31, Feb. 1–2, 6, 8, 1856. I am grateful to Guylaine Petrain for her assistance in locating these articles and for her help with searching the Toronto Jail Registers.

113. *Buffalo Courier*, Nov. 5–6, 10, 1856.

114. City of Toronto, Assessment Rolls, Ward of St. James, 1857, CTA.

115. *Commercial Advertiser Directory City of Buffalo*, 203. She is listed as "Laahceil, Mrs. Indian doctress, cor. Washington and Carroll."

CHAPTER SIX

1. Hawes, *Buffalo Fifty Years Ago*.

2. Map of the City of Buffalo, N.Y., surveyed under the direction of Quackenboss & Kennedy, Insurance Agents, New York City, 1854, Buffalo Museum.

3. *Buffalo Daily Courier*, June 11, 1862.

4. *Buffalo Daily Courier*, June 9, 1862; *Spirit of the Times*, June 14, 1862. Although she did not advertise in local papers, "Mrs. Laahceil, Indian Doctress" did appear in the city directory. *Commercial Advertiser Directory City of Buffalo*, 203.

5. "Dr. Maungwudaus, the Successful Indian Physician!" [broadside], 1862–63, New York State Archives; *Biography of Nahmeonitah,* 7.

6. Rothstein, *American Physicians in the 19th Century,* 128, 156.

7. Numbers, "Do-It-Yourself the Sectarian Way," 49–56; Starr, *Social Transformation of American Medicine,* 48–49, 51–54.

8. See, e.g., the Tubbees' ads in the *North American,* Apr. 23–Aug. 24, 1852.

9. "Chief Okah Tubbee, No. 15, Victoria Street, Toronto," [1854], Toronto Public Library.

10. Rothstein, *American Physicians in the 19th Century,* 221–25; Warner, *Therapeutic Perspective,* 4.

11. See, e.g., Ward, introduction to *Winter Quarters,* 11.

12. See Wolfe, "Steaming Saints."

13. Stapley and Wright, "Female Ritual Healing," 4–11.

14. Madame Lee-o-neeto, another Indian doctress in Buffalo several years later, also used the phrase "cases of a delicate nature" in her advertisements. She specifically indicated that she specialized in women's maladies. *Roman Citizen,* Jan. 5, 1876. As Tuchman has shown, the appellation "doctress" was seen as indicative of women's inferior position as medical practitioners, and professional women physicians worked to avoid it. Tuchman, *Science Has No Sex,* 147.

15. Other common herbal abortifacients were savin and pennyroyal. If these plant-based methods were unsuccessful, women often resorted to instrumental means of eliminating the fetus, sometimes leading to death or permanent injury. A useful case study of abortion in the colonial era is Dayton, "Taking the Trade," 19–49.

16. Starr, *Social Transformation of American Medicine,* 49–50; Brodie, *Contraception and Abortion,* 50–52; Faragher, *Sugar Creek,* 114–15.

17. Mohr, *Abortion in America,* 13–14, 65. One ethnologist also remarked on Indian women producing instrumental abortions, but it seemed to be regarded as something of an exception. Hayden, *Contributions to the Ethnography,* 280.

18. The idea of a female physician at all frequently conjured an association with abortion providers. Morantz-Sanchez, *Sympathy and Science,* 188–89.

19. Joseph, "'Pennsylvania Model,'" 284–92.

20. Reagan, *When Abortion Was a Crime,* 10–13.

21. *Buffalo Daily Courier,* Feb. 27, 1861.

22. Ibid., *Daily News & Reformer,* June 12, 1862. The last-mentioned paper suggested that Madame Laahceil was an alias, but went no further. See also *Rochester Daily Union and Advertiser,* June 9, 1862.

23. *Buffalo Medical and Surgical Journal and Reporter,* 372–73.

24. *Reproductive Control, or a Rational Guide,* vii.

25. *Buffalo Daily Courier,* June 7, 1862. On the Bonney House, see *History of the City of Buffalo and Erie County,* 268; *Umberhine & Gustin's Lake Shore Gazetteer,* 260.

26. *Buffalo Daily Courier,* June 9, 1862; *Spirit of the Times,* June 14, 1862.

27. *Buffalo Daily Courier,* June 7, 1862; *Rochester Daily Union and Advertiser,* June 7, 1862.

28. Tuchman, *Science Has No Sex*, 61; Reagan, *When Abortion Was a Crime*, 10–11.

29. Wells, *Out of the Dead House*, 7.

30. Skinner, "Domestic Medicines," 1–2.

31. Brodie, *Contraception and Abortion*, 253–55. Far from promoting greater reproductive rights, significant numbers of middle-class American women participated in the health reform movement, vigorously repudiating abortion and advocating a return to traditional feminine roles that emphasized motherhood and morality. See Morantz-Sanchez, "Nineteenth Century Health Reform and Women."

32. Morantz-Sanchez, "Negotiating Power at the Bedside," 288.

33. Morantz-Sanchez, "Feminism, Professionalism, and Germs," 463. On Restell, see also C. Browder, *Wickedest Woman in New York*.

34. Reagan, *When Abortion Was a Crime*, 11.

35. The quote comes from *Buffalo Daily Courier*, Oct. 4, 1862. The other high-profile case took place in Albany, N.Y., in 1857 and involved an Indian doctress named Mrs. Halm. *Buffalo Courier*, Sept. 7, 1857; *Daily Eagle*, Sept. 8, 1857; *New York Times*, Sept. 9, 1857; *Brockport Republic*, Sept. 11, 1857. See also Briggs, "Race of Hysteria," 251–52.

36. Because Jenny Johnson survived the ordeal, perhaps she was considered something less than a true victim. *Daily Standard*, June 9, 1862.

37. Ibid.

38. *Rochester Daily Union and Advertiser*, June 9, 1862.

39. Reagan, *When Abortion Was a Crime*, 10.

40. *Buffalo Daily Courier*, June 7, 1862.

41. *Daily News & Reformer*, June 12, 1862.

42. Cohen, *Murder of Helen Jewett*. See also Halttunen, *Murder Most Foul*.

43. On the proliferation of scandals revolving around sex and crime in Buffalo specifically, see Vogel, Patton, and Redding, *America's Crossroads*, 103–4.

44. *Buffalo Daily Courier*, June 11, 1862; *Rochester Daily Union and Advertiser*, June 9, 1862; *Spirit of the Times*, June 14, 1862; *Buffalo Daily Courier*, June 7, 1862; *Detroit Free Press*, June 10, 1862.

45. *Rochester Daily Union and Advertiser*, June 9, 1862; *Spirit of the Times*, June 14, 1862; *Morning Herald*, June 9, 1862.

46. *Rochester Daily Union and Advertiser*, June 9, 1862.

47. Ibid.

48. *Rochester Daily Union and Advertiser*, June 7, 1862; *Daily Standard*, June 9, 1862; *Daily News & Reformer*, June 12, 1862.

49. Green, "Pocahontas Perplex," 711.

50. Horsman, *Race and Manifest Destiny*, 276–301; Berkhofer, *White Man's Indian*, 155, 165–66; Hine and Faragher, *American West*, 291.

51. On the initial arrests: *Buffalo Daily Courier*, June 7, 11–12, 1862; *Rochester Daily Union and Advertiser*, June 7, 1862; *Daily Standard,* June 9, 1862; *Daily News & Reformer*, June 12, 1862; *Spirit of the Times*, June 14, 1862; *Roman Citizen*, June 20, 1862; *Buffalo Daily Courier*, June 27, 1862. Connell O'Donovan has provocatively suggested that John Craig could have been Okah Tubbee. The name John

Craig bears a similarity to other Tubbee aliases, such as James Carey and Jesus Christ, and when Madame Laahceil learned he was being interrogated, she reportedly expressed dismay. I am intrigued by the possibility but remain skeptical because Okah Tubbee was too well known in Buffalo to hide in plain sight, nor was that his modus operandi. O'Donovan, "Plural Marriage and African Americans."

52. On the charges against Craig and Kelly, see *Spirit of the Times*, June 14, 1862.

53. *Buffalo Daily Courier*, June 11, 1862.

54. Ibid., Sept. 27, Oct. 1, 1862.

55. *Buffalo Daily Courier*, June 10–22, Oct. 22, 1862.

56. List of Prisoners in Erie County Jail, October 6, 1862, Erie County Records, C00-1, box 9, folder 1, Buffalo Museum. "Celeste Laahciel"'s crime was recorded as "manslaughter, 2d degr," but this document indicates that she had only been in the jail since Sept. 27. This seems unlikely because the nature of her case suggests that she would probably not have been released on bail, and she later mentioned spending "19 weeks" in prison.

57. *Buffalo Daily Courier*, June 16, 1862.

58. U.S. Bureau of the Census, *Eighth Census of the United States, 1860*. http://www.ancestry.com.

59. *Rochester Daily Union and Advertiser*, June 9, 1862.

60. See *Proceedings of the Common Council of the City of Buffalo, From January 7th, 1861, to January 6th, 1862*; *Proceedings of the Common Council of the City of Buffalo, from January 5th, 1862, to January 6th, 1863*. Admittedly, Madame Laahceil was arrested and convicted for manslaughter, not merely abortion. But someone had recently alerted police to surveil her property, which suggests that she faced greater scrutiny even before the death of her patient.

61. The jury returned its verdict on Oct. 8, but sentencing did not take place until Oct. 22. *Evening Courier & Republic*, Oct. 7, 1862; *Buffalo Daily Courier*, Oct. 8, 22, 1862.

62. *Rochester Daily Union and Advertiser*, June 9, 1862; *Buffalo Daily Courier*, June 7, 1862.

63. Board of Prisons, New York Inspectors of Prisons Record Book, 1858–65, 1, 342, 350–51, New York State Archives. The negotiation of contracts for male and female prison labor occupies a good deal of this record. The population of the female prison (called Mt. Pleasant) at Sing Sing rose from 115 in 1862 to 182 in 1865, at which point the convicts were relocated to another facility.

64. Wood, "Abridged Sketch," 4–5. According to Wood's memoir, Solon died June 2, 1870; Ann died Sept. 14, 1871; and Daniel died Oct. 9, 1872. There is some discrepancy in the date of Solon's death because he was enumerated in the 1870 census taken on Aug. 11, 1870. U.S. Bureau of the Census, *Ninth Census, 1870*. http://www.ancestry.com.

65. Wood, "Abridged Sketch," 4–5.

66. Doctrine and Covenants 52; U.S. Bureau of the Census, *Ninth Census, 1870*. http://www.ancestry.com; Connell O'Donovan personal email communication to the author, May 12, 2012.

67. Springville Ward, Utah Stake, General Minutes, 1873, CHL.

68. *Deseret News*, Dec. 11, 1852.

69. Springville Ward, Utah Stake, Manuscript History and Historical Reports, 1875, CHL.

70. *Deseret News*, Feb. 2, 1905.

71. Springville Ward, Utah Stake, Record of Members, 1851–92, Record of Members Collection 1836–1970, CHL.

72. Laah Ceil's daughter, Semira Wood, also experienced bouts of paralysis and according to her death certificate, died from a "diabetic coma" in circumstances similar to her mother's passing. O'Donovan, personal email communication to the author, May 12, 2012.

73. Wood, "Abridged Sketch," 5.

74. In 1881, Semira indicated that Frank still lived with her, suggesting either that he may not have been capable of caring for himself as an adult or that he was integrated into the household as a servant or employee. Wood, "Abridged Sketch," 4–5. Semira's husband, Lyman, purchased the boy in 1859, when the child was about ten years old. Springville Ward, Utah Stake, Record of Members, 1851–92, Record of Members Collection 1836–1970, CHL. The Paiutes had been involved in the Indian slave trade for at least two centuries by the time this purchase took place. Ute traders were known to use various means to coerce outsiders into purchasing Paiute children. See Van Hoak, "And Who Shall Have the Children?"; Reeve, *Making Space on the Western Frontier*; Brooks, *Captives and Cousins*.

EPILOGUE

1. Jeffrey Steele notes specifically that images of American Indians in advertising increased exponentially in the period after 1870. Steele, "Reduced to Images," 45–64.

2. On late nineteenth-century representations and Native peoples' roles in shaping them, see Deloria, *Indians in Unexpected Places*; Denson, *Demanding the Cherokee Nation*; Perdue, *Race and the Atlanta Cotton States Exposition*.

3. Genetin-Pilawa, *Crooked Paths to Allotment*. Other useful studies of the various means American Indian people used to influence local, state, and federal policies in the late nineteenth and early twentieth centuries include Cahill, *Federal Fathers and Mothers*, and Lowery, *Lumbee Indians in the Jim Crow South*.

4. Maddox, *Citizen Indians*, 50.

5. Lipsitz, "Mardi Gras Indians," 223.

6. Grover, "Mormon Priesthood Revelation."

7. For example, *Companion to American Literature and Culture* describes Okah Tubbee as "an African-American who escaped slavery by passing as a Chocktaw." Foster and Jackson, "Race and Literary Politics," 318. For references to Tubbee as a slave who used claims to Native ancestry to find freedom, see also Mielke, "'Native to the Question,'" 246–70; Gilmore, *Genuine Article*; Usner, *Indian Work*, 61; King, *Stolen Childhood*, 124. References to Okah Tubbee's autobiography in critical studies of early African American literature also attest to a certain skepticism about his Native heritage and focus on the idea that he used his Indian guise to evade authori-

ties and transcend the stigma of slavery. See, e.g., *Greenwood Encyclopedia of African American Literature,* 4:1621–22. Nevertheless, the role of Indian ancestry in slave freedom suits is worthy of scholarly attention. For the few works that currently address the topic, see Wallenstein, "Indian Foremothers"; Miles, "Uncle Tom Was an Indian"; Sachs, "'Freedom by a Judgment.'"

8. Littlefield asserts, following Ceil's own claims in the autobiography, that her "mother was Delaware and whose father, she said, was Mohawk," but then further suggests that her father was instead "possibly Mahican, or Stockbridge." Littlefield, *Life of Okah Tubbee,* xvi. Following Littlefield, other authors have repeated the contention that Ceil was Stockbridge or Mahican as well as possibly Delaware. See, e.g., Gilmore, *Genuine Article, 81*; Peyer, *Tutor'd Mind,* 130. For other works that take Ceil's claims regarding Native ancestry at face value, see Brennan, *When Brer Rabbit Meets Coyote,* 25, 57, 65, 168–88; Usner, *Indian Work,* 61; Sobel, *Teach Me Dreams,* 245n13; Wong, *Sending My Heart Back across the Years,* 212n5; Otter, *Melville's Anatomies,* 129–30; Murray, "Racial Identity and Self-invention," 80–101. Most of these are very brief, passing references. Brennan is the exception, going to great lengths to argue that "the autobiography of Okah Tubbee and Laah Ceil demonstrates a fascinating merging of African American and Native American traditions. . . . Their autobiography shares with Native American collaborative autobiographies the use of prefatory and appendatory documentation, the inclusion of tribal histories, the narration of spiritual awakenings, conversion, dreams, and visions, especially through the Delaware cultural traditions with which Laah Ceil was familiar," mistaking signs of her Mormon upbringing for American Indian religious traditions. Brennan, *When Brer Rabbit Meets Coyote,* 56–57. Similarly, Arnold Krupat includes Tubbee and Ceil's coauthored narrative as an example of Indian as-told-to autobiography but asserts that it is not biculturally composed as were other Indian autobiographies because Tubbee and Ceil were both Indians. Krupat, "Indian Autobiography," 24n3.

9. The first person to link the two sets of stories was folklorist Patrick Polk in "Early Black Mormons" and "William McCarey (Alias Wm. Chubbee)."

10. I was inspired by the example of my friend and mentor George Miles in his Tanner Lecture before the Mormon History Association annual meeting in 2012. Miles, "Mormon Stories."

Bibliography

MANUSCRIPT COLLECTIONS

Albany, N.Y.

New York State Archives, Manuscripts and Special Collections
 "Dr. Maungwudaus, The Successful Indian Physician!" [broadside] 1862–63
 Board of Prisons, New York Inspectors of Prisons Record Book, 1858–65

Baltimore, Md.

Maryland Historical Society
 Alonzo May, "May's Dramatic Encyclopedia of Baltimore, 1750–1912"

Buffalo, N.Y.

Buffalo Museum
 Erie County Records, List of Prisoners in Erie County Jail, Oct. 6, 1862
 Map of the City of Buffalo, N.Y., Quackenboss & Kennedy, 1854

Jackson, Miss.

Mississippi Department of Archives and History
 Adams County Records
  Probate Cases, Estate of James McCary, Box 27, Microcopy 5646
  Deed Book K, Microcopy 5341
  Deed Book BB, Microcopy 5351
  Board of Police Minutes, Microcopy 5322

Jefferson City, Mo.

Missouri State Archives
 Lafayette County Records
  Individual Licenses Granted, 1843–50, Microcopy C53722
  Circuit Court, May Term 1848, Box 23, Microcopy C29454
  Circuit Court, 1849–51, Box 25, Microcopy C29454

New Haven, Conn.

Beinecke Rare Book and Manuscript Library, Yale Collection of Western Americana
  Oliver H. Olney Papers, 1842–43
New Haven Museum, New Haven Hotels Collection, 1847–1973
  Guest Register, Tontine Hotel, 1848

New Orleans, La.

Tulane University, Louisiana Research Collections
  Merchants of New Orleans Print Collection, 1840s–1850s
    Leed's Foundry [broadside]
  James H. Dakin Papers, 1816–1973

Ottawa, Ont.

Library and Archives Canada
  Central Toronto Superintendency, Correspondence, 1845–79, Record Group 10, Vols. 205, 207 (Microcopy C-11521), Vol. 411 (Microcopy C-9616, C-9617), Vol. 516 (Microcopy C-13346)

Provo, Utah

Brigham Young University, L. Tom Perry Special Collections
  "Autobiography of William Adams, 1844" (Typescript)
  Robert Lang Campbell Journal, 1843–48
  "A Copy of the Sketch of the Life of David Cazier as Written by Himself Dated Nephi, Utah, 1913"
  Thomas Colborn Letters, 1846
  H. H. Cole Letter, 1846
  Elias Hutchings, "Autobiography, ca. 1842"
  Charles William Mitchell, "Biographies, 1935"
  Charles Smith Papers, 1840–1905
  Nelson Wheeler Whipple Diaries, 1863–87 (Typescript by Anor Whipple)
  Samuel Whitney Richards, Diaries, 1846–76, 2 vols.

Salt Lake City, Utah

Latter-day Saints Church History Library
  Nelson W. Whipple, "Autobiography and Journal of Nelson W. Whipple"
  General Church Minutes, 1839–77, Box 1, Mar. 26, 1847–Apr. 6, 1847
  Willard Richards Papers, 1821–54, Box 2, Vol. 17–22 and Folder 6
  Springville Ward, General Minutes, 1851–1902
  Springville Ward Manuscript History and Historical Reports, 1850–1900
  Record of Members Collection 1836–1970
  Springville Ward, Utah Stake, Record of Members, 1851–92
Family History Library
  Adams County, Ill., Clerk of the Circuit Court, Chancery Case Files, 1827–54, Microcopy 1839548

Toronto, Ont.

City of Toronto Archives
  City of Toronto Records
    Assessment Rolls, St. Patrick's Ward, 1852, Microcopy 264731–54
    Assessment Rolls, Ward of St. James, 1854, Microcopy 264731–55
    Register of Criminals, 1853–57
Archives of Ontario
  Toronto Jail Registers, 1852–64, RG 20-100-1, Microcopy MS2785
Toronto Public Library
  "Chief Okah Tubbee, No. 15, Victoria Street, Toronto," [broadside], 1854

Washington, D.C.

National Archives and Records Administration
  Records of the Bureau of Indian Affairs, Letters Received by the Office of
    Indian Affairs, 1824–51, Record Group 75, Microcopy 234
Library of Congress
  Miscellaneous Manuscripts Collection
    George Copway Papers, 1858
  Patent Medicine Labels and Advertisements, http://www.loc.gov/pictures/item
    /2002696083. Mar. 16, 2012

NEWSPAPERS AND MAGAZINES

Adams Sentinel (Gettysburg, Pa.)
Baltimore Clipper (Baltimore, Md.)
Bangor Daily Whig & Courier
  (Bangor, Maine)
Barre Gazette (Barre, Mass.)
Boston Courier (Boston, Mass.)
Boston Daily Atlas (Boston, Mass.)
Boston Investigator (Boston, Mass.)
Brockport Republic (Brockport, N.Y.)
Brooklyn Daily Eagle (Brooklyn, N.Y.)
Buffalo Daily Courier (Buffalo, N.Y.)
Buffalo Commercial Advertiser
  (Buffalo, N.Y.)
Buffalo Courier (Buffalo, N.Y.)
Buffalo Evening Courier (Buffalo, N.Y.)
Carolina Observer (Fayetteville, N.C.)
Cattaraugus Republican
  (Ellicottville, N.Y.)
Choctaw Intelligencer (Doaksville,
  Choctaw Nation)
Cincinnati Commercial
  (Cincinnati, Ohio)

Cleveland Herald (Cleveland, Ohio)
Concordia Intelligencer (Vidalia, La.)
Covington Journal (Covington, Ky.)
Daily Gazette (Utica, N.Y.)
Daily Journal and Courier
  (Lowell, Mass.)
Daily Leader (Toronto, Ont., Canada)
Daily Missouri Republican
  (St. Louis, Mo.)
Daily Morning News (Savannah, Ga.)
Daily National Intelligencer
  (Washington, D.C.)
Daily National Journal
  (Washington, D.C.)
Daily News & Reformer
  (Watertown, N.Y.)
Daily Ohio Statesman (Columbus, Ohio)
Daily Picayune (New Orleans, La.)
Daily Standard (Syracuse, N.Y.)
Democratic Expounder (Marshall, Mich.)
Democratic Telegraph and Texas
  Register (Houston, Tex.)

Deseret News (Salt Lake City, Utah)

Detroit Daily Free Press (Detroit, Mich.)

Detroit Free Press (Detroit, Mich.)

Dover Gazette & Strafford Advertiser (Dover, N.H.)

Evening Courier & Republic (Buffalo, N.Y.)

Evening Journal (Albany, N.Y.)

Far West (Liberty, Mo.)

Farmer's Cabinet (Amherst, N.H.)

Farmer's Monthly Visitor (Manchester, N.H.)

Fredonia Censor (Fredonia, N.Y.)

Freemason's Monthly Magazine (Boston, Mass.)

The Gazette (St. Louis, Mo.)

The Globe (Toronto, Ont., Canada)

Gospel Herald (Voree, Wisc.)

Hartford Daily Courant (Hartford, Conn.)

Independent American (Plattesville, Wisc.)

Indian Advocate (Louisville, Ky.)

Louisville Courier (Louisville, Ky.)

Louisville Weekly Democrat (Louisville, Ky.)

Maine Farmer (Augusta, Maine)

Manchester Guardian (Manchester, U.K.)

Maryland Gazette (Annapolis, Md.)

Masonic Signet and Literary Mirror (St. Louis, Mo.)

Massachusetts Ploughman and New England Journal of Agriculture (Boston, Mass.)

Milwaukee Daily Sentinel and Gazette (Milwaukee, Wisc.)

Mississippi Free Trader and Natchez Gazette (Natchez, Miss.)

Mohawk Courier (Rockton, N.Y.)

Morning Herald (Utica, N.Y.)

Nauvoo New Citizen (Nauvoo, Ill.)

New-Bedford Mercury (New Bedford, Mass.)

New Hampshire Patriot and State Gazette (Concord, N.H.)

Newport Daily News (Newport, R.I.)

News and Reformer (Watertown, N.Y.)

New York Daily Times (New York, N.Y.)

New York Daily Tribune (New York, N.Y.)

New York Herald (New York, N.Y.)

New York Ledger (New York, N.Y.)

New-York Morning Herald (New York, N.Y.)

New York Times (New York, N.Y.)

North American (Toronto, Ont., Canada)

Norwich Courier (Norwich, Conn.)

Oneida Chief (Clinton, N.Y.)

Onondaga Gazette (Baldwinsville, N.Y.)

Providence Patriot, Columbian Phenix (Providence, R.I.)

Raleigh Register, and North Carolina Gazette (Raleigh, N.C.)

Rochester Daily Union and Advertiser (Rochester, N.Y.)

Roman Citizen (Rome, N.Y.)

Saturday Evening Post (Philadelphia, Pa.)

Schenectady Cabinet (Schenectady, N.Y.)

Semi-Weekly Eagle (Brattleboro, Vt.)

Sheboygan Mercury (Sheboygan, Wisc.)

Spectator (New York, N.Y.)

Spirit of the Times (Batavia, N.Y.)

The Sun (Baltimore, Md.)

Toronto Patriot (Toronto, Ont., Canada)

True Latter Day Saints' Herald (Cincinnati, Ohio)

Union and Advertiser (Rochester, N.Y.)

United Empire (Toronto, Ont., Canada)

Vermont Patriot & State Gazette (Montpelier, Vt.)

Vicksburg Tri-Weekly Sentinel (Vicksburg, Miss.)

Voree Herald (Voree, Wisc.)

Weekly Eagle (Brattleboro, Vt.)

Weekly Reveille (St. Louis, Mo.)

Weekly Wisconsin (Milwaukee, Wisc.)

Zion's Reveille (Voree, Wisc.)

PUBLISHED BOOKS, ARTICLES, AND ESSAYS

Alexander, Ruth M. "'We Are Engaged as a Band of Sisters': Class and Domesticity in the Washingtonian Temperance Movement, 1840–1850." *Journal of American History* 75, no. 3 (1988): 763–85.

Alford, Terry. *Prince among Slaves: The True Story of an African Prince Sold into Slavery in the American South*. 30th anniversary ed. New York: Oxford University Press, 2007.

Allen, James B. "One Man's Nauvoo: William Clayton's Experience in Mormon Illinois." *Journal of Mormon History* 6 (1979): 37–59.

Allen, L. L. *A Thrilling Sketch of the Life of the Distinguished Chief Okah Tubbee Alias, Wm. Chubbee, Son of the Head Chief, Mosholeh Tubbee, of the Choctaw Nation of Indians*. New York: Cameron's Steam Power Presses, 1848.

Anderson, Benedict. *Imagined Communities: Reflections on the Origin and Spread of Nationalism*. Rev. ed. New York: Verso, 1991.

Archer, Armstrong. *A Compendium of Slavery, as It Exists in the Present Day in the United States of America: To Which Is Prefixed, a Brief View of the Author's*. London, 1844. Sabin Americana, 1500–1926. http://galenet.galegroup.com. Feb. 25, 2013.

Aron, Stephen. *American Confluence: The Missouri Frontier from Borderland to Border State*. Bloomington: University of Indiana Press, 2006.

Asbury, Henry. *Reminiscences of Quincy, Illinois, Containing Historical Events, Anecdotes, Matters concerning Old Settlers and Old Times, Etc.* Quincy, Ill.: D. Wilcox & Sons, 1882.

Bank, Rosemary K. "Staging the 'Native': Making History in American Theatre Culture, 1828–1838." *Theatre Journal* 45 (1993): 461–86.

Bantock, Sir Granville. *Sixty Patriotic Songs of All Nations*. Vol. 1. Boston: Oliver Ditson / New York: C. H. Ditson, 1913.

Barker, Gordon S. *The Imperfect Revolution: Anthony Burns and the Landscape of Race in Antebellum America*. Kent, Ohio: Kent State University Press, 2010.

Beckert, Sven. "Bourgeois Institution Builders: New York in the Nineteenth Century." In *The American Bourgeoisie: Distinction and Identity in the Nineteenth Century*, edited by Sven Beckert and Julia B. Rosenbaum, 103–18. New York: Palgrave-Macmillan, 2010.

Bellin, Joshua David. *Medicine Bundle: Indian Sacred Performance and American Literature, 1824–1932*. Philadelphia: University of Pennsylvania Press, 2008.

Bellin, Joshua David, and Laura L. Mielke, eds. *Native Acts: Indian Performance, 1603–1832*. Lincoln: University of Nebraska Press, 2011.

Bennett, Richard E. "Lamanism, Lymanism, and Cornfields." *Journal of Mormon History* 13 (1986–87): 44–59.

———. *Mormons at the Missouri: Winter Quarters, 1846–1852*. Norman: University of Oklahoma Press, 2004.

Berkhofer, Robert F. *The White Man's Indian: Images of the American Indian from Columbus to the Present*. New York: Random House, 1978.

Berlin, Ira. *Slaves without Masters: The Free Negro in the Antebellum South.* New York: Pantheon Books, 1974.

Biography of Nahmeonitah: The Spirit of Peace and Silence: Afterwards Mrs. M. N. Gardner, Original Compounder of the Balsam of Liverwort and Hoarhound and Well Known and Justly Celebrated as the Wonderful Indian Doctress. Boston: Weeks & Potter, ca. 1856.

Bird, S. Elizabeth, ed. *Dressing in Feathers: The Construction of the Indian in American Popular Culture.* Boulder, Colo.: Westview Press, 1996.

Black, Susan Easton, and Richard E. Bennett, eds. *A City of Refuge: Quincy, IL.* Riverton, Utah: Millennial Press, 2000.

Bledstein, Burton J., ed. *The Middling Sorts: Explorations in the History of the American Middle Class.* New York: Routledge, 2001.

Bowes, John P. *Pioneers and Exiles: Eastern Indians in the Trans-Mississippi West.* New York: Cambridge University Press, 2007.

Bowers, Toni. *The Politics of Motherhood: British Writing and Culture, 1680–1760.* New York: Cambridge University Press, 1996.

Braund, Kathryn Holland, ed. *Tohopeka: Rethinking the Creek War and the War of 1812.* Tuscaloosa: University of Alabama Press, 2012.

Brazy, Martha Jane. *An American Planter: Stephen Duncan of Antebellum Natchez and New York.* Baton Rouge: Louisiana State University Press, 2006.

Brennan, Jonathan, ed. *When Brer Rabbit Meets Coyote: African-Native American Literature.* Urbana: University of Illinois Press, 2003.

Briggs, Laura. "The Race of Hysteria: 'Overcivilization' and the 'Savage' Woman in Late Nineteenth-century Obstetrics and Gynecology." *American Quarterly* 52, no. 2 (June 2000): 246–73.

Bringhurst, Newell G. "The 'Descendants of Ham' in Zion: Discrimination against Blacks along the Shifting Mormon Frontier, 1830–1920." *Nevada Historical Society Quarterly* 24, no. 3 (1981): 298–318.

———. *Saints, Slaves, and Blacks: The Changing Place of Black People within Mormonism.* Westport, Conn.: Greenwood Press, 1981.

Brinton, Daniel G. *The Lenâpé and Their Legends: With the Complete Text and Symbols of the Walam Olum, a New Translation, and an Inquiry into Its Authenticity.* Philadelphia: D. G. Brinton, 1885.

Brodie, Janet Farrell. *Contraception and Abortion in Nineteenth-century America.* Ithaca, N.Y.: Cornell University Press, 1994.

Brooks, James. *Captives and Cousins: Slavery, Kinship, and Community in the Southwest Borderlands.* Chapel Hill: University of North Carolina Press, 2002.

Brooks, Joanna. *American Lazarus: Religion and the Rise of African-American and Native American Literatures.* Oxford: Oxford University Press, 2003.

Browder, Clifford. *The Wickedest Woman in New York: Madame Restell, the Abortionist.* Hamden, Conn.: Archon Books, 1988.

Browder, Laura. *Slippery Characters: Ethnic Impersonators and American Identities.* Chapel Hill: University of North Carolina Press, 2000.

Brown, Kathleen M. *Good Wives, Nasty Wenches and Anxious Patriarchs: Gender, Race and Power in Colonial Virginia*. Chapel Hill: University of North Carolina Press, 1996.

Brown, Lorenzo. *Journal of Lorenzo Brown, 1823–1900*. 2 vols. Provo, Utah: Brigham Young University Library, 1960.

Brown's Toronto General Directory. Toronto: W. R. Brown & Maclear, 1856.

Buchanan, Thomas C. *Black Life on the Mississippi: Slaves, Free Blacks, and the Western Steamboat World*. Chapel Hill: University of North Carolina Press, 2004.

Buffalo Medical and Surgical Journal and Reporter. Buffalo: Joseph Warren, 1861–62.

Bushman, Claudia Lauper, and Richard Lyman Bushman. *Building the Kingdom: A History of Mormons in America*. New York: Oxford University Press, 1999.

Bushman, Richard Lyman. *Joseph Smith: Rough Stone Rolling*. New York: Vintage, 2007.

Buss, James J. *Winning the West with Words: Language and Conquest in the Lower Great Lakes*. Norman: University of Oklahoma Press, 2011.

Butler, Judith. *Gender Trouble: Feminism and the Subversion of Identity*. New York: Routledge, 1990.

Byars-Nichols, Keely. *The Black-Indian in American Literature*. New York: Palgrave-McMillan, 2014.

Cahill, Cathleen. *Federal Fathers and Mothers: A Social History of the United States Indian Service, 1869–1933*. Chapel Hill: University of North Carolina Press, 2013.

Camp, Stephanie. *Closer to Freedom: Enslaved Women and Everyday Resistance in the Plantation South*. Chapel Hill: University of North Carolina Press, 2004.

Campbell, Douglas. "'White' or 'Pure': Five Vignettes." *Dialogue: A Journal of Mormon Thought* 29, no. 4 (1996): 119–35.

Cannon, Donald Q., and Lyndon W. Cook, eds. *Far West Record: Minutes of the Church of Jesus Christ Latter-day Saints, 1830–1844*. Salt Lake City: Deseret Book, 1983.

Carson, James Taylor. "Greenwood LeFlore: Southern Creole, Choctaw Chief." In *Pre-removal Choctaw History: Exploring New Paths*, edited by Greg O'Brien, 221–36. Norman: University of Oklahoma Press, 2008.

———. "Native Americans, the Market Revolution, and Culture Change: The Choctaw Cattle Economy, 1690–1830." In *Pre-removal Choctaw History: Exploring New Paths*, edited by Greg O'Brien, 183–99. Norman: University of Oklahoma Press, 2008.

———. *Searching for the Bright Path: The Mississippi Choctaws from Prehistory to Removal*. Lincoln: University of Nebraska Press, 1999.

Castle Clinton National Monument. New York. http://www.nps.gov/cacl. July 13, 2013.

Chateaubriand, François-Rene. *Atala and René*. New York: Oxford University Press, 1963.

"The Chinese Collection in the Lower Saloon of the New Building at the Corner of 9th & George Street, Philadelphia . . ." Philadelphia [between 1838 and 1843].

Library of Congress. http://www.loc.gov/pictures/item/95504703/. Feb. 12, 2013.

Clapp, William W., Jr. *A Record of the Boston Stage*. Boston: J. Munroe, 1853.

Clarke, Edward. *A Treatise upon the Law of Extradition, with the Conventions upon the Subject Existing between England and Foreign Nations, and the Cases Decided Thereon*. London: Stevens & Haynes, 1874.

Clarke, John B. *Manchester, A Brief Record of Its Past, and a Picture of Its Present, including an Account of its Settlement of its Growth as Town and City, a History of its Schools, Churches, Societies, Banks, Post-Offices, Newspapers and Manufactures*. Manchester, N.H.: John B. Clarke, 1875.

Clayton, Augustin N. *A Vindication of the Recent and Prevailing Policy of the State of Georgia, Both in Reference to Its Internal Affairs, and Its Relation with the General Government*. Athens, Ga.: O. P. Shaw, Office of the Athenian, 1827.

Clayton, James D. *Antebellum Natchez*. Baton Rouge: Louisiana State University Press, 1968.

Cobbett, William. *Thirteen Sermons*. New York: J. Doyle, 1834.

Cohen, Patricia Cline. *The Murder of Helen Jewett: The Life and Death of a Prostitute in Nineteenth-century New York*. New York: Alfred A. Knopf, 1998.

The Commercial Advertiser Directory, City of Buffalo, to Which Is Added a Business Directory of the City of Buffalo. Buffalo, N.Y.: R. Wheeler, 1861.

Conyers, Josiah B. *A Brief History of the Leading Causes of the Hancock Mob, in the Year 1846*. Saint Louis: Cathcart & Prescott, 1846.

Cook, James. *The Arts of Deception: Playing with Fraud in the Age of Barnum*. Cambridge, Mass.: Harvard University Press, 2001.

Cook, Lyndon. *The Revelations of the Prophet Joseph Smith: A Historical and Biographical Commentary of the Doctrine and Covenants*. Salt Lake City: Deseret Book, 1985.

Cooper, Samuel. *A Concise System of Instructions and Regulations for the Militia and Volunteers of the United States, comprehending the Exercises and Movements of the Infantry, Light Infantry, and Riflemen; Cavalry and Artillery*. Philadelphia: Frank Desilver, 1846.

Copway, George. *Life, Letters, and Speeches*. Edited by A. LaVonne Brown Ruoff and Donald B. Smith. Lincoln: University of Nebraska Press, 1997.

Craft, William, and Ellen Craft. *Running a Thousand Miles for Freedom: The Escape of William and Ellen Craft from Slavery*. Edited by Barbara McCaskill. Athens: University of Georgia Press, 1999.

Crapo, Henry Howland. *New Bedford Directory*. New Bedford, Mass.: Press of B. Lindsey, 1849.

Curtis, Annette Wegner, comp. *1836 Clay County, Missouri State Tax List: All Taxpayers and Land Owners Are Identified including Mormons. And, The 1835 Missouri Tax Law*. Independence, Mo.: Missouri Mormon Frontier Foundation, 2003.

Davis, Hudson. "The Negro A Beast: Nachash Theology and the Nineteenth-century American Re-Making of Negro Origins." Ph.D. diss., St. Louis University, 2012.

Dayton, Cornelia. "Taking the Trade: Abortion and Gender Relations in an Eighteenth-century New England Village." *William and Mary Quarterly* 48, no. 1 (1991): 19–49.

Deloria, Philip J. *Indians in Unexpected Places*. Lawrence: University Press of Kansas, 2004.

——. *Playing Indian*. New Haven, Conn.: Yale University Press, 1998.

Deloria, Vine, Jr. "Comfortable Fictions and the Struggle for Turf." *American Indian Quarterly* 16, no. 3 (1992): 397–410.

Denson, Andrew. *Demanding the Cherokee Nation: Indian Autonomy and American Culture, 1830–1900*. Lincoln: University of Nebraska Press, 2004.

Duffy, John-Charles. "Clyde Forsberg's *Equal Rites* and the Exoticizing of Mormonism." *Dialogue: A Journal of Mormon Thought* 39, no. 1 (2006): 4–34.

——. "The Use of 'Lamanite' in Official LDS Discourse." *Journal of Mormon History* 34, no. 1 (2008): 118–67.

Easley-Houser, Arika. "The Indian Image in the Black Mind: Representing Native Americans in Antebellum African American Public Culture." Ph.D. diss., Rutgers University, 2014.

Elliott, Michael. "Telling the Difference: Nineteenth-century Legal Narratives of Racial Taxonomy." *Law and Social Inquiry* 24, no. 3 (1999): 611–36.

Epstein, Dena. *Sinful Tunes and Spirituals: Black Folk Music to the Civil War*. Urbana: University of Illinois Press, 1977.

Esplin, Ronald K. "'A Place Prepared': Joseph, Brigham and the Quest for Promised Refuge in the West." *Journal of Mormon History* 9 (1982): 71–97.

Faragher, John Mack. *Sugar Creek: Life on the Illinois Prairie*. New Haven, Conn.: Yale University Press, 1988.

Farmer, Jared. *On Zion's Mount: Mormons, Indians, and the American Landscape*. Cambridge, Mass.: Harvard University Press, 2008.

Fields, Barbara Jean. *Slavery and Freedom on the Middle Ground: Maryland during the Nineteenth Century*. New Haven, Conn.: Yale University Press, 1985.

Fluhman, J. Spencer. *'A Peculiar People': Anti-Mormonism and the Making of Religion in Nineteenth-century America*. Chapel Hill: University of North Carolina Press, 2012.

Forsberg, Clyde R. *Equal Rites: The Book of Mormon, Masonry, Gender, and American Culture*. New York: Columbia University Press, 2004.

Foster, Frances Smith, and Cassandra Jackson. "Race and Literary Politics." In *A Companion to American Literature and Culture*, edited by Paul Lauter, 316–27. Malden, Mass.: Wiley-Blackwell, 2010.

Fowler, David Henry. *Northern Attitudes towards Interracial Marriage: Legislation and Public Opinion in the Middle Atlantic and the States of the Old Northwest, 1780–1830*. New York: Garland, 1987.

Free, Joseph M. "The Ante-bellum Theatre of the Old Natchez Region." *Journal of Mississippi History* 5 (1943): 14–27.

Freemasons. African Lodge No. 459. *Proceedings of the One Hundredth Anniversary of the Granting of Warrant 459 to African Lodge, at Boston,*

Massachusetts Monday Sept. 29th, 1884, under the Auspices of the M. W. Prince Hall Grand Lodge F. and A. Masons. Boston: Franklin Press, 1885.

Fretz, Eric. "P. T. Barnum's Theatrical Selfhood and the Nineteenth-century Culture of Exhibition." In *Freakery: Cultural Spectacles of the Extraordinary Body*, edited by Rosemarie Garland-Thomson, 97–107. New York: New York University Press, 1996.

Fryer, William Kelley Frohawk, Jr. *Indian Guide to Health, or a Treatise on the Cure of Various Diseases, by Vegetable Medicines, &c.: Designed as a Guide to Young Practitioners and Private Families.* Indianapolis: Author, 1839.

Gallay, Alan. *The Indian Slave Trade: The Rise of the English Empire in the American South, 1670–1717.* New Haven, Conn.: Yale University Press, 2003.

Galloway, Patricia. "'The Chief Who Is Your Father': Choctaw and French Views of the Diplomatic Relation." In *Powhatan's Mantle: Indians in the Colonial Southeast,* edited by Peter S. Wood, Gregory A. Waselkov, and M. Thomas Hatley, 249–78. Lincoln: University of Nebraska Press, 1989.

———. *Choctaw Genesis, 1500–1700.* Lincoln: University of Nebraska Press, 1998.

Garrison, Tim Alan. *The Legal Ideology of Removal: The Southern Judiciary and the Sovereignty of Native American Nations.* Athens: University of Georgia Press, 2002.

Gatewood, Willard B., Jr. "The Perils of Passing: The McCarys of Omaha." *Nebraska History* 71 (1990): 64–70.

Gaul, Theresa Strouth. *To Marry an Indian: The Marriage of Harriett Gold and Elias Boudinot in Letters, 1823–1839.* Chapel Hill: University of North Carolina Press, 2005.

Genetin-Pilawa, C. Joseph. "'All Intent on Seeing the White Woman Married to the Red Man': The Parker/Sackett Affair and the Public Spectacle of Intermarriage." *Journal of Women's History* 20, no. 2 (2008): 57–85.

———. *Crooked Paths to Allotment: The Fight over Federal Indian Policy after the Civil War.* Chapel Hill: University of North Carolina Press, 2014.

Gilmore, Paul. *The Genuine Article: Race, Mass Culture, and American Literary Manhood.* Durham, N.C.: Duke University Press, 2001.

Gordon, Sarah. *The Mormon Question: Polygamy and Constitutional Conflict in Nineteenth-century America.* Chapel Hill: University of North Carolina Press, 2002.

Grafton, Thomas. "Natchez: Its Past, Present and Future." In *The Queen City of the South, Natchez, Mississippi, On Top Not "Under the Hill," Adams County and the Neighboring Territory,* edited by C. N. M'Cormick. Natchez: Daily Democrat Steam Print, 1880.

"Grand Exhibition: A Grand Exhibition Will Be Given at the Grand Saloon of the Arcade Chesnut Street, Every Evening This Week Commencing on Monday, Feb. 7th, 1842." Peale's Museum [Philadelphia, Pa.]: C. Alexander, 1842.

Granqvist, Raoul. *Imitation as Resistance: Appropriations of English Literature in Nineteenth-century America.* Madison, N.J.: Fairleigh Dickinson University Press, 1995.

Green, Michael D. *The Politics of Indian Removal: Creek Government and Society in Crisis*. Lincoln: University of Nebraska Press, 1985.

Green, Rayna. "The Pocahontas Perplex: The Image of Indian Women in American Culture." *The Massachusetts Review* 16, no. 4 (1975): 698-714.

———. "The Tribe Called Wannabe: Playing Indian in America and Europe." *Folklore* 99 (1988): 30-55.

Greenblatt, Stephen. *Renaissance Self-Fashioning: From More to Shakespeare*. Chicago: University of Chicago Press, 1980.

Greene, R. *Dr. R. Greene's Indianopathy, or, Science of Indian Medicine: Founded Upon the "Laws of Nature," the Principles of Which Were Obtained by Dr. Greene in His Travels among the Indians, Whereby He Is Enabled to Successfully Treat Cancers, Tumors, Scrofula, Ulcers, and All Chronic Diseases*. 14th ed. Boston: Order of the Board of Managers [Indian Medical Institute], 1858.

Grisvard, Larry Eugene. "The Final Years: The Ludlow and Smith Theatrical Firm in St. Louis, 1845-1851." Ph.D. diss., Ohio State University, 1965.

Gross, Ariela. *What Blood Won't Tell: A History of Race on Trial in America*. Cambridge, Mass.: Harvard University Press, 2008.

Grover, Mark L. "The Mormon Priesthood Revelation and the Sao Paulo, Brazil Temple." *Dialogue: A Journal of Mormon Thought* 23 (1990): 39-52.

Gutjahr, Paul C. *Book of Mormon: A Biography*. Princeton, N.J.: Princeton University Press, 2012.

Haefli, Evan. "A Note on the Use of North American Borderlands." *American Historical Review*, 104, no. 4 (1999): 1222-25.

Hallwas, John E., and Roger D. Launius, eds. *Cultures in Conflict: A Documentary History of the Mormon War in Illinois*. Logan: Utah State University Press, 1995.

Halttunen, Karen. *Confidence Men and Painted Women: A Study of Middle-class Culture in American, 1830-1870*. New Haven, Conn.: Yale University Press, 1982.

———. *Murder Most Foul: The Killer and the American Gothic Imagination*. Cambridge, Mass.: Harvard University Press, 2000.

Harmon, Reuben P. "[Statement of] Reuben P. Harmon." In *Naked Truths about Mormonism: Also a Journal for Important, Newly Apprehended Truths, and Miscellany*, edited by Arthur B. Deming, 1. Vol. 1, no. 2:2. Oakland: Deming, 1888.

Hauptman, Laurence M. *Conspiracy of Interests: Iroquois Dispossession and the Rise of New York State*. Syracuse, N.Y.: Syracuse University Press, 1999.

Hawes, Lucy Williams. *Buffalo Fifty Years Ago: A Paper Read Before the Buffalo Historical Society, April 27, 1886*. Buffalo: Courier, 1886.

Hayden, F. V. *Contributions to the Ethnography and Philology of the Indian Tribes of the Missouri Valley: Prepared under the Direction of Capt. William P. Raynolds, T.E.U.S.A., and Published by Permission of the War Department*. Philadelphia: C. Sherman & Son, 1862.

Haynes, Stephen R. *Noah's Curse: The Biblical Justification of American Slavery*. New York: Oxford University Press, 2002.

Hill, Marvin S., C. Keith Rooker, and Larry T. Wimmer. *The Kirtland Economy Revisited*. Provo, Utah: Brigham Young University Press, 1977.

Hine, Robert V., and John Mack Faragher. *The American West: A New Interpretive History*. New Haven, Conn.: Yale University Press, 2000.

Hinks, Peter P. *To Awaken My Afflicted Brethren: David Walker and the Problem of Antebellum Slave Resistance*. University Park, Pa.: Penn State University Press, 1997.

Hodes, Martha. *White Women, Black Men: Illicit Sex in the Nineteenth-century South*. New Haven, Conn.: Yale University Press, 1997.

Hodgson, Adam. *Letters from North America: Written during a Tour in the United States and Canada*. Vol. 1. London: Hurst, Robinson, 1824.

Hogan, William Ransom, and Edwin Adams Davis. Introduction to *William Johnson's Natchez: The Ante-bellum Diary of a Free Negro*. Baton Rouge: Louisiana State University Press, 1951.

Horsman, Reginald. *Race and Manifest Destiny: Origins of American Racial Anglo-Saxonism*. 2d ed. Cambridge, Mass: Harvard University Press, 1986.

The House-Keeper's Guide, and Indian Doctor: Containing the Very Best Directions for Making All Kinds of Ice Creams, Preserves, Jellies, Perfumery, and Essences, Fancy and Plain Soaps, and an Excellent System on the Treatment of the Hair; the Best Method of Cleaning Brass, Marble, Mahogany Furniture, Cutlery, Carpets, &c. &c. Also a Complete System of Genuine Indian Doctoring: To Which Is Added Directions for Letter Writing under Various Circumstances. The Book Closes with the Celebrated Chemical Washing Recipe. New York: American Family, 1856.

Howe, LeAnne. "Ohoyo Chishba Osh: Woman Who Stretches Way Back." In *Pre-removal Choctaw History: Exploring New Paths*, edited by Greg O'Brien, 26–47. Norman: University of Oklahoma Press, 2008.

Hudson, Angela Pulley. *Creek Paths and Federal Roads: Indians, Settlers, and Slaves and the Making of the American South*. Chapel Hill: University of North Carolina Press, 2010.

Huhndorf, Shari. *Going Native: Indians in the American Cultural Imagination*. Ithaca, N.Y.: Cornell University Press, 2001.

Hurt, R. Douglas. *The Ohio Frontier: Crucible of the Old Northwest, 1720–1830*. Bloomington: University of Indiana Press, 1996.

The Indian Doctor's Family Physician, comprising about Two Hundred Receipts, for the Cure of Different Diseases; an Accurate Description of the Medical Properties of the Roots and Herbs Prescribed; and Directions as to Diet, Treatment, and Cookery, for the Sick and Convalescent. With Remarks on the Asiatic Cholera. By a Celebrated Indian Doctor. 6th ed. New York: Charles C. Broadwell, 1849.

The Indian Guide to Health, or Valuable Vegetable Medical Prescriptions for the Use of Families, or Young Practitioners. St. Louis: J. H. Stevens & J. C. Cory / Lafayette, Ind.: J. Rosser & Brother, 1845.

Iowa. *[Special] Census of Iowa, 1851*. In *Iowa State Census Collection, 1836–1925*. http://www.ancestry.com. Jan. 26, 2012.

Jackson, Joseph H. *The Adventures and Experience of Joseph H. Jackson;*
   Disclosing the Depths of Mormon Villany Practiced in Nauvoo. Warsaw, Ill.:
   Author, 1846.

Jacobson, Matthew Frye. *Barbarian Virtues: The United States Encounters Foreign*
   Peoples at Home and Abroad, 1876–1917. New York: Hill and Wang, 2000.

James, D. Clayton. *Antebellum Natchez.* Baton Rouge: Louisiana State University
   Press, 1968.

Janson, Charles William. *The Stranger in America: Containing Observations*
   Made during a Long Residence in That Country. London: Albion Press / James
   Cundee, 1807.

Jennings, Warren A. "The First Mormon Mission to the Indians." *Kansas*
   Historical Quarterly 37 (1971): 288–99.

Johnson, Paul E., and Sean Wilentz. *The Kingdom of Matthias.* New York: Oxford
   University Press, 1994.

Johnson, William. *William Johnson's Natchez: The Ante-bellum Diary of a Free*
   Negro. Edited by William Ransom Hogan and Edwin Adams Davis. Baton
   Rouge: Louisiana State University Press, 1951.

Jones, Eugene H. *Native Americans as Shown on the Stage, 1753–1916.*
   Metuchen, N.J.: Scarecrow Press, 1988.

Jones, Josiah. "History of the Mormonites." *Evangelist* 9 (June 1, 1831): 134.

Joseph, Anthony M. "'Pennsylvania Model': The Judicial Criminalization of
   Abortion in Pennsylvania, 1838–1850." *American Journal of Legal History* 49,
   no. 3 (2007): 284–320.

Kappler, Charles J., ed. *Indian Affairs: Laws and Treaties.* Vol. 2, *Treaties.*
   Washington, D.C.: Government Printing Office, 1904. http://digital.library
   .okstate.edu/kappler. Sept. 10, 2013.

Kennedy, J. H. *Early Days of Mormonism: Palmyra, Kirtland, and Nauvoo.*
   New York: Charles Scribner's Sons, 1888.

Kennedy, V. Lynn. *Born Southern: Childbirth, Motherhood, and Social Networks*
   in the Old South. Baltimore: Johns Hopkins University Press, 2010.

Kettley, Marlene C., Arnold K. Garr, and Craig K. Manscill. *Mormon*
   Thoroughfare: A History of the Church in Illinois, 1830–1839. Provo, Utah:
   Brigham Young University Religious Studies Center, 2006.

Kimball, Stanley B. "The Captivity Narrative on Mormon Trails, 1846–65."
   Dialogue: A Journal of Mormon Thought 18, no. 4 (1983): 81–88.

———. *Heber C. Kimball: Mormon Patriarch and Pioneer.* Urbana: University of
   Illinois Press, 1986.

King, Wilma. *Stolen Childhood: Slave Youth in Nineteenth-century America.*
   Bloomington: University of Indiana Press, 1998.

Konkle, Maureen. *Writing Indian Nations: Native Intellectuals and the Politics of*
   Historiography, 1827–1863. Chapel Hill: University of North Carolina Press,
   2004.

Krauthamer, Barbara. *Black Slaves, Indian Masters: Slavery, Emancipation, and*
   Citizenship in the Native American South. Chapel Hill: University of North
   Carolina Press, 2013.

Krupat, Arnold. "The Indian Autobiography: Origins, Type, and Function." *American Literature* 53, no. 1 (1981): 22–42.

LaBrew, Arthur R. *The Black Swan: Elizabeth T. Greenfield, Songstress.* Detroit: s.n., 1969.

Landon, Fred. "The Negro Migration to Canada after the Passing of the Fugitive Slave Act." *Journal of Negro History* 5, no. 1 (1920): 22–36.

Larson, John Lauritz. *Internal Improvement: National Public Works and the Promise of Popular Government in the Early United States.* Chapel Hill: University of North Carolina Press, 2001.

Launius, Roger D., and John E. Hallwas. Introduction to *Kingdom on the Mississippi Revisited: Nauvoo in Mormon History,* edited by Roger D. Launius and John E. Hallwas, 1–18. Urbana: University of Illinois Press, 1996.

Laver, Harry S. "Rethinking the Social Role of the Militia: Community-Building in Antebellum Kentucky." *Journal of Southern History* 68, no. 4 (2002): 777–816.

Lee, John D. *Journals of John D. Lee, 1846–47 and 1859.* Edited by Charles Kelly. Salt Lake City: University of Utah Press, 1984.

Lenning, C. *Allgemeines Handbuch der Freimaurerei. Zweite völlig umgearbeitete Auflage von Lenning's Encyklopädie der Freimaurerei.* Vol. 2. Leipzig: F. A. Brockhaus, 1865.

LeSueur, Stephen C. *The 1838 Mormon War in Missouri.* Columbia: University of Missouri Press, 1987.

Lewis, Henry. *Das illustrirte Mississippithal: Dargestellt in 80 nach der Natur aufgenommen Ansichten vom Wasserfalle zu St. Anthony an bis zum Golf von Mexico (eine Entfernung von ungefaehr 2300 englischen Meilen).* Düsseldorf: Arnz, [1854–57].

Libby, David J. *Slavery and Frontier Mississippi, 1720–1835.* Jackson: University Press of Mississippi, 2004.

Lincecum, Gideon. *Pushmataha: A Choctaw Leader and His People.* Tuscaloosa: University of Alabama Press, 2004.

Lipsitz, George. "Mardi Gras Indians: Carnival and Counternarrative in Black New Orleans." In *When Brer Rabbit Meets Coyote: African-Native American Literature,* edited by Jonathan Brennan, 218–41. Urbana: University of Illinois Press, 2003.

Littlefield, Daniel F., Jr. *The Life of Okah Tubbee.* Lincoln: University of Nebraska Press, 1988.

Lott, Eric. *Love and Theft: Blackface Minstrelsy and the American Working Class.* New York: Oxford University Press, 1995.

Lowery, Malinda Maynor. *Lumbee Indians in the Jim Crow South: Race, Identity, and the Making of a Nation.* Chapel Hill: University of North Carolina Press, 2010.

Maddox, Lucy. *Citizen Indians: Native American Intellectuals, Race, and Reform.* Ithaca, N.Y.: Cornell University Press, 2005.

Marquardt, H. Michael, comp. *Early Patriarchal Blessings of the Church of Jesus Christ of Latter-day Saints.* Salt Lake City: Smith-Petit Foundation, 2007.

Marshall, Amani. "'They Will Endeavor to Pass for Free': Enslaved Runaways' Performances of Freedom in South Carolina." *Slavery and Abolition* 31, no. 2 (2010): 161–80.

Mason, Jeffrey D. *Performing America: Cultural Nationalism in American Theater*. Ann Arbor: University of Michigan Press, 2001.

McCloskey, John C. "The Campaign of Periodicals after the War of 1812 for National American Literature." *PMLA* 50, no. 1 (1935): 262–73.

Mielke, Laura L. "'Native to the Question': William Apess, Black Hawk, and the Sentimental Context of Early Native American Autobiography." *American Indian Quarterly* 26, no. 2 (2002): 246–70.

Mielke, Laura, and Joshua Bellin, eds. *Native Acts: Indian Performance, 1603–1832*. Lincoln: University of Nebraska Press, 2011.

Mihm, Stephen. *A Nation of Counterfeiters: Capitalists, Con Men, and the Making of the United States*. Cambridge, Mass.: Harvard University Press, 2007.

Miles, George A. "Mormon Stories: A Librarian's Perspective." *Journal of Mormon History* 38, no. 2 (2012): 47–66.

Miles, Tiya. *Ties That Bind: The Story of an Afro-Cherokee Family in Slavery and Freedom*. Berkeley: University of California Press, 2006.

———. "Uncle Tom Was an Indian: Tracing the Red in Black Slavery." In *Confounding the Color Line: The Indian-Black Experience in North America*, edited by James F. Brooks, 137–60. Lincoln: University of Nebraska Press, 2002.

Miller, David W. *Forced Removal of American Indians from the Northeast: A History of Territorial Cessions and Relocations, 1620–1854*. Jefferson, N.C.: Macfarland, 2011.

Miller, Joel. "Joel Miller's Statement." In *Naked Truths about Mormonism: Also a Journal for Important, Newly Apprehended Truths, and Miscellany*, edited by Arthur B. Deming, 2. Vol. 1, no. 2. Oakland: Deming, 1888.

Mintz, Steven, ed. *African American Voices: The Life Cycle of Slavery*. 3rd ed. St. James, N.Y.: Brandywine Press, 2004.

Mississippi, Compiled Census and Census Substitutes Index, 1805–1890. http://www.ancestry.com. June 6, 2014.

Mohr, James C. *Abortion in America: The Origins and Evolution of National Policy, 1800–1900*. New York: Oxford University Press, 1979.

Moody, Richard. *America Takes the Stage: Romanticism in American Drama and Theatre, 1750–1900*. Bloomington: Indiana University Press, 1955.

Morantz-Sanchez, Regina Markell. "Feminism, Professionalism, and Germs: The Thought of Mary Putnam Jacobi and Elizabeth Blackwell." *American Quarterly* 34, no. 5 (1982): 459–78.

———. "Negotiating Power at the Bedside: Historical Perspectives on Nineteenth-century Patients and Their Gynecologists." *Feminist Studies* 26, no. 2 (Summer 2000): 287–309.

———. "Nineteenth Century Health Reform and Women: A Program of Self-Help." In *Medicine without Doctors: Home Health Care in American History*, edited by

Guenter B. Risse, Ronald L. Numbers, and Judith Walzer Leavitt, 73–93. New York: Science History USA Publications, 1977.

———. *Sympathy and Science: Women Physicians in American Medicine*. 1985. Reprint, Chapel Hill: University of North Carolina Press, 2000.

Mulholland, James. *An Address to Americans: A Poem in Blank Verse*. Nauvoo, Ill.: E. Robinson, [1841?].

Murray, David. "Racial Identity and Self-invention in North America: The Red and the Black." In *Writing and Race*, edited by Tim Youngs, 80–101. London: Longman, 1997.

Naylor, Celia. *African Cherokees in Indian Territory: From Chattel to Citizens*. Chapel Hill: University of North Carolina Press, 2008.

Newell, Linda King, and Valeen Tippetts Avery. "Sweet Counsel and Seas of Tribulation: The Religious Life of the Women in Kirtland." *BYU Studies* 20, no. 2 (1980): 151–62.

Numbers, Ronald L. "Do-It-Yourself the Sectarian Way." In *Medicine without Doctors: Home Health Care in American History*, edited by Guenter B. Risse, Ronald L. Numbers, and Judith Walzer Leavitt, 49–72. New York: Science History Publications, 1977.

Oberg, Michael. *Professional Indian: The American Odyssey of Eleazer Williams*. Philadelphia: University of Pennsylvania Press, 2015.

O'Brien, Greg, ed. *Pre-removal Choctaw History: Exploring New Paths*. Norman: University of Oklahoma Press, 2008.

O'Brien, Jean M. *Firsting and Lasting: Writing Indians Out of Existence in New England*. Minneapolis: University of Minnesota Press, 2010.

O'Brien, Sheila Ruzycki. "Writing with a Forked Pen: Racial Dynamics and Johnson Jones Hooper's Twin Tale of Swindling Indians." *American Studies* 35, no. 2 (1994): 95–113.

O'Donovan, Connell. "'I Would Confine Them to Their Own Species': LDS Historical Rhetoric and Praxis Regarding Marriage Between Whites and Blacks." http://www.connellodonovan.com/black_white_marriage.html#17. June 10, 2011.

———. "The Mormon Priesthood Ban and Elder Q. Walker Lewis." *John Whitmer Historical Association Journal* 26 (2006): 48–100.

———. "Plural Marriage and African Americans: Race, Schism, and the Beginnings of Priesthood & Temple Denial in 1847." In *The Persistence of Polygamy: Joseph Smith and the Origins of Mormon Polygamy*, edited by Newell G. Bringhurst and Craig L. Foster. Vol. 2. Forthcoming.

Oestreicher, David M. "The Anatomy of the Walam Olum: A 19th Century Anthropological Hoax." Ph.D. diss., Rutgers University, 1995.

Ostrom, Hans J., and J. David Macey, eds. *The Greenwood Encyclopedia of African American Literature, O-T*. Vol. 4. Westport, Conn.: Greenwood Press, 2005.

Otter, Samuel. *Melville's Anatomies*. Berkeley: University of California Press, 1999.

Palmer, Grant. "Did Joseph Smith Commit Treason in His Quest for Political Empire in 1844?" *John Whitmer Historical Association Journal* 32, no. 2 (Fall–Winter 2012): 52–58.

Pascoe, Peggy. *What Comes Naturally: Miscegenation Law and the Making of Race in America*. New York: Oxford University Press, 2009.

Pearce, Roy Harvey. *Savagism and Civilization: A Study of the Indian and the American Mind*. Rev. ed. Berkeley: University of California, 1988.

Perdue, Theda. *Race and the Atlanta Cotton States Exposition of 1895*. Athens: University of Georgia Press, 2010.

Perry, Lewis. *Boats against the Current: American Culture between Revolution and Modernity, 1820–1860*. New York: Oxford University Press, 1993.

Peyer, Bernd. *The Tutor'd Mind: Indian Missionary-Writers in Antebellum America*. Amherst: University of Massachusetts Press, 1997.

Pick, Daniel. *Svengali's Web: The Alien Enchanter in Modern Culture*. New Haven, Conn.: Yale University Press, 2000.

Polk, Patrick. "Early Black Mormons and Dilemmas of Identification." Paper delivered at the Mormon History Association Annual Meeting, Sacramento, May 23, 2008.

———. "William McCarey (Alias Wm. Chubbee); Or the Magic Mulatto in Mormon Country." Paper delivered at the Sunstone Symposium, Salt Lake City, Aug. 9, 2008.

Porter, Joy. *Native American Freemasonry: Associationalism and Performance in America*. Lincoln: University of Nebraska Press, 2011.

Power, Tyrone. *Impressions of America: During the years 1833, 1834, and 1835*. 2 vols. Philadelphia: Carey, Lea & Blanchard, 1836.

Pratt, Foster. *Historical Sketch of Early Masonry in Michigan*. Grand Rapids, Mich.: I. S. Dygert, 1884. Originally printed by order of Wm. P. Innes, Grand Secretary, Grand Lodge, 1883.

Pratt, Parley P. *The Autobiography of Parley Parker Pratt, One of the Twelve Apostles of the Church of Jesus Christ of Latter-day Saints, Embracing his Life, Ministry and Travels, with Extracts, in Prose and Verse, from His Miscellaneous Writings*. New York: Russell Brothers, 1874.

———. *History of the Late Persecution Inflicted by the State of Missouri upon the Mormons: In Which Ten Thousand American Citizens Were Robbed, Plundered, and Driven from the State, and Many Others Imprisoned, Martyred, &c., for Their Religion, and All This by Military Force, by Order of the Executive*. 1839. Reprint, Mexico, N.Y.: Office of the Oswego Co. Democrat, 1840.

Proceedings of the Common Council of the City of Buffalo, from January 5th 1862, to January 6th, 1863. Buffalo: Joseph Warren, 1863.

Proceedings of the Common Council of the City of Buffalo, from January 7th, 1861, to January 6th, 1862. Buffalo: Rockwell & Baker, 1862.

Proceedings of the Grand Lodge of Freemasons of New Hampshire, from June 5842, to June 5856, Inclusive. Vol. 2. Manchester, N.H.: C. F. Livingston, 1869.

Proceedings of the Grand Lodge of the Most Ancient and Honorable Fraternity of Free and Accepted Masons of the State of Florida; at the Several Grand Communications, from Its Organization, A.D. 1830, to 1850, inclusive. New York: J. F. Brennan, 1859.

Purdy, William E. "They Marched Their Way West: The Nauvoo Brass Band." *Ensign* (July 1980): 20–23.

Pusey, Merlo J. *Builders of the Kingdom: George A. Smith, John Henry Smith, George Albert Smith*. Provo, Utah: Brigham Young University Press, 1981.

Putzi, Jennifer. *Identifying Marks: Race, Gender, and the Marked Body in Nineteenth- century America*. Athens: University of Georgia Press, 2006.

Quick, Henry, and Herbert Quick. *Mississippi Steamboatin': A History of Steamboating on the Mississippi and Its Tributaries*. New York: Henry Holt, 1926.

Quinn, D. Michael. *The Mormon Hierarchy: Origins of Power*. Salt Lake City: Signature Books, 1994.

Rafinesque, Constantine Samuel. *The American Nations, or, Outlines of Their General History, Ancient and Modern including the Whole History of the Earth and Mankind in the Western Hemisphere, the Philosophy of American History, the Annals, Traditions, Civilization, Languages, &c., of all the American Nations, Tribes, Empires and States*. Philadelphia: C. S. Rafinesque / F. Turner, 1836.

Reagan, Leslie J. *When Abortion Was a Crime: Women, Medicine, and Law in the United States, 1867–1973*. Berkeley: University of California Press, 1997.

Reeve, W. Paul. *Making Space on the Western Frontier: Mormons, Miners, and Southern Paiutes*. Urbana: University of Illinois Press, 2006.

———. *Religion of a Different Color: Race and the Mormon Struggle for Whiteness*. New York: Oxford University Press, 2015.

Regina v. Tubbee, 1 P.R. 98, 1851. Westlaw Canada, http://canada.westlaw.com. June 15, 2011.

Reiss, Benjamin. "P. T. Barnum, Joice Heth, and Antebellum Spectacles of Race," *American Quarterly* 51, no. 1 (1999): 78–107.

———. *The Showman and the Slave: Race, Death, and Memory in Barnum's America*. Cambridge, Mass.: Harvard University Press, 2001.

Reproductive Control, or a Rational Guide to Matrimonial Happiness, the Right and Duty of Parents to Limit the Number of Their Offspring According to Their Circumstances Demonstrated . . . By an American Physician. Cincinnati, 1855. Reprinted in *Birth Control and Family Planning in Nineteenth-century America*, edited by Charles Rosenberg and Carroll Smith-Rosenberg, i–xi. New York: Arno Press, 1974.

Richards, Mary Haskin Parker. *Winter Quarters: The 1846–1848 Life Writings of Mary Haskin Parker Richards,* edited by Maurine Carr Ward. Logan: Utah State University Press, 1996.

Richards, Samuel W. *Diary of Samuel Whitney Richards*. Provo, Utah: Brigham Young University Library, 1946.

Roach, Joseph R. "Slave Spectacles and Tragic Octoroons: A Cultural Genealogy of Antebellum Performance." *Theatre Survey* 33 (1992): 167–87.

Robinson, Charles F., II. *Dangerous Liaisons: Sex and Love in the Segregated South*. Fayetteville: University of Arkansas Press, 2003.

Rosaldo, Renato. "Imperialist Nostalgia." *Representations* 26 (Spring 1989): 107–22.

Rothstein, William G. *American Physicians in the 19th Century: From Sects to Science*. Baltimore: Johns Hopkins University Press, 1985.

Rottenberg, Catherine. "Passing: Race, Identification, and Desire." *Criticism* 45, no. 4 (2003): 435–52.

Round, Philip H. *Removable Type: Histories of the Book in Indian Country, 1663–1880*. Chapel Hill: University of North Carolina Press, 2010.

Rourke, Constance. *American Humor: A Study of the National Character*. New York: Doubleday Anchor Books, 1953.

Rousey, Dennis C. "Aliens in the WASP Nest: Ethnocultural Diversity in the Antebellum Urban South." *Journal of American History* 79, no. 1 (1992): 152–64.

Sachs, Honor. "'Freedom by a Judgment': The Legal History of an Afro-Indian Family." *Law and History Review* 30, no. 1 (2011): 173–203.

A Sanitary Survey of St. Louis: Being a Series of Short Papers on Leading Public Health Topics Contributed by City Officials and Local Sanitarians. Concord, N.H.: Republican Press Association, 1884–85.

Satz, Ronald N. "The Mississippi Choctaw: From the Removal Treaty to the Federal Agency." In *After Removal: The Choctaw in Mississippi*, edited by Samuel J. Wells and Roseanna Tubby, 3–32. Jackson: University Press of Mississippi, 1986.

Saunt, Claudio. *Black, White, and Indian: Race and the Unmaking of an American Family*. New York: Oxford University Press, 2005.

Sayre, Gordon. *The Indian Chief as Tragic Hero: Native Resistance and the Literatures of America, from Moctezuma to Tecumseh*. Chapel Hill: University of North Carolina Press, 2005.

Scheckel, Susan. *The Insistence of the Indian: Race and Nationalism in Nineteenth-century American Culture*. Princeton, N.J.: Princeton University Press, 1998.

Schlicher, John J. "Terre Haute in 1850." *Indiana Magazine of History* 12, no. 1 (1916): 245–70.

Schulz, Christian. Letter 28. Baton Rouge, West Florida, April 13, 1808. In *Travels on an Inland Voyage through the States of New-York, Pennsylvania, Virginia, Ohio, Kentucky and Tennessee: Performed in the Years 1807 and 1808; Including a Tour of Nearly Six Thousand Miles*. Vol. 2. New York: Isaac Riley, 1810, Sabin Americana, http://galenet.galegroup.com. April 4, 2012.

Schwartz, Marie Jenkins. *Birthing a Slave: Motherhood and Medicine in the Antebellum South*. Cambridge, Mass.: Harvard University Press, 2010.

———. *Born in Bondage: Growing Up Enslaved in the Antebellum South*. Cambridge, Mass.: Harvard University Press, 2001.

Schweninger, Loren. "Prosperous Blacks in the South, 1790–1880." *American Historical Review* 95, no. 1 (1990): 31–56.

Scully, Arthur, Jr. *James Dakin, Architect, His Career in New York and the South*. Baton Rouge: Louisiana State University Press, 1973.

Seeman, Erik. "Native Spirits, Shaker Visions: Speaking with the Dead in the Early Republic." Paper delivered at the Society for the History of Early America. Philadelphia, Penn. July 2014.

Sellers, Charles. *The Market Revolution, 1815-1848*. New York: Oxford University Press, 1991.

Shank, Theodore J. "Theatre for the Majority: Its Influence on a Nineteenth Century American Theatre." *Educational Theatre Journal* 11, no. 3 (1959): 188-99.

Sheriff, Carol. *The Artificial River: The Erie Canal and the Paradox of Progress, 1817-1862*. New York: Hill and Wang, 1996.

Silverman, David J. *Red Brethren: The Brothertown and Stockbridge Indians and the Problem of Race in Early America*. Ithaca, N.Y.: Cornell University Press, 2010.

Simms, William Gilmore. "Oakatibbee; or the Choctaw Sampson." *The Wigwam and the Cabin, 176-208*. New York: Wiley and Putnam, 1845.

Skinner, J. F. "Domestic Medicines." *Boston Medical and Surgical Journal* 40, no. 16 (1849): 1-4.

Smith, Christopher C. "Playing Lamanite: Ecstatic Performance of American Indian Roles in Early Mormon Ohio." *Journal of Mormon History* 40, no. 3 (2015): 132-67.

Smith, Donald. *Mississauga Portraits: Ojibwe Voices from Nineteenth-century Canada*. Toronto: University of Toronto Press, 2013.

———. *Sacred Feathers: The Reverend Peter Jones (Kahkewaquonaby) and the Mississauga Indians*. Toronto: University of Toronto, 1988.

Smith, George A. "Historical Discourse. Delivered by Elder George A. Smith, in the Tabernacle, Ogden City, on Tuesday, November 15, 1864." *Journal of Discourses by President Brigham Young, His Two Counsellors, the Twelve Apostles, and Others. Reported by G. D. Watt, E. L. Sloan, and D. W. Evans, and Humbly Dedicated to the Latter-day Saints in All the World*. Vol. 11. London: Latter-day Saints' Book Depot, 1867.

Smith, H. Perry, ed. *History of the City of Buffalo and Erie County, with Illustrations and Biographical Sketches of Some of Its Prominent Men and Pioneers*. Vol. 2. Syracuse, N.Y.: D. Mason, 1884.

Smith, Joseph. *The Personal Writings of Joseph Smith*, edited by Dean C. Jessee. Salt Lake City: Deseret Book, 1984.

Smith, Joseph, Jr. *History of the Church of Jesus Christ of Latter Day Saints*, edited by B. H. Roberts. 2nd ed. 7 vols. Salt Lake City: Deseret Book, 1959-60.

Smith, Solomon. *The Theatrical Journey-Work and Anecdotical Recollections of Sol Smith, Comedian, Attorney at Law, Etc. Etc.: Comprising a Sketch of the Second Seven Years of his Professional Life; Together with Sketches of Adventure in After Years*. Philadelphia: T. B. Peterson, 1854.

———. *Theatrical Management in the West and South for Thirty Years*. New York: Harper and Brothers, 1868.

Snow, Eliza Roxcy. *The Personal Writings of Eliza Roxcy Snow*. Edited by Maureen Ursenbach Beecher. Salt Lake City: University of Utah Press, 1995.

Snyder, Christina. *Slavery in Indian Country: The Changing Face of Captivity in Early America*. Cambridge, Mass.: Harvard University Press, 2010.

Sobel, Mechal. *Teach Me Dreams: The Search for Self in the Revolutionary Era*. Princeton, N.J.: Princeton University Press, 2002.

Speek, Vickie Cleverley. *"God Has Made Us a Kingdom": James Strang and the Midwest Mormons*. Salt Lake City: Signature Books, 2007.

Spencer, Thomas M., ed. *The Missouri Mormon Experience*. Columbia: University of Missouri Press, 2010.

Staker, Mark Lyman. *'Hearken, O Ye People': The Historical Setting of Joseph Smith's Ohio Revelations*. Salt Lake City: Greg Kofford Books, 2009.

Stapley, Jonathan A., and Kristine Wright. "Female Ritual Healing in Mormonism." *Journal of Mormon History* 37, no. 1 (2011): 1–85.

Starr, Paul. *The Social Transformation of American Medicine*. New York: Basic Books, 1982.

Steele, Jeffrey. "Reduced to Images: American Indians in Nineteenth-century Advertising." In *Dressing in Feathers: The Construction of the Indian in American Popular Culture*, edited by S. Elizabeth Bird, 45–64. Boulder, Colo.: Westview Press, 1996.

Stenhouse, T. B. H. *The Rocky Mountain Saints: A Full and Complete History of the Mormons: from the First Vision of Joseph Smith to the Last Courtship of Brigham Young; including the Story of the Hand-cart Emigration; the Mormon War; the Mountain-Meadow Massacre; the Reign of Terror in Utah; the Doctrine of Human Sacrifice; the Political Domestic, Social, and Theological Influences of the Saints; the Facts of Polygamy; the Colonization of the Rocky Mountains: and the Development of the Great Mineral Wealth of the Territory of Utah*. New York: D. Appleton, 1873.

Stout, Hosea. *On the Mormon Frontier: The Diary of Hosea Stout, 1844–1861*. Edited by Juanita Brooks. Vol. 1. Salt Lake City: University of Utah Press, 1982.

Streeby, Shelley. *American Sensations: Class, Empire, and the Production of Popular Culture*. Berkeley: University of California Press, 2002.

Sullivan, Lester. "Composers of Color of Nineteenth-century New Orleans: The History behind the Music." *Black Music Research Journal* 8, no. 1 (1988): 51–82.

Taves, Ann. *Fits, Trances, and Visions: Experiencing Religion and Explaining Experience from Wesley to James*. Princeton, N.J.: Princeton University Press, 1999.

———. "Sex, Race, Gender, and Religion in the Eighteenth and Nineteenth Centuries." In *Retelling U.S. Religious History*, edited by Thomas A. Tweed, 38–56. Berkeley: University of California Press, 1997.

Taylor, George Rogers. *The Transportation Revolution, 1815–1860*. New York: Rinehart, 1951.

Thomas, James. *From Tennessee Slave to St. Louis Entrepreneur: The Autobiography of James Thomas*. Edited by Loren Schweninger. Columbia: University of Missouri Press, 1984.

Thrush, Coll. *Indigenous London: Native Travellers at the Heart of Empire*. New Haven, Conn.: Yale University Press. Forthcoming 2016.

Trachtenberg, Alan. *Shades of Hiawatha: Staging Indians, Making Americans, 1880–1930*. New York: Hill and Wang, 2004.

Transactions of the Grand Lodge of Ancient York Masons, of the State of Michigan, at its Annual Grand Communication, January 8, A.L. 5851.

Convened at 'Mason's Hall,' in the City of Detroit. Reprint, Grand Rapids, Mich.: Grand Lodge, 1883.

Truettner, William H. *Painting Indians and Building Empires in North America, 1710–1840*. Berkeley: University of California Press, 2010.

Tubbee, Laah Ceil Manatoi Elaah. *A Sketch of the Life of Okah Tubbee, (Called) William Chubbee, Son of the Head Chief, Mosholeh Tubbee, of the Choctaw Nation of Indians. By Laah Ceil Manatoi Elaah Tubbee, His Wife*. Springfield, Mass.: H. S. Taylor, 1848.

——. *A Sketch of the Life of Okah Tubbee, (Called) William Chubbee, Son of the Head Chief, Mosholeh Tubbee, of the Choctaw Nation of Indians. By Laah Ceil Manatoi Elaah Tubbee, His Wife*. Toronto: Henry Stephens, 1852.

Tuchman, Arleen M. *Science Has No Sex: The Life of Marie Zakrzewska, M.D.* Chapel Hill: University of North Carolina Press, 2006.

Turner, John G. *Brigham Young: Pioneer Prophet*. Cambridge, Mass.: Harvard University Press, 2012.

U.S. Bureau of the Census. *Eighth Census of the United States, 1860*. http://www.ancestry.com. Feb. 3, 2013.

——. *Fifth Census of the United States, 1830*. http://www.ancestry.com. Sept. 21, 2012.

——. *Fourth Census of the United States, 1820*. http://www.ancestry.com. Sept. 24, 2012.

——. *Ninth Census of the United States, 1870*. http://www.ancestry.com. Jan. 26, 2012.

——. *Seventh Census of the United States, 1850*. http://www.ancestry.com. June 15, 2011.

——. *Sixth Census of the United States, 1840*. http://www.ancestry.com. Sept. 2, 2014.

U.S. Congress. House. 26th Congress, 2nd session, no. 22. "'Latter-day Saints,' alias Mormons: The Petition of the Latter-day Saints, Commonly Known as Mormons." [1840].

Umberhine & Gustin's Lake Shore Gazetteer and Business Directory, For 1861–2. Indianapolis: Indianapolis Journal, 1861.

Usner, Daniel. *Indian Work: Language and Livelihood in Native American History*. Cambridge, Mass.: Harvard University Press, 2009.

——. *Indians, Settlers, and Slaves in a Frontier Exchange Economy: The Lower Mississippi Valley before 1783*. Chapel Hill: University of North Carolina Press, 1992.

Utah State Historical Society, comp. *Utah Cemetery Inventory*. http://www.ancestry.com. Jan. 26, 2012.

Van Hoak, Stephen P. "And Who Shall Have the Children? The Indian Slave Trade in the Southern Great Basin, 1800–1865." *Nevada Historical Quarterly* 41 (1998): 3–25.

VanDerBeets, Richard. *Held Captive by Indians: Selected Narratives, 1642–1836*. Knoxville: University of Tennessee Press, 1973.

The Village Doctor; or, The Art of Curing Diseases Rendered Familiar and Easy.
London: Knight and Lacey, 1825.

Vogel, Dan. *Indian Origins and the Book of Mormon: Religious Solutions from
Columbus to Joseph Smith.* Salt Lake City: Signature Books, 1986.

Vogel, Dan, and Scott C. Dunn. "'The Tongue of Angels': Glossalalia among
Mormonism's Founders." *Journal of Mormon History* 19, no. 2 (Fall 1993):
1–34.

Vogel, Michael N., Edward J. Patton, and Paul F. Redding. *America's Crossroads:
Buffalo's Canal Street/Dante Place—The Making of a City.* Buffalo, N.Y.:
Heritage Press, 1993.

Walker, Robert J. "Public Dinner Given in Honor of the Chickasaw and Choctaw
Treaties: At Mr. Parker's Hotel, in the City of Natchez, on the 10th day of
October, 1830." [Mississippi?: s.n., 1830?]. Sabin Americana. http://galenet
.galegroup.com. April 10, 2012.

Walker, Ronald W. "Seeking the 'Remnant': The Native American during the
Joseph Smith Period." *Journal of Mormon History* 19, no. 1 (Spring 1993): 1–33.

Wallenstein, Peter. "Indian Foremothers: Race, Sex, Slavery, and Freedom in
Early Virginia." In *The Devil's Lane: Sex and Race in the Early South,* edited by
Catherine Clinton and Michele Gillespie, 57–73. New York: Oxford University
Press, 1997.

Ward, Maurine Carr. Introduction to *Winter Quarters: The 1846–1848 Life
Writings of Mary Haskin Parker Richards,* edited by Maurine Carr Ward, 1–48.
Logan: Utah State University Press, 1996.

Warner, John Harley. *The Therapeutic Perspective: Medical Practice, Knowledge,
and Identity in America, 1820–1885.* Cambridge, Mass.: Harvard University
Press, 1986.

Waselkov, Gregory A. *A Conquering Spirit: Fort Mims and the Redstick War of
1813–1814.* Tuscaloosa: University of Alabama Press, 2009.

Watson, Harry L. *Liberty and Power: The Politics of Jacksonian America.* New
York: Noonday Press, 1990.

Weaver, Jace. *Red Atlantic: American Indigenes and the Making of the Modern
World, 1000–1927.* Chapel Hill: University of North Carolina Press, 2014.

Wells, Samuel J. Introduction to *After Removal: The Choctaw in Mississippi,*
edited by Samuel J. Wells and Roseanna Tubby, vii–x. Jackson: University of
Mississippi Press, 1986.

Wells, Susan. *Out of the Dead House: Nineteenth-century Women Physicians and
the Writing of Medicine.* Madison: University of Wisconsin Press, 2001.

Westbrook, G. W. *Mormonism: Embracing the Origin, Rise and Progress of the
Sect, with an Examination of the Book of Mormon; Also, Their Troubles in
Missouri and Final Expulsion from the State.* St. Louis: Ustick and Davies,
1844.

*The Western Farmer and Gardener, Devoted to Agriculture, Horticulture, and
Rural Economy.* Vol. 2. Edited by Thomas Affleck. Cincinnati: Charles Foster
/ R. P. Brooks, 1841.

Wimsatt, Mary Ann. Introduction to *Tales of the South*, edited by Mary Ann Wimsatt, 1–16. Columbia: University of South Carolina Press, 1996.

Winn, Kenneth H. "The Missouri Context of Antebellum Mormonism and Its Legacy of Violence." In *The Missouri Mormon Experience*, edited by Thomas M. Spencer III, 19–26. Columbia: University of Missouri Press, 2010.

Wong, Hertha Dawn. *Sending My Heart Back across the Years: Tradition and Innovation in Native American Autobiography*. New York: Oxford University Press, 1992.

Woodruff, Wilford. *Wilford Woodruff's Journal, 1833–1898*. Edited by Scott G. Kenney. Vol. 3. Midvale, Utah: Signature Books, 1983.

Woods, Fred E. "Between the Borders: Mormon Transmigration through Missouri, 1838–1868." In *The Missouri Mormon Experience*, edited by Thomas M. Spencer, 151–78. Columbia: University of Missouri Press, 2010.

———. "Two Sides of a River: Mormon Transmigration through Quincy, Illinois, and Hannibal, Missouri." *Mormon Historical Studies* 2 (2001): 119–47.

Young, Brigham. *The Journal of Brigham: Brigham Young's Own Story in His Own Words*. Compiled by Leland R. Nelson. Provo, Utah: Council Press, 1980.

Young, Mary E. *Redskins, Ruffleshirts, and Rednecks: Indian Allotments in Alabama and Mississippi, 1830–1860*. Norman: University of Oklahoma Press, 1961.

Acknowledgments

My first word of gratitude is for Daniel F. Littlefield Jr. and his book *Life of Okah Tubbee* (1988). He recovered, compiled, edited, and annotated the three editions of Okah Tubbee and Laah Ceil's remarkable autobiography, resurrecting their experiences for a new generation of scholars. His volume was my constant companion as I traveled around North America in search of the elusive and electric people at the center of this book.

And what a journey it has been. Researching and writing this book introduced me to unfamiliar fields of study and made me rethink familiar ones. In each case, however, I have been fortunate to have the help of friends, both new and old. Each had a hand in crafting this book. Despite the heroic efforts of these guides, mentors, and advisers, some mistakes and misinterpretations surely remain, for which I take full responsibility.

I will always be grateful for the generosity of the Mormon history scholars I met during the course of this project. Spencer Fluhman carefully read the middle chapters and gently corrected my many missteps, while encouraging me in my first tentative interpretations. Connell O'Donovan befriended me at the Latter-day Saints Church History Library, introduced me to other scholars in the field, and graciously shared his copious research materials on William McCary and Lucy Stanton. His work on the pair has been incredibly influential in my efforts to follow them. I benefited from collaborations with Quincy Newell, Paul Reeve, and Max Mueller, each of whom offered useful guidance and probing questions. David Whittaker of the L. Tom Perry Special Collections at the Brigham Young University Library gave me sage advice about navigating the vast Mormon historiography. William Slaughter and Michael Landon at the LDS Church History Library handled my considerable ignorance with grace and patience, educating me on basic aspects of church organization and theology while directing me to a treasure trove of sources. I must also gratefully acknowledge Hudson Davis for providing me my first glimpse of Okah Tubbee's other life as a Lamanite prophet and Patrick Polk for sharing his important insights.

Scholars from a wide variety of subfields also contributed to this book's development, suggesting leads, offering counter interpretations, and supporting me through a vibrant and far-flung intellectual community. In addition to the anonymous reader who offered incisive and generous commentary on the manuscript, Daniel Usner's careful review of the manuscript on behalf of University of North Carolina Press was indispensable. He has been a steadfast supporter of this project from an early stage and his mentorship, including a timely invitation to the Vanderbilt Americanist Seminar, has meant a great deal to me personally and intellectually. Michael Oberg read the entire draft and not only offered me feedback but also shared his work on Eleazer Williams, which catalyzed my thinking on a number of topics. Ashley Riley Sousa read early chapters and gave me the kind of tough critique that only close friends can do with grace. Dan Shaule and Guylaine Petrain went out of their way to help me find vital sources relating to the history of Ontario, and like my new Mormon history friends, they patiently oriented me to places and events. I am sincerely grateful for their time, assistance, and kindness.

In addition to the folks already mentioned, a long list of friends and colleagues have listened patiently to me ramble on about Okah Tubbee and Laah Ceil in conferences, classrooms, cafés, and kitchens. Their enthusiasm for the project has been a source of inspiration and motivation. For this, I would like to thank Eric Anderson, Jessi Bardill, Carlos Blanton, Cathleen Cahill, Boyd Cothran, Qwo-Li Driskill, Tasha Dubriwny, Tom Dunlap, Arika Easly-Houser, Robbie Ethridge, Andrew Frank, C. Joseph Genetin-Pilawa, Rayna Green, Tammy Ingram, Shona Jackson, Harold Livesay, Paula Madden, Robin Morris, Alyssa Mt. Pleasant, Jason Parker, Theda Perdue, Kristan Poirot, Kristofer Ray, Honor Sachs, Nancy Shoemaker, Rose Stremlau, Jeff Winking, Marisa Winking, and Matt Woods.

Researching this book often felt like a wild chase, as I followed clues about Okah Tubbee and Laah Ceil from Mississippi to Ontario to Utah and down plenty of rabbit holes. I was supported in my peripatetic research by a Franklin Grant from the American Philosophical Society and a Ballard Breaux Fellowship at the Filson Library, as well as several grants from Texas A&M University, including awards from the Melbern G. Glasscock Center for Humanities Research, the College of Liberal Arts, and the Department of History. The Ray A. Rothrock '77 Fellowship enabled me to conduct final research and prepare the manuscript. I am grateful for the generous support of these institutions.

Although the locations are too numerous to list in these acknowledgments, I imposed myself on librarians, archivists, and government employees in nearly every locale that Okah Tubbee and Laah Ceil lived or visited. I am thankful for their assistance and their patience as I tried to explain my research topics. In addition to the knowledgeable staff at the LDS Church History and Brigham Young University Libraries, I would especially like to thank George Miles at the Beinecke Rare Book and Manuscript Library and Cynthia Van Ness at the Research Library of the Buffalo History Museum. And although authors rarely thank people they do not actually know, I would also like to acknowledge the hundreds of librarians, archivists, and digital media experts who make it possible to access literally millions of records through their digital collections. The work of these individuals has revolutionized the way we do historical research, and I am deeply grateful for their efforts.

The writing phase of any project is in some ways the hardest and the loneliest. When the excitement of the hunt gives way to the solitude of a writer and her computer, the allure of the archives can be irresistible. Thankfully, I had the firm discipline and steady guidance of an incomparable writing group to keep me focused, even when life made that difficult. April Hatfield, James Rosenheim, Cynthia Bouton, Rebecca Hartkopf Schloss, and Julia Blackwelder are imaginative, passionate, and generous scholars, which of course makes them incisive critics. They read every chapter multiple times, traveling with me down every new path and into more than a few briar patches. I am so very lucky not only to write with them, but also to call them colleagues, mentors, and friends.

I have also benefited tremendously from participation in the Indigenous Studies Working Group at Texas A&M University and from the intellectual stimulation provided by the Melbern G. Glasscock Center for Humanities Research. And I would like to thank Tyler Thompson for his essential bibliographic help near the end of the project, as well as the staff of the Interlibrary Loan Office at Sterling Evans Library to whom I owe a pie. I want to offer a word of gratitude to my undergraduate students, who have (sometimes unwittingly) suggested new perspectives and inspired my work. Mark Simpson-Vos deserves special acknowledgment not only as an excellent editor, but also as a mentor who helped me refocus when I wanted to give up, always reminding me to "trust the process." I am grateful for his patience and support.

Throughout the process of writing this book, my family has been a source of inspiration and support. Linda and Phil Pulley, Tina Robinette, Kym Lawrence, Carolyn and Fritz Korte, and my wonderful nieces and nephews have been terrific cheerleaders. Connie Hudson and my late father-in-law Bill Hudson, as well as my sister-in-law Jody Hudson, provided amazing encouragement, even in difficult times. My cousins Joannah and Robert Powers and Ginny Graunke offered me welcome respite during my research travels.

My sons Hayden and Cameron have lived with this book most of their lives. Their curiosity, their silliness, and their unconditional love and affection, even when my research kept me far from home or my writing kept me deep in my head, means more to me than I can say. Finally, this work is dedicated to my husband Jonathan, who has never wavered in his support. He made it possible for me to write this book, encouraging me, reassuring me, reminding me of what is important and what is not, when to keep going and when to stop.

Index

Bassett, Semira La Celestine, 60, 64, 116, 120, 153, 165, 168–69, 192 (n. 97), 193 (n. 105), 214 (nn. 72, 74)

Bassett, Solon, 57, 153, 165, 168, 191 (n. 71), 192 (n. 97), 193 (n. 105), 204 (n. 107), 213 (n. 64)

"Big Family," 47–49, 53, 78

Bishop, Anna, 129, 144, 205 (n. 29)

Blackface minstrelsy, 5, 6, 97, 108, 131, 200 (nn. 20, 21)

Black Hawk, 66, 96

"Black Pete," 48, 50, 53–54, 56, 168, 190 (nn. 56, 57)

Bochsa, Nicholas-Charles, 129, 144, 205 (n. 29)

Boggs, Lilburn, 61

Bonney House Hotel (Buffalo, N.Y.), 158, 211 (n. 25)

Book of Mormon, 66, 67, 85, 188 (n. 9), 202 (n. 80)

Boston, Mass., 10, 109, 110–11, 121, 139, 150, 159, 160, 185 (n. 85), 199 (n. 18)

Boudinot, Elias, 95, 132

Brown, Samuel, 58

Bruce Peninsula, Ont., 146–47

Bsuba, Luceil. See Tubbee, Laah Ceil Manatoi Elaah

Buffalo, N.Y., 128–31, 134–37, 154, 211 (n. 14), 212–13 (n. 51), 213 (n. 56); economic development, 152–53; fugitive slave controversies, 130–31, 134–36, 139, 206 (n. 35); canal district, 153; medical reform, 157; crime, 166, 212 (n. 43); free blacks, 206 (n. 33)

Burnett, Aaron, 165

Byer, Mary Louisa, 158, 160–61, 164–66

Cain, mark of, 81

Caldwell, James, 34, 185 (n. 85)

Caldwell County, Mo., 57

California, 78, 114, 157, 164, 168

Calkins, Sylvanus, 198 (n. 94)

Campbell, Alexander, 43, 47

Campbell, Robert, 78

Campbellites, 43, 44, 70

Canada, 1, 3, 9, 13, 130, 131, 139–42, 145, 149, 153, 154, 155, 156, 173, 206 (n. 33)

Canadian National Exhibition (1852), 142

Captivity narratives, 4, 23, 138. See also American Indians: in antebellum literature

Carey, Andrew. See Tubbee, Okah

Carey, James. See Tubbee, Okah

Carey, William. See Tubbee, Okah

Castle Garden, 107–9, 201 (n. 58), 202 (n. 62)

Catlin, George, 39, 140, 179 (n. 16), 187 (n. 111)

Cattaraugus, N.Y., 43

Ceil, Laah. See Tubbee, Laah Ceil Manatoi Elaah

Chase, Sisson, 90, 168

Chateaubriand, François-Rene de, 19, 180 (n. 15)

Cherokees, 23, 37, 38, 39, 95, 132; Trail of Tears, 61–62

Choctaws, 19–20, 23, 99, 104, 108, 134, 143, 172, 180 (nn. 10, 14), 180–81 (n. 15), 181 (nn. 16, 21), 195 (n. 17); in Natchez, 16–17, 30–32, 78; owning slaves, 22; perceptions of Okah Tubbee, 31, 127–28; removal, 32–33, 37–39, 43, 75, 186 (n. 109); gender and kinship, 182 (n. 42)

Chubbee, Okah. See Tubbee, Okah

Chubbee, William. See Tubbee, Okah

Church of Jesus Christ of Latter-day Saints, 3, 55–56, 192–93 (n. 99); ban on blacks in priesthood, 12, 91, 174–75; establishment of, 43–48; position of women, 53, 59–60, 64, 155; participation of African Americans, 54, 84, 91, 174; consolidation of authority, 58–60, 70, 191 (n. 75); Quorum of the Twelve, 63, 70; succession crisis, 70–71, 79, 85; schismatic controversies, 79–80, 82,